HORSE

THE FAMILY LEISURE GUIDE

A comprehensive guide to the racecourses of the United Kingdom and the major leisure attractions around them

m Robertson McCarta

Published in association with the National Tourist Boards of England, Scotland, Wales and Northern Ireland

First published in the UK by Robertson McCarta Ltd., 122 Kings Cross Road, London WC1X 9DS

Published in association with the National Tourist Boards of England, Scotland, Wales and Northern Ireland.

First published 1990
© Research and text – J & J Entertainment Ltd
© Design and production – The Pen & Ink Book Company Ltd., Whitwell Chambers, Ferrars Road, Huntingdon, Cambs PE18 6DH

British Library Cataloguing in Publication Data

Horse racing leisure guide. – (Sporting and leisure directories).
  1. Great Britain. Racecourses – Visitors' guides
  I. English Tourist Board II. Series
  798.4006841

  ISBN 1–85365–249–0

Research – Gill Lloyd and Catherine Hutton
Cartography – Lovell Johns Ltd., Oxford
Photographs
BTA/Britain in View
All Sport
Braybrook Racing, Huntingdon
The Trustees of the Goodwood Collection

Design and production – PEN & INK

Printed and bound in Great Britain

GUIDE TO SYMBOLS

☎	telephone	🚌	guided tours	⛳18	18-hole golf course
i	tourist information	✕	catering	⛳9	9-hole golf course
P	car parking	♿	disabled access	⇥A	nearest 'A' road
🏠	admission charged	♿	disabled facilities		
✗	no charge	🏇	racecourses		

Please note that within the calendar of events for each racecourse, national hunt meetings are represented by bold italic script and evening meetings by the asterisk symbol.

This is the first edition of _HORSE RACING – THE FAMILY LEISURE GUIDE_. It has been produced in association with the four National Tourist Boards to serve as a practical information source for racing enthusiasts who like to combine the enjoyment of their favourite sport with holiday breaks around the country for the whole family.

The first part of the Guide is a detailed description in alphabetical order of all 61 professional racecourses in the United Kingdom. Each racecourse entry includes details on road and rail access, parking, facilities in the different enclosures and costs, a brief guide to major events and a complete 1991 calendar of meetings.

The second part of the Guide is again organised alphabetically by racecourse name and contains information about major sporting, leisure and recreational facilities that can be found within approximately 15 miles of the racecourse. Up to 50 different leisure facilities are covered ranging from historic houses and museums through golf clubs and fishing locations to ballooning and hang gliding.

All the information on the racecourses has been researched during 1990 and is as accurate and up-to-date as possible. The information on the cost of day tickets has been provided by the racecourses and it is possible during 1991 some racecourses may increase these costs.

The information on leisure facilities around each racecourse has also been researched during 1990. This information is not intended to be exhaustive, merely to show the range of leisure activities available in each area. If you feel that we have missed out a major facility that should be included please let us know and we will include it in next year's Guide.

The 'how–to' of on-course betting has been compiled from information supplied by the Tote, to whom we are most grateful. We are indebted to the Jockey Club who provided the 1991 calendar of meetings. The Racecourse Association has also been very helpful in providing information as have the Clerks of the individual racecourses to whom we are also most grateful.

CONTENTS

CONTENTS

ON COURSE BETTING

WHAT YOU NEED

A *racecard* or *newspaper* to give the horses' numbers. The Tote stores the numbers on a computer, this enables them to show the dividends on Tote television straight after a race has finished.

WHERE TO GO

To place your bet find the nearest kiosk, counter or Tote building; the Tote staff can be recognised by their red uniforms.

WHAT BET TO MAKE

Win: You can make a bet to Win on all races. Minimum state £2.

Place: You can make a bet for a Place on all races with five or more horses running. A place dividend is paid according to the number of horses in the race.

Runners	Dividend
5–7	1st and 2nd horses
8+	1st, 2nd and 3rd horses
16+	1st, 2nd, 3rd and 4th
(handicap)	horses

Place only betting is a unique feature of the Tote service and usually there is no limit on the bet or stake you can place. **Minimum stake £2.**

Each Way: You can make a bet Each Way which combines a Win and a Place. **Minimum stake £2.** Silver Ring/Course Enclosures £1 each way bets accepted.

Dual Forecast: You can make a bet on two horses to come in first and second. The Tote Dual Forecast pays out whichever order they come in. **Minimum stake £2.** All enclosures accept £1 permutations.

Tote Jackpot: You are asked to select the winners of the first six races. **Minimum stake £1.**

Tote Placepot: You are asked to select the horses that will be placed in the first six races. Any horse on which a dividend is paid counts towards a winning line; in races where fewer than five horses run the winner must be selected. **Minimum stake £1** for a single line (one horse in each leg).

HOW TO BET

Give the amount of your bet	£2 £2.50 £4 £5 etc
Give the type of bet	Win Place Each Way Dual Forecast
Give the number of the horse(s)	3 6 8 etc.

Pay the stake:

£2	Win Number 3		Pay £2
£2	Place Number 6		Pay £2
£2	Each Way Number 8		Pay £4
£2	Dual Forecast 5 and 11		Pay £2

TOTE PLACEPOT AND JACKPOT

Take a Tote Jackpot or Tote Placepot entry form. Mark your selection as shown on the sample ticket using any colour except red and keeping your mark within the brackets.

Indicate your unit stake at the top of the form beside the section marked *Bet Stake*.

Use the section at the foot of the form to calculate permutation bets or let the machine do it for you.

Take your receipt from the operator and check that all your selections are correctly printed on it, mistakes will not be corrected once the race has been run.

```
Jackpot 20p        1111
0200271            0501
1:10 28 50
2:11 42
3:35 53
4:01
5:04 14 32 56
6:03 12


TOTAL £19.20
```

What You Win

Win, Place, Each Way and Dual Forecast
A Win dividend declared, for example, at £11.50 will pay:

Bet	Dividend declared	Winnings	Profit
£2	£11.50	£23	£21

Your profit will be your winnings (£23) less your bet (£2).

Jackpot and Placepot
A permutation bet in the Placepot could win several dividends. When the Jackpot or Placepot pool is not won, or only partly won, the stake money is carried over to the next days racing.

ON COURSE BETTING

EXAMPLE 96 line perm at 20p per line

tote JACKPOT

BET STAKE P (10) 20 (25) (30) (40) (50)
£ (1) (2) (5) (10) (20) (50)

MINIMUM STAKE £1.00

HORSE SELECTIONS

Leg 1		Leg 2		Leg 3		Leg 4		Leg 5		Leg 6	
1	31	1	31	1	31	1	31	1	31	1	31
2	32	2	32	2	32	2	32	2	32	2	32
3	33	3	33	3	33	3	33	3	33	3	33
4	34	4	34	4	34	4	34	4	34	4	34
5	35	5	35	5	35	5	35	5	35	5	35
6	36	6	36	6	36	6	36	6	36	6	36
7	37	7	37	7	37	7	37	7	37	7	37
8	38	8	38	8	38	8	38	8	38	8	38
9	39	9	39	9	39	9	39	9	39	9	39
10	40	10	40	10	40	10	40	10	40	10	40
11	41	11	41	11	41	11	41	11	41	11	41
12	42	12	42	12	42	12	42	12	42	12	42
13	43	13	43	13	43	13	43	13	43	13	43
14	44	14	44	14	44	14	44	14	44	14	44
15	45	15	45	15	45	15	45	15	45	15	45
16	46	16	46	16	46	16	46	16	46	16	46
17	47	17	47	17	47	17	47	17	47	17	47
18	48	18	48	18	48	18	48	18	48	18	48
19	49	19	49	19	49	19	49	19	49	19	49
20	50	20	50	20	50	20	50	20	50	20	50
21	51	21	51	21	51	21	51	21	51	21	51
22	52	22	52	22	52	22	52	22	52	22	52
23	53	23	53	23	53	23	53	23	53	23	53
24	54	24	54	24	54	24	54	24	54	24	54
25	55	25	55	25	55	25	55	25	55	25	55
26	56	26	56	26	56	26	56	26	56	26	56
27	57	27	57	27	57	27	57	27	57	27	57
28	58	28	58	28	58	28	58	28	58	28	58
29	59	29	59	29	59	29	59	29	59	29	59
30	FV	30	FV	30	FV	30	FV	30	FV	30	FV

3 X 2 X 2 X 1 X 4 X 2 ■

= 96 BETS AT 20p

= £ 19-20 **TOTAL STAKE**

INTERNATIONAL TOTALIZATOR SYSTEMS INC. 0738-00111B HBH LTD.

Advance Betting

You can make advance bets on the day's card at all major race fixtures. Please check that you have the correct race number and horse numbers on your ticket as mistakes will not be corrected after a race has been run.

Betting Vouchers

You can purchase £2, £5 and £10 vouchers (valid on any racecourse and in any pool) from the Tote, in advance. At Festival meetings and big fixtures on Saturdays vouchers are on sale at the Tote Information Kiosk and cheques backed by a banker's card are accepted up to a maximum of £50.

HISTORY OF THE TOTE

1929–1960

The Tote opened for business on July 2nd 1929 at Newmarket and Carlisle. Its inauguration was the result of fierce campaigning by the Jockey Club who felt that betting should contribute towards the maintenance of the sport. In August 1928 the Racecourse Betting Act became law. Under this act the Racecourse Betting Control Board was created, its objectives were to provide backers with an alternative to betting with bookmakers and to generate money to support the sport of horseracing.

The fledgling Tote financed itself with difficulty and operated on the courses in competition with the bookmakers who also operated in the off course betting market, an advantage denied to the Tote. In order to gain access to this lucrative market, a group of racehorse owners formed a private company, Tote Investors Ltd., who channeled off course credit bets to the Tote's racecourse pools on a commission basis. This arrangement existed between 1929 and 1960 and during this 30 year period £9 million was contributed to racing.

1960–1972

Cash betting away from the course, although illegal, was common and in response to police pressure the Betting and Gaming Act was passed in 1960 – off course betting was made legal. Bookmakers rapidly expanded their off course business, new betting shops opened and off course betting boomed. The Tote, however, was still prevented from offering starting price betting, so it lost its competitive position; its finances dwindled during the sixties and into the early seventies.

1972–

In 1972 the Tote was empowered to accept bets at starting price as well as Tote odds so restoring its position. The Tote has since divided into three sectors; the *Racecourse Cash Division* which runs pool betting on Britain's 59 racecourses, *Tote Credit* which offers its 45,000 members credit facilities to bet at Tote odds and starting price and *Tote Bookmakers* which runs 140 off course and 20 on course betting shops.

ASCOT

The Racecourse
Ascot
Berkshire
☎ 0990 22211

A right-handed, 14 furlong, triangular course, it stages 13 flat and 10 national hunt race days each year. The racecourse was founded in 1711 by Queen Anne but the present course is more modern, dating from 1955. The Royal Meeting held in June is both an important race meeting and a prestigious social event. The daily procession of the royal family along the course and the display of exotic hats and costumes make it the most fashionable race meeting of the year. The other important flat race meetings staged at Ascot are the Diamond Day meeting in July and the Brent Walker Festival of British Racing held in late September.

1990 saw the introduction of the Ascot Spring Evening Meeting at the end of April, a meet that marks the end of the National Hunt season at Ascot.

✦ CALENDAR OF EVENTS ✦

January	**11**	**Friday**
	12	**Saturday**
February	**6**	**Wednesday**
April	**10**	**Wednesday**
	13	**Saturday**
	30	**Tuesday***
May	1	Wednesday
June	18	Tuesday
	19	Wednesday
	20	Thursday
	21	Friday
	22	Saturday
July	26	Friday
	27	Saturday
September	26	Thursday
	27	Friday
	28	Saturday
October	11	Friday
	12	Saturday
	23	**Wednesday**
November	**15**	**Friday**
	16	**Saturday**
December	**14**	**Saturday**

MAJOR EVENTS

The major races held during the flat race season are the Gold Cup, the Royal Hunt Cup, the Coronation Stakes during the Royal Meeting in June; the King George VI and Queen Elizabeth Diamond Stakes during the Diamond Day meeting and the Queen Elizabeth II Stakes during the Brent Walker Festival of British Racing. The two most important national hunt races are the H & T Walker Gold Cup and the SGB Handicap Chase.

June
The Royal Meeting is a four day event during which several important races are run including The Gold Cup, a $2\frac{1}{2}$ mile race for 4 year olds and upwards, first run in 1807; the Royal Hunt Cup, a 1 mile handicap for 3 year olds and upwards, first run in 1843 and the Coronation Stakes, a 1 mile race for 3 year old fillies, first run in 1870.

July
The Diamond Day Meeting is held at the end of July, its most important race being the King George VI and Queen Elizabeth Stakes, a $1\frac{1}{2}$ mile race for 3 year olds and upwards first run at the Festival of Britain Meeting in 1951.

September
The Brent Walker Festival of British Racing Meeting held in late September hosts the Queen Elizabeth II Stakes, a 1 mile race for 3 year olds and upwards.

October
The National Hunt season begins in late October.

November
The H & T Walker Gold Cup, an important national hunt race is held in mid-November.

December
The SGB Handicap Chase, another important national hunt race is held in mid-December.

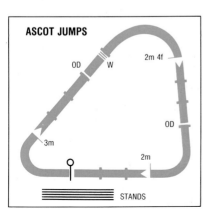

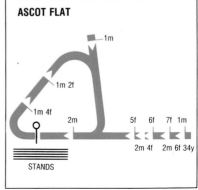

ASCOT

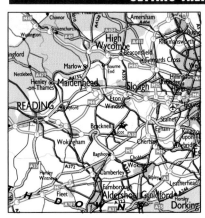

Rail: Ascot B.R. station, ½ mile from the course
Road: On Ascot High Street, (the A329)
P Ample space for cars ⬥ £3
Royal Meeting in June ⬥ £5–£7
50% of car space reserved for Royal Enclosure badge holders only
Ample space for coaches ⬥
Royal Meeting, Diamond Day Meeting and Festival of British Racing Meeting
⬥ £10–£20

Enclosures

Members Enclosure and Paddock: full viewing facilities; betting facilities; numerous bars and restaurants; shops and a bank.
Royal Meeting in June: the Members Enclosure becomes the **Royal Enclosure**; admission is strictly restricted to invitation only.
Diamond Day, July 27th, Day Members tickets must be purchased in advance, no tickets are available on the day, no transfers are allowed.
Grandstand and Paddock Enclosure (Tattersalls): paddock viewing facilities; full betting facilities; numerous bars and restaurants; a bank.
Royal Meeting: Tattersalls tickets must be purchased in advance on the Wednesday and Thursday; no tickets are available on the day, no transfers are allowed.
Silver Ring: full betting facilities; bars and snack bars.
Heath Enclosure: Public enclosure, open for the Royal Meeting only; snack bars; picnic area; childrens playground.

Costs

Annual membership

Adult	⬥ £75
Ladies	⬥ £40
Junior	⬥ £35

Note: annual membership does not give admission to the Members Enclosure during the Royal Meeting.

Day tickets
Members Enclosure

Not available during Royal Meeting.	
Diamond Day, pre-booking only	⬥ £18
Festival of British Racing	⬥ £16
All other race days	⬥ £10–£12

Tattersalls Enclosure

Royal Meeting, Wednesday and Thursday, pre-booking only	⬥ £19
Rest of Royal Meeting	⬥ £17
Diamond Day	⬥ £12
Festival of British Racing	⬥ £10
All other race days	⬥ £6.50–£8

Methods of payment: cash/cheque with valid bankers card

AYR

THE COURSE

The Racecourse
Whitletts Road
Ayr
☎ 0292 264179
Ayr is the premier racecourse in Scotland; a left-handed 1½ mile, oval course, it stages 1 mixed, 16 flat and 14 national hunt races each year. National hunt racing has been recorded at Ayr since 1871.

✦ CALENDAR OF EVENTS ✦

Jan	2	W	July	13	Sa
	3	Th		15	M
	26	Sa		16	Tu
	28	M		19	Fr
Feb	9	Sa		20	Sa
	13	W		22	M
Mar	9	Sa	Sept	18	W
	11	M		19	Th
Apr	17	W		20	F
	18	Th		21	Sa
	19	F	Oct	12	Sa
	20	Sa		14	M
June	21	F		15	Tu
	22	Sa	Nov	14	Th
				15	F
				16	Sa

MAJOR EVENTS

January
The West of Scotland Pattern Chase.

April
The Scottish Grand National, first staged in 1867 at the Bogside Course and run at Ayr since 1966; a four day meeting during which the Scottish Champions Hurdle is also run.

July
The William Hill Classic.

September
The Western Meeting, first run in 1804. A four day meeting during which the Ladbroke Ayr Gold Cup, a 6 furlong handicap for 3 year olds and upwards is staged.

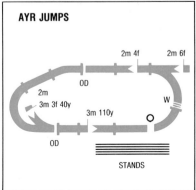

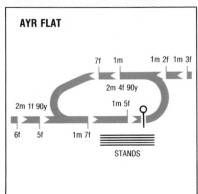

AYR

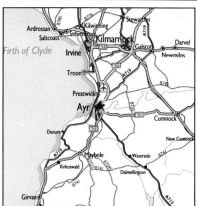

Rail: Ayr B.R. station, 1 mile from the course
Road: Off the A70, east of Ayr town centre, signposted
P ☙ Ample space for cars and coaches

Enclosures

Club Enclosure members only; viewing; full betting facilities; bars; members clubhouse and restaurant.
Eglinton Stand and Paddock (Tattersalls) viewing; full betting facilities; bars; Eglinton Room restaurant; snack bars.
Carrick and Craigie Stands (Silver Ring) betting facilities; bars; snack bar; childrens playground.

Costs

Annual membership
Couple ☙ £115

Day tickets
Club enclosure

Ayr Gold Cup Day ☙ £15
Scottish Grand National Day ☙ £15
Other days of both these ☙ £12
meetings
All other race days ☙ £10
Four day badge for Western ☙ £45
Meeting

Eglinton

Ayr Gold Cup and Scottish ☙ £7
Grand National Days
All other race days ☙ £5–£6
Four day badge for Western ☙ £22
Meeting

Carrick and Craigie ☙ £1–£2.50
Method of payment: cash/cheque with valid bankers card

11

BANGOR-ON-DEE

THE COURSE

Overton Road
Bangor-on-Dee
Wrexham
Clwyd
☎ 0948 860438

Bangor-on-Dee, founded in 1859, is a delightful, rural racecourse. A left-handed, 12 furlong, triangular course, it stages 13 national hunt days each year. There is no grandstand but its geographical setting ensures that the whole course is visible.

MAJOR EVENTS

April
The McAlpine Day during which the Alfred McAlpine Handicap Chase is run.

☆ CALENDAR OF EVENTS ☆

February	1	Friday
March	6	Wednesday
	23	Saturday
April	20	Saturday
May	18	Saturday
August	2	Friday
	17	Saturday
September	14	Saturday
October	12	Saturday
November	1	Friday
	18	Monday
	29	Friday
December	18	Wednesday

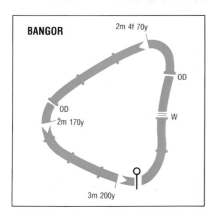

BANGOR

2m 4f 70y

OD

OD
2m 170y

W

3m 200y

GETTING THERE/GETTING IN

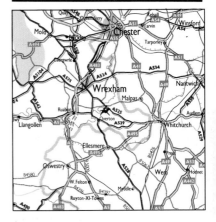

Rail: Wrexham B.R. station, 6 miles from the course
Road: Off the A525 Whitchurch to Wrexham road; Overton Road is the B5069
P 🅿 4000 car spaces, 24 coach spaces

Enclosures

Paddock Enclosure: access to Paddock and Parade Ring; betting facilities including Tote; owners, trainers and members bar; refreshment building comprising a buffet bar, a cafeteria-style restaurant and public bar.
Course Enclosures: betting facilities; vans serving fast food, soft drinks and alcohol.

Costs

Annual membership
Adult   🎟 £55

Day tickets
Paddock Enclosure   🎟 £7

Course Enclosure   🎟 £3

Methods of payment: cash/cheques with valid bankers card

BATH

THE COURSE

The Racecourse
Landsdown
Bath
Avon
☎ 0225 24609

Bath's pleasant left-handed, 1½ mile oval course stages 12 flat race days each year.

MAJOR EVENTS

April–October
All Bath's meetings are one day events except one evening meeting in late June. The most important race in its calendar is the Somerset Stakes.

☆ CALENDAR OF EVENTS ☆

April	30	Thursday
May	11	Saturday
	20	Monday
June	15	Saturday
	28	Friday*
July	6	Saturday
	10	Wednesday
	22	Monday
August	13	Tuesday
September	16	Monday
	30	Monday
October	28	Monday

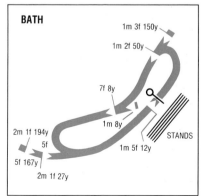

GETTING THERE/GETTING IN

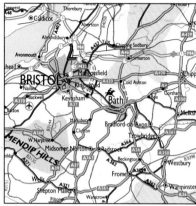

Rail: Bath B.R. station 2 miles from the course
Road: Off the A431, 2 miles north-west of Bath city centre, well signposted
P 🛇 Ample space for cars and coaches

Enclosures

Members Enclosure: viewing; betting facilities; bar, bar snacks and Members Restaurant.
Tattersalls Enclosure: viewing; betting facilities including betting shop; bars; restaurant and snack bars.
Silver Ring Enclosure: betting facilities; bar and snack bars.
Course Enclosure: betting facilities; bar and snacks.

Costs

Annual membership
Adult	🎫	£50
Couples	🎫	£100
Junior (under 21)	🎫	£15

Day tickets
Members Enclosure	🎫	£9
Tattersalls Enclosure	🎫	£6
Silver Ring Enclosure	🎫	£2
Course Enclosure	🎫	£1

Methods of payment: cash/cheque with valid bankers card

BEVERLEY

THE COURSE

The Racecourse
Westwood
Beverley
North Humberside
☎ 0482 882645

Beverley's right-handed, 1 mile 3 furlong, oval course stages 18 flat racing days each year.

MAJOR EVENTS

April–September
Seven two day meetings are held during these months.

July
One meeting features a Friday evening meeting followed by a Saturday race card.

✦ CALENDAR OF EVENTS ✦

Apr	12	F	July	5	F*
	13	Sa		6	Sa
	25	Th		15	M*
May	10	F		16	Tu
	11	Sa		30	Tu
	21	Tu	Aug	14	W
June	5	W*		15	Th
	6	Th	Sept	18	W
	12	W		19	Th

BEVERLEY

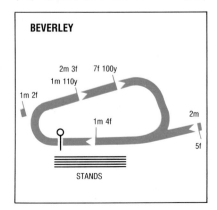

2m 3f 7f 100y
1m 110y
1m 2f
1m 4f 2m
5f
STANDS

GETTING THERE/GETTING IN

Rail: Beverley B.R. station 1 mile from the course
Road: Off the A1035 just to the west of Beverley
P 🚌 Ample space for cars and coaches

Enclosures

Members Enclosure: viewing; betting facilities; bars; restaurant and snack bar.
Tattersalls Enclosure: viewing; betting facilities; bars; restaurant and snack bars.
Silver Ring Enclosure: betting facilities; bar and snack bars.
Course Enclosure: betting facilities; bar and snack bars.

Costs

Annual membership

Adult	🎫	£55
Membership closed for 1990		
Couples	🎫	£85
Waiting list for 1990		

Day tickets

Members Enclosure	🎫	£10
Tattersalls Enclosure	🎫	£6
Silver Ring Enclosure	🎫	£2.50
Course Enclosure	🎫	£1

Methods of payment: cash/cheque with valid bankers card

BRIGHTON

THE COURSE

The Racecourse
Freshfield Road
Brighton
Sussex
☎ 0273 682912

Brighton's left-handed, 1½ mile, U-shaped course stages 18 flat race days each year.

MAJOR EVENTS

March
Flat racing commences at Brighton.

May/June/July
A popular two day meeting is staged at the end of May.

August
A well attended three day meeting is held in early August.

✮ CALENDAR OF EVENTS ✮

Mar	28	Th	Aug	6	Tu
Apr	4	Th		7	W
	22	M		8	Th
May	9	Th		28	W
	29	W	Sept	3	Tu
	30	Th		25	W
June	10	M	Oct	1	Tu
	17	M			
	25	Tu			
July	4	Th*			
	25	Th			

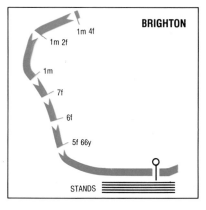

BRIGHTON

1m 4f
1m 2f
1m
7f
6f
5f 66y
STANDS

GETTING THERE/GETTING IN

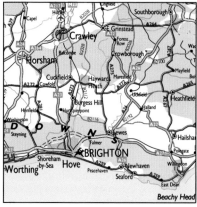

Rail: Brighton B.R. station, 2 miles from the course
Road: Just to the east of Brighton town centre between the A27 and the A259, signposted
P 🅿 2000 car spaces; 200 coach spaces

Enclosures

Club Enclosure: members only; viewing; betting facilities; bars; restaurant and snack bars.
Tattersalls Enclosure: viewing; betting facilities including betting shop; bars and snack bars.
Grandstand (Silver Ring) Enclosure: betting facilities; bars and snack bars.

Costs

Annual membership
Adult   🎟 £80

Day tickets
Members Enclosure   🎟 £10

Tattersalls Enclosure   🎟 £7

Grandstand   🎟 £3
Methods of payment: cash only

CARLISLE

THE COURSE

Burdar Road
Carlisle
Cumbria
☎ 0228 22973

Carlisle's right-handed, 1 mile 4 furlong, oval course stages 9 flat and 11 national hunt racing days each year. The course was founded in 1849 but has not been in continuous use since then.

MAJOR EVENTS

June
The major two day flat meeting of the year includes the 1½ mile Cumberland Plate and the 1 mile Carlisle Bell.

☆ CALENDAR OF EVENTS ☆

January	14	Monday
February	5	Tuesday
March	8	Friday
	30	Saturday
April	1	Monday
	26	Friday
May	9	Thursday
	10	Friday
	30	Thursday
June	8	Saturday*
	26	Wednesday
	27	Thursday
July	26	Friday
September	10	Tuesday
	28	Saturday
	30	Monday
October	11	Friday
November	11	Monday
	28	Thursday
December	30	Monday

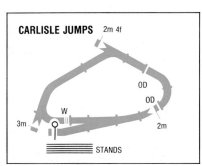

CARLISLE JUMPS 2m 4f

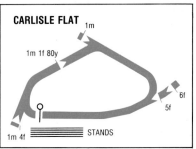

CARLISLE FLAT 1m

GETTING THERE/GETTING IN

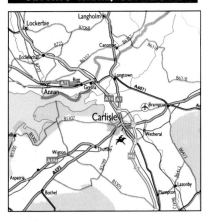

Rail: Carlisle B.R. station, 2 miles from the course
Road: 1½ miles from the M6, jct 42, signposted
P ☒ 1000 car spaces; 40 coach spaces

Enclosures

Club Enclosure: members only; viewing; betting facilities; Lucius bar and restaurant.
Tattersalls Enclosure: viewing; betting facilities; Red Rum, Lowther and Tattersalls Bars; Old Tote Restaurant and self service cafeteria.

Costs
Annual membership

Adult	☐	£50
Couple	☐	£75

May be increased in 1991

Day tickets
Club Enclosure

Saturdays and Bank Holidays	☐	£10
All other days	☐	£8

Tattersalls Enclosure

Premium meetings	☐	£5
All other meetings	☐	£4

Methods of payment: cash only

CARTMEL

THE COURSE

Cartmel Racecourse
Near Grange-over-Sands
Cumbria
☎ 044854 340

Cartmel, founded in 1880, is a left-handed,
1 mile, oval course. It stages 5 national
hunt race days over just two meetings held
around the May/Whitsun Bank Holiday and
the August Bank Holiday each year.

MAJOR EVENTS

May
Racing takes place on the Saturday, Bank
Holiday Monday and the following
Wednesday of the Bank Holiday weekend –
a three day meeting that offers a five day
break in the Lake District.

August
Racing on the Saturday and the Bank
Holiday Monday gives the option for a long
Lakeland weekend.

☀ CALENDAR OF EVENTS ☀

May	25	Saturday
	27	Monday
	29	Wednesday
August	24	Saturday
	26	Monday

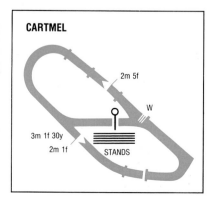

CARTMEL

2m 5f

W

3m 1f 30y
2m 1f

STANDS

GETTING THERE/GETTING IN

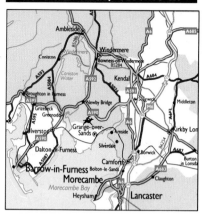

Rail: Cark B.R. station, 2 miles from the
course
Road: Off the B5278, 2 miles to the west of
Grange-over-Sands
P Ample car space
Paddock 🎟 £5
Course 🎟
Ample coach space 🎟 £3

Enclosures

Members Enclosure: restricted to annual
members and their guests only.
Paddock Enclosure: viewing; betting
facilities; bars and snack bars.
Course Enclosure: betting facilities; bars
and snack bars.
Funfair and Sideshows: at all race days.

Costs

Annual membership
Couples 🎟 £42

Day tickets
Paddock Enclosure 🎟 £7
OAPs 🎟 £4
Under 14s 🎟

Course Enclosure 🎟 £3
OAPs 🎟 £1.50
Under 14s 🎟
Methods of payment: cash only

17

CATTERICK

THE COURSE

The Racecourse
Catterick
Richmond
North Yorkshire
☎ 0748 811478

Catterick, founded in 1867, is a left-handed, 1 mile, oval course that stages 14 flat and 12 national hunt race days each year including a popular New Year's Eve/New Year's Day Meeting.

MAJOR EVENTS

Catterick hosts race meetings throughout the year.

December/January
A popular New Years two day national hunt meeting is staged.

✯ CALENDAR OF EVENTS ✯

January	1	*Tuesday*
	18	*Friday*
	19	*Saturday*
February	9	*Saturday*
	20	*Wednesday*
March	6	*Wednesday*
	27	Wednesday
April	24	Wednesday
May	23	Thursday
June	7	Friday
	8	Saturday
July	3	Wednesday
	4	Thursday
	17	Wednesday
	18	Thursday
	31	Wednesday
August	13	Tuesday*
September	21	Saturday
October	18	Friday
	19	Saturday
	26	*Saturday*
November	16	*Saturday*
	25	*Monday*
December	4	*Wednesday*
	13	*Friday*
	31	*Tuesday*

CATTERICK BRIDGE JUMPS

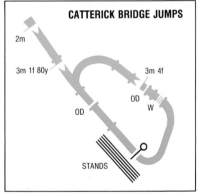

2m
3m 1f 80y
3m 4f
OD
OD
W
STANDS

CATTERICK BRIDGE FLAT

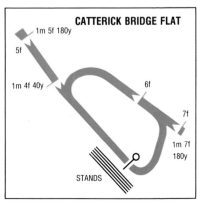

1m 5f 180y
5f
1m 4f 40y
6f
7f
1m 7f 180y
STANDS

CATTERICK

GETTING THERE/GETTING IN

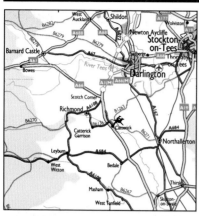

Rail: Darlington B.R. station, 14 miles from the course
Road: Off the A6136 between Catterick and Catterick Bridge
P Ample space for cars 🛈 £1.50
Ample space for coaches 🚌

Enclosures

Members Enclosure: viewing; betting facilities; bar and dining room.
Tattersalls Enclosure: viewing; betting facilities; bar and snack bars.
Course Enclosure: betting facilities; bar and snacks.

Costs

Annual membership
Adult	🛈	£50
Couple	🛈	£85
Junior (16–21)	🛈	£25

Day tickets
Members Enclosure	🛈	£8
Tattersalls Enclosure	🛈	£5
Course Enclosure	🛈	£2

Methods of payment: cash only

CHELTENHAM

THE COURSE

Prestbury Park
Cheltenham
Gloucestershire
☎ 0242 513014

Cheltenham racecourse is a left-handed, 1 mile 3 furlong oval course which hosts 16 national hunt race days each year including the important three day Cheltenham National Hunt Festival. Founded in 1831, its present course at Prestbury Park dates from 1902 and was rebuilt in 1966.

✯ CALENDAR OF EVENTS ✯

January	1	Tuesday
	26	Saturday
March	12	Tuesday
	13	Wednesday
	14	Thursday
April	17	Wednesday
	18	Thursday
May	1	Wednesday*
October	2	Wednesday
	3	Thursday
	16	Wednesday
November	8	Friday
	9	Saturday
December	6	Friday
	7	Saturday
	31	Tuesday

MAJOR EVENTS

Cheltenham's most important event is the Cheltenham National Hunt Festival, its three most important races being the Champion Hurdle, the Queen Mother Champion Chase and the Tote Cheltenham Gold Cup.

January
The Arlington Premier Series Chase Final is held in late January.

March
The Cheltenham National Hunt Festival, 18 races worth nearly £1 million in prize money run over three days in March each year. The Tote Cheltenham Gold Cup, a 3 mile 2 furlong race for 5 year olds and upwards was first run in 1924 and is one of the most prestigious races in the country.

April
The Steel Plate & Sections Young Chasers Final is held in mid April.

November
The Mackeson Gold Cup is held in early November.

December
The BMW Series Final and the A F Budge Gold Cup are both run in early December.

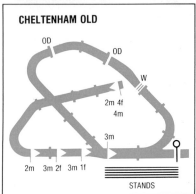

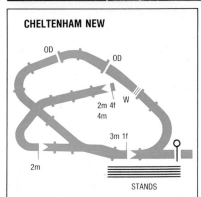

CHELTENHAM OLD

OD
OD
W
2m 4f
4m
3m
2m   3m 2f   3m 1f
STANDS

CHELTENHAM NEW

OD
OD
W
2m 4f
4m
3m 1f
2m
STANDS

CHELTENHAM

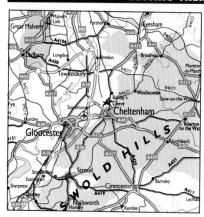

Rail: Cheltenham Spa B.R. station, 4 miles from the course
Road: A435, 1 mile north of Cheltenham
P 14,000 car spaces 🏍
Cheltenham National Hunt Festival
All cars 🎫 £5
350 coach spaces 🏍

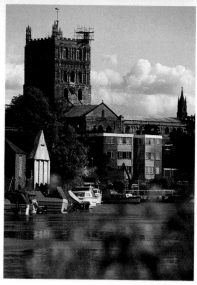

Enclosures

Club Enclosure: access to Paddock and refreshment areas, the Lawn and Grandstand; full betting facilities including Tote, bookmakers and betting shop; bars and buffets in enclosure.
Tattersalls Enclosure: viewing either side of Club Enclosure and access to Paddock; full betting facilities; bars and refreshments in enclosure.
Fosters Enclosure: National Hunt Festival only; viewing opposite main Grandstand; full betting facilities and bars. Large screen TV, food hall and bars at National Hunt Festival.
Restaurants: Gold Cup Restaurant, carvery-style, booking suggested, telephone reservations.
☎ 0242 523203
Mandarin Restaurant: hot meals 🎫 £5–£7.

Note: Cheltenham National Hunt Festival; 3 days in March each year climaxing in the Gold Cup; advance booking for Club and Tattersalls essential to be made: in person at the course or the Jockey Club; by post to the course; by telephone to 0242 226226 (credit card booking only)

Costs

Annual membership
Full membership:
Enrolment fee 🎫 £70
Season fee 🎫 £110
Senior membership:
Enrolment fee 🎫 £10
Season fee 🎫 £25
Junior membership:
Under 25s season fee 🎫 £55

Day tickets
Club Enclosure 🎫 £9–£15
Junior badge (16–24) 🎫 £5–£8

Tattersalls Enclosure 🎫 £6–£8

Fosters Enclosure 🎫 £3–£5
Under 16s 🏍
Note: full rates apply during National Hunt Festival.

National Hunt Festival:
Club Enclosure
Daily 🎫 £30
Three-day badge 🎫 £80
Note: no discount for Junior badges.

Tattersalls Enclosure
Daily 🎫 £15

Fosters Enclosure
Daily 🎫 £5

Festival Grandstand Seats
Daily 🎫 £15 extra
Gold Cup Day 🎫 £20 extra

Methods of payment: cash/cheque with valid bankers card/Visa/Access/Mastercard

CHEPSTOW

THE COURSE

Chepstow Racecourse
Piercefield Park
Chepstow
Gwent
☎ 0291 622260

Chepstow is one of the two racecourses remaining in Wales. It is a left-handed, 2 mile oval course that hosts 12 national hunt and 11 flat race days each year. Founded in 1880 and best known as a national hunt course, flat racing was introduced in 1926.

✿ CALENDAR OF EVENTS ✿

Jan	8	Tu	Oct	5	Sa
	22	Tu		15	Tu
Feb	2	Sa		22	Tu
	16	Sa	Nov	2	Sa
Mar	9	Sa		30	Sa
	16	Sa	Dec	21	Sa
Apr	1	M			
	2	Tu			
May	7	Tu			
	27	M			
June	13	Th*			
	29	Sa			
July	2	Tu			
	11	Th			
	18	Th			
Aug	26	M			
Sept	14	Sa			

MAJOR EVENTS

The Coral Welsh National is the most famous race held at Chepstow; other important races include the Aynsley China Chase, the Crown Paints Hurdle, the Welsh Champion Hurdle and the Welsh Derby.

February
The Aynsley China Chase.

March/April
The Crown Paints Hurdle is held in early March and the Welsh Champion Hurdle on Easter Monday.

July
The Welsh Derby.

December
The Coral Welsh National, a 3 mile 6 furlong race, is the successor to the Welsh Grand National first run in 1895; this race is held just before Christmas each year.

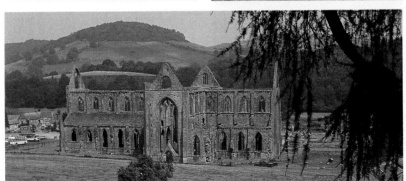

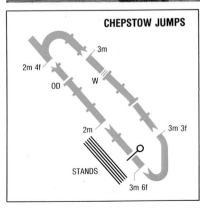

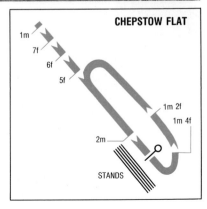

CHEPSTOW

GETTING THERE/GETTING IN

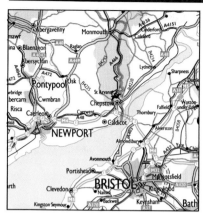

Rail: Chepstow B.R. station, 1½ miles from the course

Road: Off the A466 Chepstow to Monmouth road, 1 mile from the centre of Chepstow

P Ample space for cars 🎟 £2
Coaches 🎟

Enclosures

Club Enclosure: viewing; betting facilities including Tote and betting shop; bars and a restaurant.

Tattersalls Enclosure: viewing; betting facilities; bars; restaurant and snack food.

Silver Ring Enclosure: betting facilities; bar and snack food.

Centre Course: a car park with picnic facilities is open during the summer months in the centre of the course.

Costs

Annual membership
Adult   🎟 £66

Day tickets
Club Enclosure   🎟 £8

Tattersalls Enclosure   🎟 £5

Silver Ring Enclosure   🎟 £3

Centre Course
Summer only   🎟 £3
P included

Methods of payment: cash/cheque with valid bankers card

23

CHESTER

THE COURSE

The Racecourse
Chester
Cheshire
☎ 0244 323170

The Roodee course at Chester, founded in 1540, is the oldest surviving racecourse in the country. A left-handed, plate shaped, 1 mile course; it hosts 10 flat racing days each year.

MAJOR EVENTS

The three most important races held at Chester, the Ladbroke Chester Cup, the Dalham Chester Vase and the Ormonde EBF Stakes are all run during the Chester Cup Meeting.

May
The three day Chester Cup Meeting during which the Ladbroke Chester Cup, first run in 1824, a 2 mile 2 furlong 97 yard handicap for 4 year olds and over; the Dalham Chester Vase, first run in 1907, a 1 mile 4 furlong and 65 yard race for 3 year olds, an important Derby trial run 29 days before the Derby; and the Ormonde EBF Stakes are all staged.

⚞ CALENDAR OF EVENTS ⚟

May	7	Tuesday
	8	Wednesday
	9	Thursday
June	26	Wednesday*
July	12	Friday*
	13	Saturday
August	30	Friday
	31	Saturday
October	22	Tuesday
	23	Wednesday

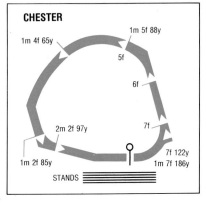

CHESTER

1m 5f 88y
1m 4f 65y
5f
6f
2m 2f 97y
7f
7f 122y
1m 2f 85y
1m 7f 186y
STANDS

GETTING THERE/GETTING IN

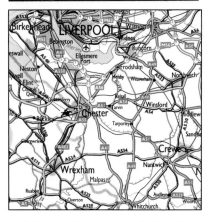

Rail: Chester B.R. station, 1 mile from the course
Road: South-east of Chester city centre, signposted from the M56, jct 14
P Ample space for cars ⌂ £1
Three day pass ⌂ £2.50
Coaches ⌂ £2.50

Enclosures

County Enclosure: viewing; betting facilities including Tote and betting shops; bank; bars and restaurant.
Tattersalls Enclosure: viewing; betting facilities including betting shops; bars; restaurant and snack bar.
Dee Stands: betting facilities; bars and snack bars.

Costs

Annual membership		
Adult	⌂	£60

Day tickets		
County Enclosure		
Chester Cup day	⌂	£15
Other race days	⌂	£12
Three day badge	⌂	£30
Tattersalls Enclosure		
Chester Cup day	⌂	£8
Other race days	⌂	£7
Dee Stands		
Chester Cup day	⌂	£3
Other race days	⌂	£2
Open Course	⌂	£1

Methods of payment: cash/cheque with valid bankers card

DEVON AND EXETER

THE COURSE

The Racecourse
Kennford
Exeter
☎ 0392 832599

There is evidence of racing at the Devon and Exeter course from 1840 onwards, the present course dating from 1898. A right-handed, oval, 2 mile course, it hosts 15 national hunt race days each year.

MAJOR EVENTS

The most important race is the Plymouth Gin Haldon Gold Challenge Cup.

January
The New Year's Day meeting, another very popular meeting, is held.

August
A popular early August Meeting is held.

October
The Plymouth Gin Haldon Gold Challenge Meeting is run.

✯ CALENDAR OF EVENTS ✯

January	1	Tuesday
March	21	Thursday
April	5	Friday
May	6	Monday
	27	Monday
August	7	Wednesday
	8	Thursday
	13	Tuesday
	23	Friday
September	11	Wednesday
	18	Wednesday
October	1	Tuesday
	25	Friday
November	5	Tuesday
December	6	Friday

GETTING THERE/GETTING IN

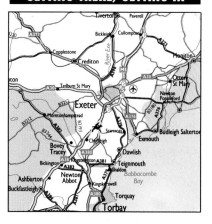

Rail: St Davids B.R. station, Exeter, 10 miles from the course
Road: 5 miles from the end of the M5 on the A38 Plymouth to Exeter road
P Ample space for cars
On the rails 🎫 £1
Members car park 🎫 £1
Exeter car park 🎫 £1
Coaches 🚌

Enclosures

Paddock/Grandstand Enclosure: open to both members and Tattersalls; viewing; betting facilities; two bars and one restaurant.
Course Enclosure: betting facilities, one bar and numerous snack bars.

Costs

Annual membership
Adult 🎫 £55
Couple 🎫 £80

Day tickets
Paddock Enclosure 🎫 £7.50

Course Enclosure 🎫 £3
Under 16s accompanied 🚌

Methods of payment: cash/cheque with valid bankers card

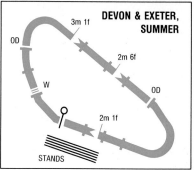

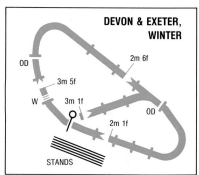

DONCASTER

THE COURSE

Doncaster Racecourse
Leger Way
Doncaster
South Yorkshire
☎ 0302 320066/67/68

Doncaster racecourse was founded in 1778 on the Town Moor site which was vested to Doncaster corporation by Henry VIII. A left-handed, pear-shaped, 2 mile course, it hosts 19 flat and 7 national hunt race days each year.

☈ CALENDAR OF EVENTS ☈

January	25	*Friday*
	26	*Saturday*
February	*23*	*Saturday*
	25	*Monday*
March	*9*	*Saturday*
	21	Thursday
	22	Friday
	23	Saturday
May	6	Monday
	25	Saturday
	27	Monday
June	14	Friday*
	28	Friday
	29	Saturday*
July	24	Wednesday
	25	Thursday*
September	11	Wednesday
	12	Thursday
	13	Friday
	14	Saturday
October	25	Friday
	26	Saturday
November	8	Friday
	9	Saturday
December	*6*	*Friday*
	7	*Saturday*

MAJOR EVENTS

Doncaster is best known for its flat racing and the most important flat races of its season are the Lincoln Handicap, the William Hill November Handicap, the St. Leger Stakes and the Doncaster Cup.

March
The first race of the flat season is the Lincoln Handicap; first run in 1853, it is a 1 mile race for 4 year olds and over.

September
The oldest and last Classic of the flat season is the St. Leger Stakes; first run in 1776, it is a 1 mile 6 furlong 127 yard race for 3 year old colts and fillies. The oldest race still run annually under the Rules of Racing is the Doncaster Cup, a 2½ mile race first run in 1766, it is still run during the St. Leger Festival Meeting.

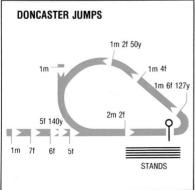

DONCASTER JUMPS

1m 2f 50y
1m
1m 4f
1m 6f 127y
5f 140y
2m 2f
1m 7f 6f 5t
STANDS

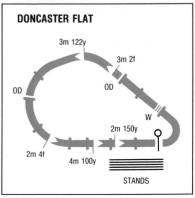

DONCASTER FLAT

3m 122y
3m 2f
OD
OD
W
2m 150y
2m 4f
4m 100y
STANDS

26

DONCASTER

Rail: Doncaster B.R. station, 1 mile from the course
Road: M18 spur to the A630 Doncaster to Bawtry road
P 🅿 3000 car spaces
Ample spaces for coaches

Enclosures

Members Enclosure: viewing; betting facilities; bars; Lonsdale Rooms; Nijinsky Rooms (Members Club only); restaurant (Grandstand); banking facilities (St. Leger Festival Meeting only).
Tattersalls Enclosure: viewing; betting facilities; bars; restaurant and snack bars.
Second Enclosure: betting facilities; bars and snack bars.
Tented Village: St. Leger Festival Meeting only.

Costs

Annual membership

Adult	🎫	£130
Couple	🎫	£150

Day tickets

Members Enclosure	🎫	£12–£22
Tattersalls Enclosure	🎫	£6–£11
Second Enclosure	🎫	£2–£5

Note: ticket prices vary according to the meeting.

Methods of payment: cash/cheque with valid bankers card/Visa/Access/American Express

DOWNPATRICK

THE COURSE

Downpatrick Racecourse
Ballydugan Road
Downpatrick
County Down
Northern Ireland
☎ 0396 612054

Downpatrick, a right-handed, 1 mile 3 furlong course, was founded in 1685; it hosts 8 race days each year.

MAJOR EVENTS

The most important races run at Downpatrick are the Ulster Harp National and the SP Graham Memorial INH Flat Race.

February
The Ulster National Meeting during which the Ulster Harp National is run.

March
The SP Graham Memorial INH Flat Race.

✵ CALENDAR OF EVENTS ✵

February	21	Wednesday
March	28	Wednesday
May	11	Friday
	12	Saturday
August	27	Monday
September	29	Saturday
November	14	Wednesday

All dates are mixed race days and refer to 1990 as the new calendar is not yet available.

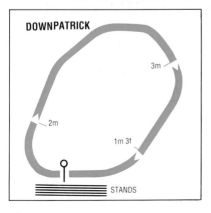

GETTING THERE/GETTING IN

Rail: Belfast N.R. station, 23 miles from the course
Road: Off the A25 Belfast to Downpatrick road
P ⛟ Ample space for cars and coaches

Enclosures

Unrestricted access to the Grandstand, and Parade Ring; betting facilities including Tote; 2 bars, the Supporters and Bottom bars and a snack bar.

Costs
Annual membership
Adult   🎟 £45

Day tickets
Special days   🎟 £5

All other days   🎟 £4
Methods of payment: cash only

DOWN ROYAL

THE COURSE

The Maze
Lisburn
County Antrim
Northern Ireland
☎ 0846 621256

The 'Down Royal Corporation of Horse-breeders', controllers of the racecourse, were founded by Royal Charter from James II in 1685. The present course, a right-handed, rectangular course, was founded in 1790, and hosts 11 race days each year.

MAJOR EVENTS

March
A major race day is held on March 17th.

July
The Ulster Harp Derby Day held on July 13th is the most important event in the Down Royal season.

December
A major meeting is held on Boxing Day.

✵ CALENDAR OF EVENTS ✵

February	7	Wednesday
March	17	Saturday
April	7	Saturday
May	7	Monday
	28	Monday
July	13	Friday
	14	Saturday
September	22	Saturday
October	13	Saturday
November	3	Saturday
December	26	Wednesday

All dates are mixed race days and refer to 1990 as the new calendar is not yet available.

GETTING THERE/GETTING IN

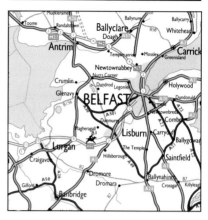

Rail: Lisburn N.R. station, 5 miles from the course
Road: Off the A1 at Sprucefield roundabout
P ⛽ 1500 car spaces, 20 coach spaces

Enclosures

Unrestricted access to 2 Grandstands, the Parade Ring and Winner's Enclosure; betting facilities including Tote; 5 bars and a snack bar.

Costs

Annual membership
Adult	🎫	£45

Day tickets
Ulster Harp Derby Day	🎫	£5
Boxing Day Meeting	🎫	£5
All other race days	🎫	£4

Methods of payment: cash only

DOWN ROYAL

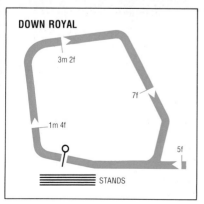

3m 2f
7f
1m 4f
5f
STANDS

29

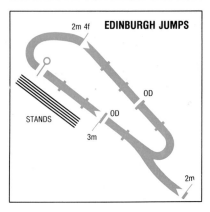

EDINBURGH MUSSELBURGH

THE COURSE

Musselburgh Racecourse
Linkfield Road
Musselburgh
Lothian
☎ 031 665 2859

Edinburgh Musselburgh opened a new national hunt course alongside its existing flat racecourse in 1987; a 1¼ mile, oval course, it hosts 12 flat and 8 national hunt race days each year.

MAJOR EVENTS

December–February
Musselburgh hosts national hunt racing over the winter months.

April–October
One day flat race meetings are held throughout the summer with two evening meetings in June and August.

✷ CALENDAR OF EVENTS ✷

January	4	*Friday*
	11	*Friday*
	31	*Thursday*
February	15	*Friday*
	23	*Saturday*
April	15	Monday
May	13	**Monday**
June	1	Saturday
	3	Monday*
	17	Monday
	24	Monday
July	1	Monday
	8	Monday
August	2	Friday*
September	16	Monday
October	23	Wednesday
November	7	Thursday
December	9	*Monday*
	14	*Saturday*
	21	*Saturday*

GETTING THERE/GETTING IN

Rail: Edinburgh Waverley B.R. station, 6 miles from the course
Road: Off the A199, 6 miles east of Edinburgh in the seaside town of Musselburgh
P 🚲 Ample space for cars and coaches

Enclosures

Club Enclosure: viewing; betting facilities; bars; restaurant and snack bars.
Paddock Enclosure: viewing; betting facilities including betting shop; bars and snack bars.

Costs

Annual membership

Adult	🎟	£55
Couple	🎟	£100

Day tickets

Club Enclosure	🎟	£8
Paddock Enclosure	🎟	£4
OAPs and unemployed	🎟	£2

Methods of payment: cash only

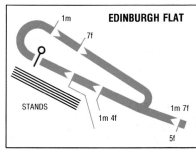

EPSOM

Racecourse Paddock
Epsom
Surrey
☎ 0372 726311

Epsom Downs has been the venue for horse racing since the 1640s. A 1½ mile, left-handed, horseshoe course. it is one of the best known racecourses in the world, it hosts only 6 flat race days each year, a two day meeting in April and a four day meeting in June yet stages two of the English Classics, the Derby and the Oaks. The Derby Week meeting in June provides a highlight in the flat season calendar, the Downs become transformed with funfairs and festivities and Derby Day sees the crowds arrive, everyone from horse racing experts to parties of office staff in open-topped coaches out the enjoy a day at the races.

☆ CALENDAR OF EVENTS ☆

June		
	5	Wednesday
	6	Thursday
	7	Friday
	8	Saturday

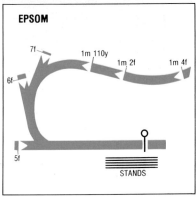

MAJOR EVENTS

The two classics, the Derby and the Oaks are the two most celebrated races run at Epsom during Derby week; the highlights of the April meeting are the Princess Elizabeth Stakes and the Racal Vodafone Blue Riband Trial.

April
A two day meeting during which the Princess Elizabeth Stakes and the Racal Vodafone Blue Riband Trial are run.

Note: there will be no April meeting in 1991.

June
The four day Derby week meeting runs from Wednesday to Saturday. The Ever Ready Derby Stakes, run on the first day of Derby week, is a 1½ mile race for 3 year old colts; fillies may also run but rarely do so, the last Derby won by a filly was in 1900.

First run in 1780, it is regarded as one of the world's greatest tests of a horse's combined speed and stamina, it was described by the Victorian prime minister, Disraeli, as 'the blue riband of the turf', an epithet still applicable today. The Coronation Cup is run on Thursday and International Day is held on Friday whilst the second classic, the Gold Seal Oaks is held on Saturday. A 1½ mile race restricted to 3 year old fillies, it was first run in 1779 and is the second oldest classic in the country, Doncaster's St. Leger being the oldest.

EPSOM

GETTING THERE/GETTING IN

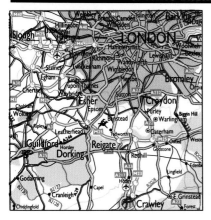

Rail: Tattenham Corner B.R. station from London Charing Cross, ½ mile from the course
Road: Off the B290, leave the M25 at jct 9, take the A24 towards London, the B290 is a right hand turn
P ☎ 0372 726311 for details and prices

Enclosures

Club Enclosure: excellent facilities including viewing, betting, banking, bars and restaurants.
Note: on Ever Ready Derby Day admission to this enclosure is restricted to annual members and their guests only (maximum two); morning dress must be worn.
Grandstand Enclosure: viewing; betting facilities; bars; restaurants and snack bars.
Note: on Ever Ready Derby Day admission to the Paddock and the Grandstand Anglesey Seating from this enclosure are both subject to supplementary charges.
Lonsdale Enclosure: inside the course opposite the Grandstand; full facilities including viewing from the winning post.
Tattenham Enclosure: Derby Week only – enclosure running from Grandstand towards Tattenham Corner; betting facilities; bars and snack bars.
Walton Enclosure: Derby Week only – inside course opposite Tattenham Enclosure; betting facilities; bars and snack bars.
Note: transfer between any of the enclosures is impossible.

Costs

Annual membership

Adult	🎟	£70
Members car park label	🎟	£10
Junior member (16–25)	🎟	£35

Day tickets

Enclosure	Derby Day	Oaks Day	All other days
Club	£40*	£20	£12
Grandstand	£16	£12	£8
Paddock entry	£4		
Anglesey seats	£35		
Lonsdale	£9	£6	£4
Tattenham and Walton	£5	£4	£3
Paddock only	£9	£6	£4

*Annual members guests only
Accompanied children under 16 🎟 except to Club Enclosure on Ever Ready Derby Day
Methods of payment: cash/cheque with valid bankers card

33

FAKENHAM

THE COURSE

The Racecourse
Fakenham
Norfolk
☎ 0328 862388

Fakenham racecourse was founded in 1883
at East Winch and moved to Fakenham in
1905. It is a left-handed, 1 mile, square
course that hosts 6 national hunt race days
each year. A traditional rural jumps course
it combines a relaxed family atmosphere
with competitive racing.

MAJOR EVENTS

The most important races run at Fakenham
are the Coral Bookmakers Handicap Hurdle,
the Queen's Cup Chase and the Prince of
Wales Cup.

April
The Easter Monday Meeting hosts the Coral
Bookmakers Handicap Hurdle and the
Queens Cup Chase.

May
The Spring Bank Holiday Meeting is held
during which the Prince of Wales Cup is
run.

⚞ CALENDAR OF EVENTS ⚟

February	15	Friday
March	15	Friday
April	1	Monday
May	27	Monday
October	21	Monday
December	13	Friday

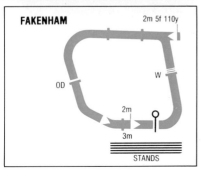

FAKENHAM

GETTING THERE/GETTING IN

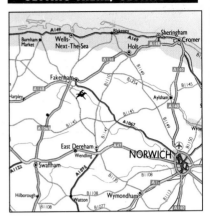

Rail: Kings Lynn B.R. station, 22 miles
from the course
Norwich B.R. station, 25 miles from the
course
Road: Off the B1146 heading south out of
Fakenham, signposted
P 🚌 Ample space for cars and coaches
Members car park, per day 🎫 £4
Bank Holidays 🎫 £5

Enclosures

Members Enclosure: viewing; betting
facilities; bar and restaurant.
Paddock Enclosure: viewing; betting
facilities; bar and restaurant.
Course Enclosure: betting facilities; bar;
snack bar.
Picnic Area: in centre of the course.

Costs

Annual membership
| Adult | 🎫 £25 |
| Couple | 🎫 £36 |

Day tickets
| Members Enclosure | 🎫 £8 |

Paddock Enclosure
| Bank Holiday meetings | 🎫 £6 |

Course Enclosure
| Bank Holiday meetings | 🎫 £3 |

Combined Paddock and Course Badge
| All other days | 🎫 £3.50 |

Methods of payment: cash/cheque with valid
bankers card

FOLKESTONE

THE COURSE

Folkestone Racecourse
Hythe
Kent
☎ 0303 66407

Folkestone racecourse, the only racecourse
in Kent, was officially founded in 1898 even
though there is some evidence of there
having been racing there in 1849 and 1876.
A right-handed, 1 mile 3 furlong, oval
course, it hosts 14 flat and 8 national hunt
race days each year.

MAJOR EVENTS

The three most important races run at
Folkestone are the Kent Marathon, the
Metropole Stakes and the Whitelaw Gold
Cup.

May
The United Hunts meeting, held in mid–
May, is the most popular of the national
hunt meetings.

September
The Garden of England Day meeting held in
early September, is the most popular of the
flat meetings.

☀ CALENDAR OF EVENTS ☀

January	15	Tuesday
February	13	Wednesday
	21	Thursday
March	6	Wednesday
	25	Monday
April	15	Monday
May	14	Tuesday*
	20	Monday
June	4	Tuesday
July	2	Tuesday
	16	Tuesday*
	23	Tuesday
August	14	Wednesday
	20	Tuesday
September	12	Thursday
	23	Monday
October	8	Tuesday
	21	Monday
November	11	Monday
	25	Monday
December	17	Tuesday
	28	Saturday

GETTING THERE/GETTING IN

Rail: Westenhanger B.R. station next to the
course
Road: Signposted from M20, jct 11
P 1500 car spaces 🚗
50 coach spaces 🚌
Cars with picnics 🚗 £3

Enclosures

Members Enclosure: access to Paddock and
viewing from Members Stand; full betting
facilities including Tote; restaurant and bars
in the enclosure.
Tattersalls Enclosure: access to Paddock and
viewing from new Grandstand; full betting
facilities including Tote; restaurant and bars
in the enclosure. Private boxes and rooms
available from September 1990 when the
new Glover Stand opens.
Course Enclosure: viewing from ground and
stand; bars and catering facilities available;
full betting facilities including Tote.

Costs

Annual membership
Adult	🎫	£90
Couple	🎫	£180

Day tickets
Members Enclosure	🎫	£9
Tattersalls Enclosure	🎫	£7
Course Enclosure	🎫	£2.50

Methods of payment: cash/cheque with valid
bankers card

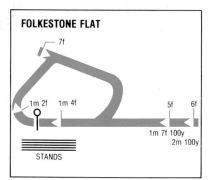

FOLKESTONE JUMPS   FOLKESTONE FLAT

35

FONTWELL PARK

THE COURSE

Fontwell Park Racecourse
Eastergate
Arundel
West Sussex
☎ 0243 543335

Fontwell Park, founded in 1924, is a 1 mile, figure of eight course. It hosts 15 national hunt race days each year.

MAJOR EVENTS

May
The two May Bank Holiday Meetings are the most popular events of Fontwell Park's calendar.

✻ CALENDAR OF EVENTS ✻

January	14	Monday
February	4	Monday
	18	Monday
March	19	Tuesday
April	16	Tuesday
May	6	Monday
	27	Monday
August	13	Tuesday*
	21	Wednesday
September	4	Wednesday
	30	Monday
October	14	Monday
	30	Wednesday
December	4	Wednesday
	30	Monday

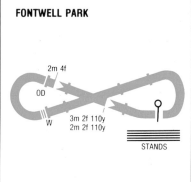

FONTWELL PARK

2m 4f
OD
3m 2f 110y
2m 2f 110y
W
STANDS

GETTING THERE/GETTING IN

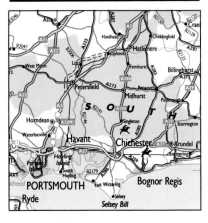

Rail: Barnham B.R. station, courtesy coach runs on race days
Road: between Chichester and Arundel at the jct of the A27 and A29
P 🅿 Ample space for cars

Enclosures

Club Enclosure: viewing; betting facilities including betting shops; Members Bar and Salmon Spray Bar; restaurant.
Tattersalls Enclosure: viewing; betting facilities; bars and snack bars.
Silver Ring Enclosure: betting facilities; bars and snack bars; picnic car park.

Costs

Annual membership
Adult	🎫	£75
Couple	🎫	£150
Annual car parking badge	🎫	£5

Day tickets
Club Enclosure	🎫	£10
Juniors (12–15)	🎫	£2
Tattersalls Enclosure	🎫	£7
Under 16s accompanied	🎫	
Silver Ring Enclosure	🎫	£3
Under 16s accompanied	🎫	
Picnic Car Park	🎫	£3 per car
plus/per person	🎫	£3

Methods of payment: cash/cheque with valid bankers card

GOODWOOD

THE COURSE

Goodwood Racecourse
Goodwood House
Chichester
West Sussex
☎ 0243 774107

Goodwood racecourse is part of the
Goodwood House estate and was created by
the third Duke of Richmond in 1801; a
right-handed, loop course, it hosts 18 flat
racing days each year. 'Glorious Goodwood'
is renowned for its summer race season,
particularly the five day Goodwood Festival
Meeting – strawberries, champagne and the
finest in horse racing blended with the
heady delights of high summer.
Goodwood hosts meetings every month
from May to October, the most important
races of the season are the Black Bottle
Whisky Prestige Stakes and the Beefeater
Gin Celebration Mile run during the August
Meeting and the William Hills Stewards
Cup, the Leslie and Godwin Stakes
Handicap, the Schweppes Golden Mile and
the Sussex Stakes held during the Festival
Meeting.

MAJOR EVENTS

May–June
Four popular evening meetings.

July–August
The Festival Meeting is held over five
days during which 31 races are run. The
most notable races are the William Hill
Stewards Cup, a 6 furlong race first run in
1840; the Leslie and Godwin Stakes
Handicap, a 1¼ mile race for 3 year olds;
the Schweppes Golden Mile and the Sussex
Stakes, a 1 mile race for 3 year olds and
upwards with a prize of £200,000 making it
the richest race of its kind in Europe.

August
The August Meeting features the Black
Bottle Whisky Prestige Stakes and the
Beefeater Gin Celebration Mile.

⚞ CALENDAR OF EVENTS ⚞

May	21	Tuesday
	22	Wednesday
	23	Thursday
	31	Friday*
June	7	Friday*
	14	Friday*
	28	Friday*
July	30	Tuesday
	31	Wednesday
August	1	Thursday
	2	Friday
	3	Saturday
	23	Friday
	24	Saturday
September	13	Friday
	14	Saturday
October	4	Friday
	5	Saturday

GETTING THERE/GETTING IN

See map for Fontwell Park on page 36.

Rail: Chichester B.R. station, 3½ miles
from the course
Road: Off the A285 Chichester to Haslemere
road, signposted
P 9000 car spaces
Long walk 🏁
Short walk 🏁 £2
July Goodwood Festival 🏁 £5
200 coach spaces 🏁

Enclosures

Richmond Enclosure: members enclosure
including access to the Paddock and Parade
Ring; full betting facilities; numerous bars
and restaurants including the Charlton
Hunt Restaurant; the Parade Ring Lawn
Restaurant and, for seafood, the Rendezvous
Restaurant.
Note: during the July Goodwood Festival
this enclosure is only available to annual
members and their guests.
Grandstand & Paddock Enclosure: viewing,
including Parade Ring; betting facilities;
bars; restaurant (July Goodwood Festival
only) and snack bars.
Public Enclosure: betting facilities; bars and
snack bars.
Other facilities: picnic car park and
childrens playground.

Costs
Annual membership
Adult	🏁	£105
Second annual badge	🏁	£95
Junior (13–21)	🏁	£55

Day tickets
Richmond Enclosure
July Goodwood Festival 🏁 £29
Annual members only plus a maximum of 4
guests per member per day
All other meetings 🏁 £12

Grandstand & Paddock Enclosure
Pre-July Festival 🏁 £6
July Goodwood Festival 🏁 £15
Post-July Festival 🏁 £8

Public Enclosure 🏁 £3

Methods of payment: on the day strictly
cash only; prior bookings: cash/cheque with
valid bankers card/Visa/Access/Mastercard

GOODWOOD

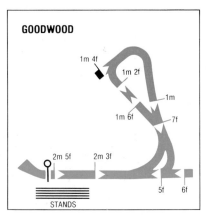

GOODWOOD

1m 4f
1m 2f
1m
1m 6f
7f
2m 5f
2m 3f
5f
6f
STANDS

HAMILTON PARK

THE COURSE

Hamilton Park
Bothwell Road
Hamilton
Lanarkshire
☎ 0698 283806

Hamilton Park was a venue for racing in the 1780s but the racecourse was not founded until 1888, the present course being built in 1926. A right-handed, 6 furlong, loop course, it hosts 17 flat racing days each year. The pioneer of evening racing in the UK, it staged its first evening meeting in 1947 and now holds four evening meetings in May, June and July every year.

MAJOR EVENTS

Hamilton Park hosts flat race meetings from April to November.

June
The Saints and Sinners evening meeting, a major meeting of the year, is held in mid-June.

✦ CALENDAR OF EVENTS ✦

April	3	Wednesday
	22	Monday
May	3	Friday
	18	Saturday*
	20	Monday
	31	Friday
June	12	Wednesday*
	13	Thursday
July	11	Thursday*
	12	Friday*
	17	Wednesday
	18	Thursday
	27	Saturday
August	19	Monday
September	9	Monday
	30	Monday
November	5	Tuesday

HAMILTON PARK

1m 40y
1m 1f 10y
1m 5f 1m 4f 1m 3f
5f 6f
STANDS

GETTING THERE/GETTING IN

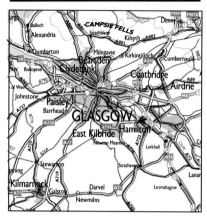

Rail: Hamilton West B.R. station, 1 mile from the course
Road: On the B7071 Hamilton to Bothwell road; access from the M74, jct 5, signposted
P 🚌 Ample space for cars and coaches

Enclosures

Club Enclosure: viewing; full betting facilities; bars; snack bar and full restaurant service in the Dining Room.

Grandstand & Paddock Enclosure: viewing; betting facilities; bar and a snack bar.

Costs

Annual membership
Adult	🎫	£70
Couple	🎫	£110

Day tickets
Club Enclosure	🎫	£10

Grandstand & Paddock Enclosure
🎫 £5

Methods of payment: cash only

HAYDOCK PARK

THE COURSE

Haydock Park
Newton-le-Willows
Lancashire
☎ 0942 725963

Haydock Park was founded in 1883; a left-handed, oval, 1 mile 5 furlong course, it hosts 1 mixed, 18 flat and 9 national hunt race days each year including evening meetings between June and August.

✦ CALENDAR OF EVENTS ✦

January	5	*Saturday*
	19	*Saturday*
March	1	*Friday*
	2	*Saturday*
	30	Saturday
May	4	Saturday
	6	Monday
	24	Friday
	25	Saturday
June	7	Friday*
	8	Saturday
July	4	Thursday*
	5	Friday
	6	Saturday
August	9	Friday*
	10	Saturday
	16	Friday*
September	6	Friday
	7	Saturday
	27	Friday
	28	Saturday
October	9	Wednesday
	10	Thursday
November	13	*Wednesday*
	20	*Wednesday*
	21	*Thursday*
December	11	*Wednesday*
	12	*Thursday*

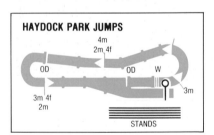

HAYDOCK PARK JUMPS

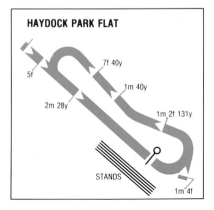

HAYDOCK PARK FLAT

MAJOR EVENTS

Haydock Park's two most important races are the Lancashire Oaks and the Ladbroke Sprint Cup.

January
The Peter Marsh Chase is run in late January.

March
The Greenall Whitley Gold Cup is run in early March.

May
The Swinton Insurance Hurdle is run on the May Bank Holiday.

July
The Lancashire Oaks, run in early July and first run in 1939, is a 1½ mile race for 3 year old fillies. The Old Newton Cup is run at the same meeting.

September
The Ladbroke Sprint Cup, first run in 1966 and a Group 1 race run over 6 furlongs for 3 year olds and over, has one of the highest sprint prizes in Europe.

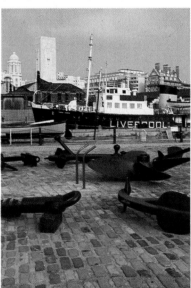

HAYDOCK PARK

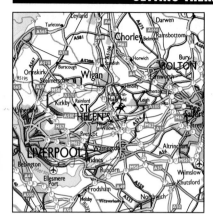

Rail: Warrington Bank Quay B.R. station or Wigan B.R. station, both approximately 5 miles from the course

Road: On the A49 between the M6, jct 23, and Ashton-in-Makerfield

P ⚿ 3000 car spaces; 1000 coach spaces

Enclosures

County Enclosure: access to Paddock and Parade Ring, Tommy Whittle Stand, and for a supplementary charge, the Park Suite on the top floor of the Makerfield Grandstand; full betting facilities including Tote, bookmakers and betting shop; bars in the enclosure; Lancaster Restaurant and the Park Suite Dining Room.

Tattersalls Enclosure: viewing from the Makerfield and Tattersalls Grandstands and terraces; betting facilities; buffet bars and bars in the enclosure and Punters fast food restaurant.

Newton Enclosure (Silver Ring): viewing from the terraces; betting facilities; bar and cafeteria in the enclosure.

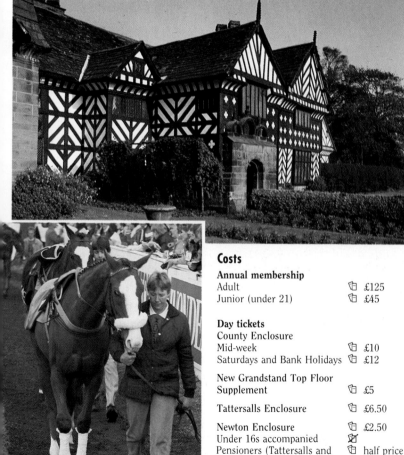

Costs

Annual membership

Adult	🎫	£125
Junior (under 21)	🎫	£45

Day tickets
County Enclosure

Mid-week	🎫	£10
Saturdays and Bank Holidays	🎫	£12

New Grandstand Top Floor Supplement	🎫	£5
Tattersalls Enclosure	🎫	£6.50
Newton Enclosure	🎫	£2.50
Under 16s accompanied	🎫	
Pensioners (Tattersalls and Newton only)	🎫	half price

Methods of payment: cash/cheque with valid bankers card

41

HEREFORD

THE COURSE

The Racecourse
Roman Road
Hereford
☎ 0432 273560

Hereford, a right-handed, 1½ mile course
founded in 1842 hosts 15 national hunt
race days each year. Hereford racecourse is
the only racecourse in the country to hold a
'rival' national hunt meeting on Grand
National Day.

MAJOR EVENTS

April/May
Two popular meetings are held on Easter
Monday and the Whitsun Bank Holiday.

✾ CALENDAR OF EVENTS ✾

February	11	Monday
March	2	Saturday
April	1	Monday
	6	Saturday
May	4	Saturday
	15	Wednesday
	27	Monday
August	24	Saturday
	31	Saturday
September	27	Friday
October	25	Friday
November	5	Tuesday
	27	Wednesday
December	13	Friday
	20	Friday

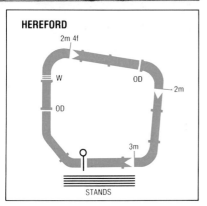

HEREFORD

GETTING THERE/GETTING IN

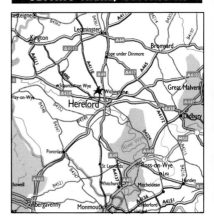

Rail: Hereford B.R. station, 1 mile from the
course
Road: On the northern outskirts of
Hereford, ½ mile west of the A49,
signposted
P 🚲 3000 car spaces; 100 coach spaces

Enclosures

Club Enclosure: access to Paddock and
Parade Ring; complete view of the
racecourse; betting facilities including Tote;
A La Carte restaurant plus well stocked
bars.
Tattersalls Enclosure: complete view of the
racecourse; betting facilities including
betting shop; bar and a snack bar.
Course Enclosure: betting facilities; bar and
snack bar.
Other facilities: 9-hole golf course in the
middle of the racecourse.

Costs

Day tickets

Club Enclosure	🎫	£9
Tattersalls Enclosure	🎫	£6
Course Enclosure	🎫	£3

Methods of payment: cash only

Note: there is no annual membership

HEXHAM

THE COURSE

The Racecourse
High Yarridge
Hexham
Northumberland
☎ 0434 603738

A left-handed, 1½ mile, conical course; it was founded in 1869 and hosts 14 national hunt race days each year.

MAJOR EVENTS

The most popular race held at Hexam is the Heart of all England Hunters Steeplechase.
May
The Spring Bank Holiday Meeting hosts the Heart of All England Hunters Steeplechase.

✶ CALENDAR OF EVENTS ✶

March	14	*Thursday*
	23	*Saturday*
	25	*Monday*
	27	*Saturday*
	29	*Monday**
May	4	*Saturday**
	25	*Saturday*
	27	*Monday**
September	2	*Monday*
October	4	*Friday*
	17	*Thursday*
November	8	*Friday*
	27	*Wednesday*
December	20	*Friday*

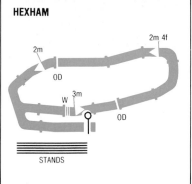

HEXHAM

GETTING THERE/GETTING IN

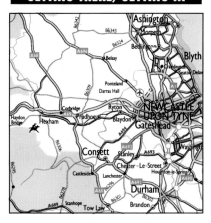

Rail: Hexham B.R. station, 1½ miles from the course
Road: 1½ miles south of Hexham off the B6306, signposted from the A69 Newcastle to Carlisle road
P 🏁 2000 car spaces; 25 coach spaces

Enclosures

Club Enclosure: viewing; betting facilities; bar serving hot snacks and a Wine and Seafood Bar.
Tattersalls Enclosure: vewing; betting facilities; bar and snack bar.

Costs

Annual membership
| Adult | 🎫 | £45 |
| Couple | 🎫 | £70 |

Day tickets
Club Enclosure	🎫	£8
Tattersalls Enclosure	🎫	£5
OAPs	🎫	£3

Methods of payment: cash only

HUNTINGDON

THE COURSE

The Racecourse
Brampton
Huntingdon
Cambridgeshire
☎ 0480 453373

A right-handed, 1½ mile, oval track; it was founded in 1886 and hosts 15 national hunt race days each year.

MAJOR EVENTS

The most important races run at Huntingdon are the Peterborough Chase; the Coral Hurdle and the Sidney Banks Memorial Hurdle.

April
The Easter Monday Meeting is a very popular event in Huntingdon's calendar.

May
Two evening meetings are held in May.

December
The Boxing Day meeting is another popular meeting.

☆ CALENDAR OF EVENTS ☆

January	24	Thursday
February	7	Thursday
	20	Wednesday
April	1	Monday
	15	Monday
May	9	Thursday*
	16	Thursday*
	27	Monday
August	26	Monday
September	20	Friday
October	26	Saturday
November	15	Friday
	26	Tuesday
December	4	Wednesday
	26	Thursday

HUNTINGDON

GETTING THERE/GETTING IN

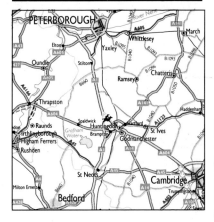

Rail: Huntingdon B.R. station, 2 miles from the course
Road: Off the A604 Cambridge to Kettering road, 1 mile before the A604/A1 jct
P ⛽ Ample space for cars and coaches
Cars to picnic on rails 🎫 £1

Enclosures
Members Enclosure: viewing; full betting facilities; bar; snack bars and Members Dining Room.
Tattersalls Enclosure: viewing; betting facilities; bars; restaurant and snack bars.
Course: betting facilities; bar and snack bars.

Costs
Annual membership
Adult	🎫	£50
Couple	🎫	£85

Day tickets
Members Enclosure	🎫	£8
Tattersalls Enclosure	🎫	£6
Course	🎫	£3
Picnic cars	🎫	£1

Methods of payment: cash/cheque with valid bankers card

Desert Orchid

KEMPTON PARK

THE COURSE

Kempton Park
Sunbury on Thames
Middlesex
☎ 0932 782292

A right-handed, 1 mile 5 furlong, triangular course; it was founded in 1878 and hosts 16 flat and 9 national hunt race days each year. A Gala Evening held at the end of June includes a spectacular firework display and musical programme.

✯ CALENDAR OF EVENTS ✯

January	18	*Friday*
	19	*Saturday*
February	22	*Friday*
	23	*Saturday*
March	30	Saturday
April	1	Monday
	5	Friday
	23	Tuesday
	24	Wednesday
May	6	Monday
	15	Wednesday*
	25	Saturday
June	12	Wednesday*
	26	Wednesday*
July	10	Wednesday*
	11	Thursday
August	7	Wednesday*
September	6	Friday
	7	Saturday
	24	Tuesday
October	19	*Saturday*
	31	*Thursday*
November	20	*Wednesday*
December	26	*Thursday*
	27	*Friday*

MAJOR EVENTS

Kempton Park holds a spectacular two day Rank sponsored national hunt Christmas Festival where the two feature races are the King George VI Rank Chase and the Top Rank Christmas Hurdle. The two major flat races are the Jubilee Handicap at the May Spring Bank Holiday meeting and the Bonusprint September Stakes in early September. Five evening meetings are held between May and August.

These are the most important races in Kempton Park's calendar.

January
The Bic Razor Lanzarote Handicap Hurdle is run in late January.

February
The Racing Post Chase is run at the end of February.

May
The Jubilee Handicap.

June
The Racal Electronics Gala Evening is held; an evening of racing accompanied by music, fireworks, fun fairs and a barbecue.

September
The Bonusprint September Stakes is run.

October
The Charisma Gold Cup is run in late October.

December
The Rank sponsored, two day, national hunt Christmas Festival is held during which the King George VI Rank Chase is run on Boxing Day and the Top Rank Christmas Hurdle is run on December 27th.

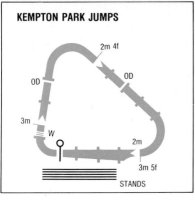

KEMPTON PARK JUMPS

2m 4f
OD
OD
3m
W
2m
3m 5f
STANDS

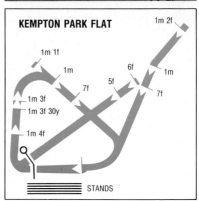

KEMPTON PARK FLAT

1m 2f
1m 1f
1m
6f
1m
7f
5f
1m 3f
7f
1m 3f 30y
1m 4f
STANDS

KEMPTON PARK

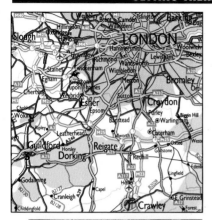

Rail: Kempton Park B.R. station, 1 minute from the course on race days only
Road: Off the A308, nr the M3, jct 1
P Main car park 1000 spaces 🅿 £2
Centre of course 🅿
Silver ring 🅿
30 coach spaces 🅿

Enclosures

Clubhouse: complete range of exclusive viewing, betting, drinking and dining facilities – reserved exclusively for annual members and their guests.
Members Enclosure: viewing terrace covering both the Parade Ring and Winners Enclosure; full betting facilities; bars; restaurants and snack bars.
Grandstand Enclosure: use of viewing terrace; betting facilities; bars; restaurant and snack bars.
Silver Ring: betting facilities; bars and snack bars.

Costs

Annual membership

Adult	🅿	£135
Junior membership (16–25)	🅿	£60

Day tickets

Clubhouse – not available, annual members and their guests only

Members Enclosure		
Boxing Day meeting	🅿	£18
Premium days	🅿	£12
All other days	🅿	£10
Junior members (16–25)	🅿	£7–£13

Grandstand Enclosure		
Boxing Day meeting	🅿	£12
Premium days	🅿	£8
All other days	🅿	£6

Silver Ring		
Boxing Day meeting	🅿	£5
All other days	🅿	£4

Methods of payment: cash/cheque with valid bankers card/Visa/Access/Mastercard

47

KELSO

THE COURSE

The Racecourse
Kelso
Roxburghshire
☎ 0573 24767

A left-handed, 1 mile 2 furlong, squarish course; it was founded in 1869 and hosts 12 national hunt race days each year. Kelso is regarded as one of the loveliest small racecourses in the UK.

MAJOR EVENTS

The most valuable race at Kelso is the Hamilton Memorial Trophy.

☚ CALENDAR OF EVENTS ☛

January	9	Wednesday
February	1	Friday
	22	Friday
March	20	Wednesday
April	8	Monday
May	1	Wednesday
October	5	Saturday
	19	Saturday
November	6	Wednesday
	20	Wednesday
December	2	Monday
	19	Thursday

GETTING THERE/GETTING IN

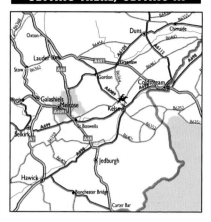

Rail: Berwick Upon Tweed B.R. station, 22 miles from the course
Road: Off the A698, just north of Kelso
P 🚗 500 car spaces; 100 coach spaces.

Enclosures

Club Enclosure: members only, viewing; full betting facilities; 3 bars and a lunch room.
Paddock Enclosure (Tattersalls): viewing; full betting facilities; large combined bar and snack bar; dining room.

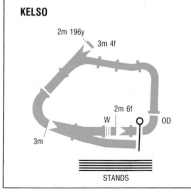

KELSO

Costs

Annual membership

Adult	🎫	£45
Couple	🎫	£80

Day tickets
Club Enclosure

Saturday meetings	🎫	£10
All other meetings	🎫	£8
Paddock Enclosure	🎫	£5
OAPs	🎫	£2.50

Methods of payment: cash/cheque with valid bankers card

LEICESTER

THE COURSE

The Racecourse
London Road
Leicester
☎ 0533 716515

A right-handed, 2 mile, rectangular course;
it was founded in 1870 and hosts 17 flat
and 11 national hunt race days each year.

MAJOR EVENTS

The most important race in Leicester's
calendar is the Leicestershire Silver Fox
Handicap Steeplechase run during
November.

☆ CALENDAR OF EVENTS ☆

Jan	1	Tu	July	8	M
	8	Tu		16	Tu*
	21	M		30	Tu*
	29	Tu	Aug	12	M*
Feb	14	Th	Sept	10	Tu
	25	M		16	M
Mar	4	M	Oct	14	M
	25	M		15	Tu
	26	Tu		28	M
Apr	27	Sa		29	Tu
May	27	M	Nov	18	M
	28	Tu		22	F
June	3	M	Dec	3	Tu
	8	Sa*		31	Tu

GETTING THERE/GETTING IN

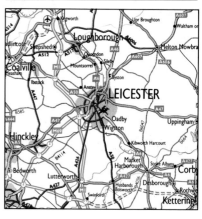

Rail: Leicester B.R. station, 2 miles from
the course
Road: Off the A6 Leicester to Market
Harborough road
P ⛺ Ample space for cars and coaches

Enclosures

Members Enclosure: viewing; betting
facilities; bars; snack bar and a lunch room.
Tattersalls Enclosure: viewing; betting
facilities; bar and snack bars.
Silver Ring: betting facilities; bar and snack
bars.

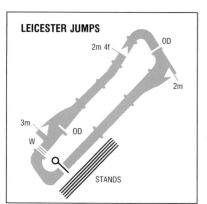

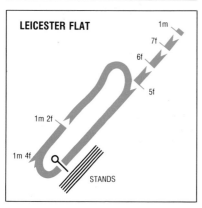

Costs

Annual membership

Adult	🎫	£90

Day tickets

Members Enclosure	🎫	£9
Tattersalls Enclosure	🎫	£6
Silver Ring	🎫	£3

Methods of payment: cash/cheque with valid
bankers card

LINGFIELD PARK

THE COURSE

Lingfield Park
Racecourse Road
Lingfield
Surrey
☎ 0342 834966

A left-handed, 10 furlong, triangular course,
it was founded in 1890. The new all weather
track (AWT) at Lingfield Park has
transformed the course and it now hosts
68 race days each year, 39 of them on the
AWT; there are 45 flat racing days and
23 national hunt days. The facilities at
Lingfield Park have also been expanded and
improved, it now has an associated golf
course and is developing into a major
leisure centre.

MAJOR EVENTS

   The introduction of the AWT at Lingfield
Park has transformed its racing calendar,
during the winter months a total of 39 race
days are on the AWT. Traditionally, a
number of important races, including two
Classics trials, have been hosted here.
   These are the most important races in
Lingfield's calendar.

March
The Bic Razor Gold Cup, run in mid-March.

May
The Calor Gas Lingfield Derby Trial and the
Marley Roof Tile Oaks Trial are both run in
early May, 25 days before the Derby.

December
The Lingfield Park Handicap Chase is run
in early December.

✦ CALENDAR OF EVENTS ✦

Jan	1	Tu			26	Tu	Sept	11	W
	3	Th			28	Th		19	Th
	5	Sa	Mar	2	Sa		Oct	3	Th
	7	M		5	Tu			28	M
	9	W		7	Th		Nov	7	Th
	10	Th		9	Sa			14	Th
	12	Sa		12	Tu			28	Th
	16	W		15	F		Dec	5	Th
	17	Th		16	Sa			7	Sa
	19	Sa		23	Sa			14	Sa
	21	M	Apr	6	Sa			18	W
	22	Tu	May	10	F			21	Sa
	24	Th		11	Sa			27	F
	26	Sa		18	Sa*				
	29	Tu		25	Sa*				
	31	Th	June	1	Sa				
Feb	1	F		15	Sa*				
	2	Sa		22	Sa*				
	5	Tu		28	F				
	7	Th		29	Sa*				
	9	Sa	July	12	F				
	12	Tu		13	Sa				
	14	Th		20	Sa				
	16	Sa		29	M				
	19	Tu	Aug	10	Sa*				
	21	Th		17	Sa*				
	23	Sa		29	Th*				
	25	M							

GETTING THERE/GETTING IN

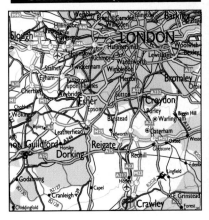

Rail: Lingfield Park B.R. station, ½ mile
from the course
Road: Off the B2028
P 🚲 Ample space for cars and coaches
Members car park 🎫 £2

Enclosures

Members Enclosure: viewing; full betting
facilities; bars; The Derby Restaurant; the
Silks Restaurant; brasserie and snack bars.
Grandstand Enclosure: viewing; full betting
facilities; bars; cocktail bar and snack bars.

Costs

Annual membership
Under review.

Day tickets
Members Enclosure	🎫	£10
Derby Trials	🎫	£15
Grandstand Enclosure	🎫	£6
Derby Trials	🎫	£8

Methods of payment: cash/cheque with valid
bankers card/Visa/Access/Mastercard

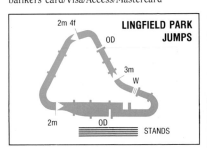

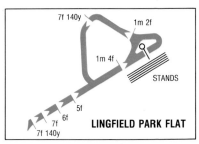

LIVERPOOL GRAND NATIONAL

Canal turn
Becher's Brook

Valentine's Brook

The Chair

2m 6f

STANDS

Red Rum

Statue of Red Rum at Aintree

LIVERPOOL – AINTREE

THE COURSE

The Racecourse
Aintree
Liverpool
☎ 051 523 2600

The Grand National course at Aintree was founded in 1839 and is a left-handed, 2¼ mile, triangular course. There are two other courses, the Mildmay and the Hurdles, all three courses are used during the Grand National Festival. Aintree hosts only 3 race days each year, all national hunt.

MAJOR EVENTS

Aintree is a major event in its own right, it only hosts one three day meeting a year but this meeting, and particularly one race, the Grand National, is the focus of world attention.

The entire meeting is sponsored by Seagrams and over the three days the most important races are The Martell Cup staged on Thursday; The Glenlivet Anniversary Hurdle race on Friday and The Seagram Grand National run on Saturday.

The Seagram Grand National is regarded as the greatest steeplechase in the world, the 4 mile 4 furlong race takes the horses round the Grand National Course twice as they jump world famous obstacles such as Becher's Brook, Valentine's, The Chair and the Water Jump. The race was first run in 1839 although it did not become known by the name "The Grand National" until 1847. Successful horses and jockeys become much loved household names, none more so than triple Grand National winning horse Red Rum and jockeys such as Bob Champion.

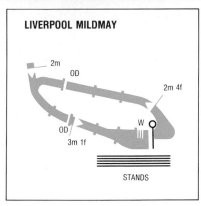

LIVERPOOL MILDMAY

2m
OD
2m 4f
OD
3m 1f
W
STANDS

⚞ CALENDAR OF EVENTS ⚟

April	4	*Thursday*
	5	*Friday*
	6	*Saturday*

LIVERPOOL – AINTREE

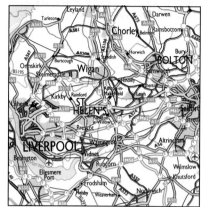

Rail: Direct express link from Liverpool Lime Street B.R. station to the course

Road: 6 miles north of Liverpool city centre in Aintree, signposted

P Ample space for cars and coaches £5–£15

Enclosures

There are two enclosures in use for the entire Festival and an extra three enclosures open for Grand National Day. There is also a general Course badge which includes access to the Embankment.

Costs

Day tickets
County Enclosure
Thursday and Friday £10–£15
Saturday, Grand National Day £25–£40

Aintree & Paddock Enclosure
Thursday and Friday £6
Saturday £13

Central Enclosure/Western Enclosure/ Steeplechase Enclosure
Grand National Day only £20
(includes parking)

Course Ticket
(includes access to the £5
Embankment)

Methods of payment: cash/cheque with valid bankers card/Visa/Access/Mastercard

The facilities are magnificent with bars and snack bars throughout the area, many shops and trade stands, two banks, giant closed circuit vision screens, side shows and exhibitions. There are major restaurants in a number of the enclosures but pre-booking of tables is essential, the caterers may be contacted on 051 523 2600.

LUDLOW

THE COURSE

Ludlow Racecourse
Bromfield
Ludlow
Shropshire
☎ 058477 221

A right-handed, 1½ mile, oval course founded in 1868, it hosts 12 national hunt race days each year. Ludlow is a small rural racecourse with an active following in the local community, 8 of its 12 race days are mid-week meetings.

MAJOR EVENTS

The most important races it hosts are the Forbra Gold Cup in March and a notable amateur race, the Prince and Princess of Wales Hunter Chase.

☆ CALENDAR OF EVENTS ☆

January	16	Wednesday
February	6	Wednesday
	28	Thursday
March	22	Friday
April	10	Wednesday
	25	Thursday
May	6	Monday
September	25	Wednesday
October	18	Friday
November	21	Thursday
December	4	Wednesday
	16	Monday

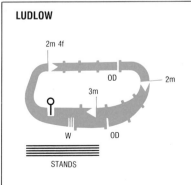

LUDLOW

GETTING THERE/GETTING IN

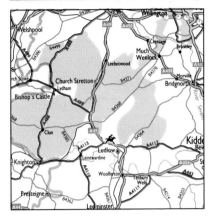

Rail: Ludlow B.R. station, 2 miles from the course
Road: On the A49, 2 miles north-west of Ludlow
P 🚫 Ample space for cars and coaches

Enclosures

Members Enclosure: viewing; betting facilities; bars and Members Restaurant.
Tattersalls Enclosure: viewing; betting facilities; bars and snack bars.
Silver Ring: betting facilities; bars and snack bars.

Costs

Annual membership
Adult   🎫 £45

Day tickets
Members Enclosure   🎫 £8

Tattersalls Enclosure   🎫 £6

Silver Ring   🎫 £3

Methods of payment: cash/cheque with valid bankers card

MARKET RASEN

THE COURSE

The Racecourse
Legsby Road
Market Rasen
Lincolnshire
☎ 0673 843434

A right-handed, 1¼ mile, oval course; it hosts 17 national hunt race days each year.

MAJOR EVENTS

All Market Rasen's 17 race days are Fridays or Saturdays apart from two very popular Bank Holiday meetings on Easter Monday and Boxing Day. It holds four evening meetings between May and August.

✦ CALENDAR OF EVENTS ✦

January	5	Saturday
	12	Saturday
March	2	Saturday
	8	Friday
April	1	Monday
	27	Saturday
May	11	Saturday*
June	1	Saturday*
August	3	Saturday*
	9	Friday
	17	Saturday*
	24	Saturday
September	21	Saturday
October	11	Friday
November	8	Friday
	23	Saturday
December	26	Thursday

GETTING THERE/GETTING IN

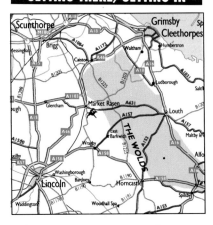

Rail: Market Rasen B.R. station, 1½ miles from the course
Road: Off the A631
P 🏕 2000 car spaces; 60 coach spaces

Enclosures

Club Enclosure: members and daily members access to Paddock and viewing from Members Stand; full betting facilities including Tote, bookmakers and betting shop; bars in the enclosure; Champagne and Seafood Restaurant and Silks Dining Room.
Tattersalls Enclosure: viewing; Tote and bookmakers betting facilities; Paddock and Tattersalls bars; Silks Dining Room and Paddock Buffet.
Silver Ring: viewing; Tote and bookmakers betting facilities; bars; Willingham Buffet and a fish and chip shop.
Other facilities: golf course in the centre of the racecourse; childrens playground; caravan park and camp site.

MARKET RASEN

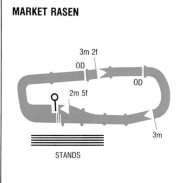

3m 2f
OD
OD
2m 5f
3m
STANDS

Costs

Annual membership
Adult	🎟	£80
Associate (member plus partner)	🎟	£140

Day tickets
Club Enclosure	🎟	£8
16–21 year olds	🎟	£5
Tattersalls Enclosure	🎟	£6
Silver Ring	🎟	£3.50

Methods of payment: cash/cheque with valid bankers card

NEWBURY

THE COURSE

The Racecourse
Newbury
Berkshire
☎ 0635 40015

Newbury racecourse was founded in 1906 by
John Porter with the support of King
Edward VII. A left-handed, 1 mile 7 furlong,
pear shaped course; it hosts 15 flat and 13
national hunt race days each year.

✦ CALENDAR OF EVENTS ✦

February	8	*Friday*
	9	*Saturday*
March	1	*Friday*
	2	*Saturday*
	22	*Friday*
	23	*Saturday*
April	19	Friday
	20	Saturday
May	17	Friday
	18	Saturday
June	12	Wednesday
	13	Thursday
	25	Tuesday*
July	19	Friday
	20	Saturday
August	16	Friday
	17	Saturday
September	20	Friday
	21	Saturday
October	24	Thursday
	25	*Friday*
	26	Saturday
November	6	*Wednesday*
	13	*Wednesday*
	22	*Friday*
	23	*Saturday*
December	28	*Saturday*
	30	*Monday*

MAJOR EVENTS

Newbury's 28 race days are grouped into 15
meetings between February and December;
a three day mixed meeting in October, 4
two day national hunt meetings, 6 two day
flat meetings, 4 one day national hunt
meetings and 1 evening flat meeting in
June. The best known meeting is probably
the Hennessy Cognac Gold Cup Meeting in
late November but during the course of the
year Newbury offers fine racing both
national hunt and on the flat and is the
host to three important national hunt races
and seven major flat races.

These are the most important races in
Newbury's calendar.

February
The Tote Gold Trophy Hurdle, run in
mid-February.

March
The Philip Cornes Saddle of Gold Hurdle,
run in early March.

April
The two Guinea trials, the Gainsborough
Stud Fred Darling Stakes and the Lanes
End John Porter EPF Stakes are staged at
the same meeting in late April.

August
The Gardner Merchant Hungerford Stakes
and the Walmac International Geoffrey
Freer Stakes are run at the same meeting
in mid-August.

September
The Rokeby Farms Mill Reef Stakes, run in
late September.

October
The Racal Vodaphone Horris Hill Stakes,
run in late October.

November
The Hennessy Cognac Gold Cup Chase, run
during the Hennessy Cognac Gold Cup
Meeting in late November.

Note: Newbury Racecourse Authority are
building a new stand during 1991, this may
cause some disruption in the enclosures,
the racing programme should be unaffected.

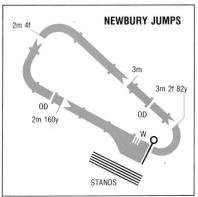

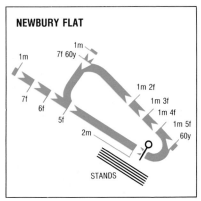

NEWBURY

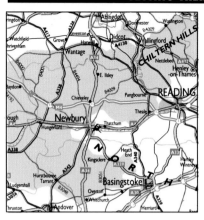

Rail: Newbury Racecourse B.R. station, adjoins the course
Road: Off the A4 and A34, east of Newbury, signposted
P ⛟ Ample space for cars and coaches

Enclosures

Members Club Enclosure: viewing including Parade Ring and Winners Enclosure; entrance to Hampshire Stand; full betting facilities; wide range of bars and self-service restaurants; Champagne and Seafood Bar and the Club Restaurant.
Tattersalls Enclosure and Paddock: viewing; full betting facilities; Paddock Bar and Chalet Bar; Tattersalls Grill Room and snack bars.
Silver Ring: betting facilities; bars and snack bars.
Geoffrey Freer Stand & Picnic Car Park: betting facilities; bars and snack bars.

Costs

Annual membership

Adult	🎫	£100
Couple	🎫	£200

Day tickets

Members Enclosure	🎫	£11–£15
Tattersalls Enclosure	🎫	£6–£8
Silver Ring	🎫	£2

Geoffrey Freer Stand & Picnic Car Park

Per car	🎫	£2
Per adult	🎫	£2

Methods of payment: cash/cheque with valid bankers card

NEWCASTLE

THE COURSE

The Racecourse,
High Gosforth Park
Newcastle Upon Tyne
☎ 091 236 2020

Horse racing in Newcastle began in 1839,
the course was moved to the present
Gosforth Park site in 1882. A left-handed,
1 mile 6 furlong, triangular course; it hosts
12 flat and 11 national hunt race days each
year.

✯ CALENDAR OF EVENTS ✯

January	12	*Saturday*
February	16	*Saturday*
March	16	*Saturday*
	18	*Monday*
	30	Saturday
April	1	Monday
	8	Monday
May	6	*Monday*
	11	*Saturday**
	31	Friday
June	28	Friday*
	29	Monday
July	27	Saturday
	29	Monday
August	24	Saturday
	26	Monday
October	1	Tuesday
	23	*Wednesday*
November	4	Monday
	9	*Saturday*
	23	*Saturday*
December	3	*Tuesday*
	28	*Saturday*

MAJOR EVENTS

There is racing at Newcastle every month of
the year except September. The
Northumberland Plate Meeting and the
Fighting Fifth Day, a national hunt meeting
at the end of November, are the two most
important meetings of the year.

These are the most important races in
Newcastle's calendar.

February
The Tote Eider Handicap Chase, run in
mid-February.

May
The Federation Brewery Novices Chase
Final, run in early May.

June
The Newcastle Brown Ale Northumberland
Plate, run at the end of June.

July
The Federation Brewery Beeswing Stakes,
run at the end of July.

October
The Ekbalco Hurdle Race, run in late
October.

November
The Dipper Novices Chase, run in mid
November and the Fighting Fifth Hurdle
Race run at the end of November.

December
The Novices, 2 mile, Champion Chase, run
at the end of December.

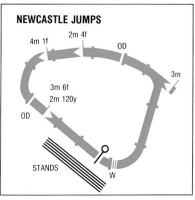

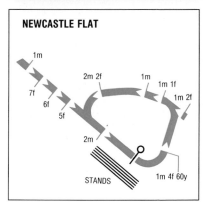

NEWCASTLE

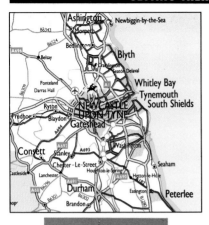

Rail: Newcastle Central B.R. station, 4 miles from the course
Road: Off the A189 or the A6125
P 🎫 6000 car spaces; 200 coach spaces

Enclosures

Club Enclosure: access to Paddock and Parade Ring; full betting facilities including Tote; Members Suite with self service meals available; Cocktail and Champagne Bar; a fast food snack bar and two bars.
Tattersalls Enclosure: access to Paddock and Parade Ring, viewing from stand with full betting facilities including betting office and Tote; two restaurants with waitress service; two bars, and a fast food snack bar. All Tattersalls facilities are available to Club members and visitors.
Silver Ring: full bar and cafeteria service; full betting facilities including Tote.
Other facilities: bank.

Costs

Annual membership

Adult	🎫	£75
Couple	🎫	£110
Junior (under 21)	🎫	£40

Day tickets
Club Enclosure

Plate and Fighting Fifth meetings	🎫	£15
All other meetings	🎫	£12
Junior club visitors (16–20)	🎫	£5
Tattersalls Enclosure	🎫	£7
OAPs	🎫	£3
Silver Ring	🎫	£2.50

Methods of payment: cash/cheque with valid bankers card

59

NEWMARKET

THE COURSE

Rowley Mile Racecourse/July Racecourse
Rowley Mile
Newmarket
Suffolk
☎ 0638 662762

There are two racecourses at Newmarket, the Rowley Mile Course, used for Spring and Autumn meetings, and the July Course, used for meetings between June and August. The Rowley Mile Course is named after Charles II and was founded in the 1660s; it hosts 31 flat race days each year over 3 spring and 3 autumn meetings. The July Course hosts 6 meetings.

⚞ CALENDAR OF EVENTS ⚟

Apr	16	Tu		3	Sa
	17	W		9	F*
	18	Th		10	Sa
May	2	Th		23	F
	3	F		24	Sa
	4	Sa	Oct	2	W
	11	Sa		3	Th
	17	F		4	F
June	28	F		5	Sa
	29	Sa		17	Th
July	9	Tu		18	F
	10	W		19	Sa
	11	Th		31	Th
	19	F*	Nov	1	F
	20	Sa		2	Sa
Aug	2	F*			

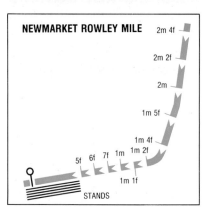

NEWMARKET ROWLEY MILE

2m 4f
2m 2f
2m
1m 5f
1m 4f
1m 2f
5f 6f 7f 1m
1m 1f
STANDS

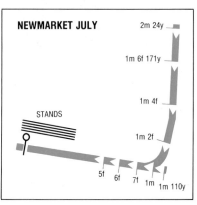

NEWMARKET JULY

2m 24y
1m 6f 171y
1m 4f
STANDS
1m 2f
5f 6f 7f 1m
1m 110y

MAJOR EVENTS

Newmarket is very much the home of horse racing, the 12 meetings at the two courses involve two classics and a total of 21 important flat races.

All the meetings are worth attending, but these are the most important meetings and races in Newmarket's calendar.

April
The three day Craven Meeting in mid April during which the Nell Gwyn Stakes; the Ladbroke European Free Handicap and the Charles Heidsieck Champagne Craven Stakes are run.

May
The three day Guineas Meeting at the start of May during which the General Accident 1000 Guineas Stakes, a 1 mile race for 3 year old fillies, first run in 1814 and the first of the English Classics is run as well as the General Accident Jockey Club Stakes and the General Accident 2000 Guineas Stakes, a 1 mile race for 3 year old colts, first run in 1809. Another English Classic, The Coral Bookmakers Handicap, a two day meeting, is run in mid-May.

June
The Van Geest Criterion Stakes is run during a two day meeting at the end of June.

July
The Princess of Wales's Stakes, the Child Stakes, the Carroll Foundation July Cup and the July Stakes, a race first held in 1786, are all run during a three day summer meeting in mid-July. The Food Brokers Trophy is staged during a two day meeting in late July.

August
The Brierley Group New Zealand Handicap is run during a two day meeting in mid-August, and the Philip Cornes Nursery Handicap is run during a two day meeting in late August.

October
The four day Cambridgeshire Meeting at the start of October hosts the Tattersalls Cheveley Park Stakes, the Middle Park Stakes and the William Hill Cambridgeshire Handicap, a 1 mile 1 furlong race for 3 year olds and upwards first run in 1839.

In late October the three day Cesarewitch Meeting hosts the Three Chimneys Dewhurst Stakes and the Tote Cesarewitch, a 2¼ mile handicap, first run in 1839.

November
The Mail on Sunday Handicap Final is run during a three day meeting at the start of November.

NEWMARKET

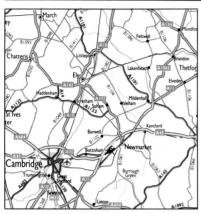

Rail: Newmarket B.R. station, 8 miles from the course

Road: From the M11, jct 9 along A1303 and A1304 or A1 then A45 towards Newmarket

P ⊠ 8000 car spaces; 200 coach spaces
Day members car park 🎫 £1

Enclosures

Members Enclosure: access to Paddock and Parade Ring; full betting facilities including Tote; restaurants; luncheon rooms; bars; private rooms and private boxes.

Grandstand & Paddock Enclosure: access to Paddock and Parade Ring; full betting facilities including Tote; restaurants and bars.

Silver Ring: viewing from the terraces; full betting facilities including Tote; bars and snacks available in the enclosure.

Other facilities: childrens play area, banks.

Costs

Annual membership	🎫 £35–£115

Day tickets	
Members Enclosure	🎫 £12–£20
Grandstand & Paddock Enclosure	🎫 £7.50–£9
Silver Ring	🎫 £3–£4

Methods of payment: cash/cheque with valid bankers card/Visa

NEWTON ABBOT

THE COURSE

The Racecourse
Kingsteignton Road
Newton Abbot
Devon
☎ 0626 53235

A left-handed, 1 mile, rectangular course founded before 1880, it hosts 21 national hunt race days each year.

MAJOR EVENTS

Newton Abbot hosts three Bank Holiday meetings on Boxing Day, Easter Monday and a three day meeting over the August Bank Holiday. There are two popular evening meetings in May.

The two most important races staged at Newton Abbot are the Hare and Hound West Country Cup and the Courage South West Steeplechase.

✱ CALENDAR OF EVENTS ✱

January	4	Friday
	24	Thursday
February	12	Tuesday
March	13	Wednesday
	30	Saturday
April	1	Monday
May	2	Thursday*
	3	Friday
	14	Tuesday
	15	Wednesday*
August	3	Saturday
	5	Monday
	15	Thursday
	26	Monday
	27	Tuesday
	28	Wednesday
September	5	Thursday
October	8	Tuesday
November	19	Tuesday
December	16	Monday
	26	Thursday

NEWTON ABBOT

3m 2f 100y
2m 150y
W
2m 5f
STANDS

GETTING THERE/GETTING IN

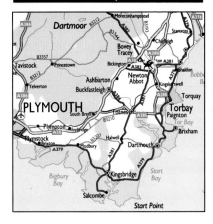

Rail: Newton Abbot B.R. station, 1 mile from the course
Road: Off the A380 Exeter road just north of Newton Abbot
P 🚌 Ample space for cars and coaches

Enclosures

Tattersalls Enclosure: Grandstand viewing; betting facilities; bars with hot snacks and a restaurant.
Silver Ring (Course Enclosure): Grandstand viewing; betting facilities; bar and snack bars.

Costs

Annual membership
Members Lounge   🎫 £80

Day tickets
Tattersalls Enclosure   🎫 £7

Silver Ring   🎫 £3
Methods of payment: cash only

NOTTINGHAM

THE COURSE

Nottingham Racecourse
Colwick Park
Nottingham
☎ 0602 580620

A left-handed, 1½ mile, oval course,
founded in 1867, it hosts 17 flat and 10
national hunt race days each year.

MAJOR EVENTS

Nottingham stages national hunt racing
from November until March. Important
national hunt races at Nottingham include
the Nottinghamshire Champion Novices
Steeplechase, the Holsten Pils City Trial
Hurdle and the Stan Mellor Handicap
Chase; Mellor rode his 1000th winner in
December 1971, when he rode Ouzo at
Nottingham.

The two most important flat races at
Nottingham are the Home Brewery Gold
Tankard and the Nottingham Stewards Cup.

February
The Nottinghamshire Champion Novices
Steeplechase run in mid February is the
most important race in Nottingham's
calendar.

✣ CALENDAR OF EVENTS ✣

January	3	*Thursday*
	22	*Tuesday*
	30	*Wednesday*
February	16	*Saturday*
	26	*Tuesday*
March	19	*Tuesday*
April	1	Monday
	15	Monday
	30	Tuesday
May	14	Tuesday*
	31	Friday
June	10	Monday
	15	Saturday*
	24	Monday
July	6	Saturday*
	22	Monday*
August	5	Monday*
	6	Tuesday*
September	2	Monday
	23	Monday
	24	Tuesday
October	21	Monday
	23	Wednesday
November	6	*Wednesday**
	19	*Tuesday*
	30	*Saturday*
December	14	*Saturday*

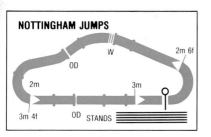

NOTTINGHAM JUMPS

GETTING THERE/GETTING IN

Rail: Nottingham B.R. station, 2 miles from
the course
Road: Off the B686 Colwick road, east of
Nottingham city centre
P ⛟ Ample space for cars and coaches

Enclosures

Tattersalls Enclosure: viewing; betting
facilities including betting shop; bars;
restaurant and snack bars.
Silver Ring: viewing, including Parade Ring
and Winner's Enclosure; betting facilities
including betting shop; bars; snack bars and
childrens playground.

Costs

Day tickets

Tattersalls Enclosure	🎫	£8
Silver Ring	🎫	£4

Note: there is no Members Enclosure and
no annual membership.

Methods of payment: cash/cheque with valid
bankers card

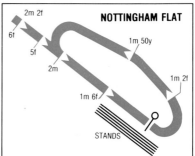

NOTTINGHAM FLAT

PERTH

THE COURSE

The Racecourse
Scone Palace Park
Perth
☎ 0738 51577

The racecourse is in the beautiful wooded
grounds of Scone Palace. A right-handed,
1 mile 2 furlong, rectangular course, it
hosts 10 national hunt race days each year.
Perth, a delightful rural course, is the
northernmost racecourse in the UK but on
racedays it attracts good crowds from the
Scottish cities.

MAJOR EVENTS

The 10 race days are organised into 5
meetings, the Perth Festival Meeting, a
three day meeting at the end of April, two
day meetings in mid-May and mid-August, a
one day meeting in mid-September and a
two day meeting at the end of September.

September
The Highland Spring Handicap Chase run
in September is the highest valued race.

☆ CALENDAR OF EVENTS ☆

April	23	Tuesday
	24	Wednesday
	25	Thursday
May	15	Wednesday*
	16	Thursday
August	16	Friday
	17	Saturday
September	11	Wednesday
	25	Wednesday
	26	Thursday

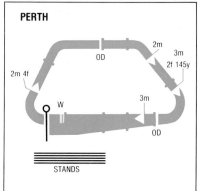

```
PERTH

                    2m
              0D        3m
                        2f 145y
2m 4f

        W           3m

                        0D


        STANDS
```

GETTING THERE/GETTING IN

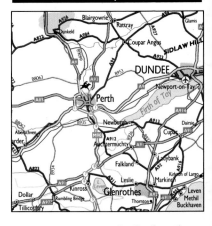

Rail: Perth B.R. station, 4 miles from the
course
Road: Off the A93 Perth to Blairgowrie
road, just north of Perth
P 🚌 Ample space for cars and coaches

Enclosures

Club Enclosure: viewing; full betting
facilities; bar and restaurant.
Paddock Enclosure: viewing; betting
facilities; bar and self-service snack bar.
Course Enclosure: betting facilities; bar and
snacks.

Costs

Annual membership
Adult	🎫	£45
Couple	🎫	£70

Day tickets
Club Enclosure	🎫	£10
Paddock Enclosure	🎫	£6
Course Enclosure	🎫	£2

Methods of payment: cash only

PLUMPTON

THE COURSE

Plumpton Racecourse
Plumpton Green
Sussex
☎ 0273 890383

A left-handed, 1 mile 1 furlong, oval course,
it was founded in 1890 and hosts
17 national hunt race days each year.

MAJOR EVENTS

Plumpton's season runs from early August
to April, all its race days are one day
meetings. The three most popular meetings
of the year are on Easter Monday, August
Bank Holiday and New Year's Eve.

✦ CALENDAR OF EVENTS ✦

January	9	Wednesday
	28	Monday
February	11	Monday
	27	Wednesday
March	11	Monday
	30	Saturday
April	1	Monday
	12	Friday
August	9	Friday
	26	Monday
September	16	Monday
October	9	Wednesday
	22	Tuesday
November	4	Monday
	27	Wednesday
December	10	Tuesday
	31	Tuesday

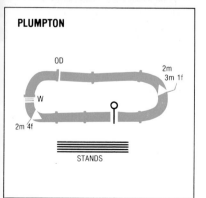

PLUMPTON

GETTING THERE/GETTING IN

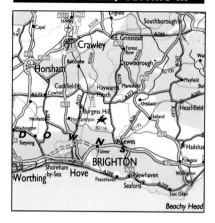

Rail: Plumpton Green B.R. station adjoins
the course
Road: Off the A276 approximately 6 miles
north of Lewes
P Ample parking for cars 🎫 50p
Picnic cars by rails 🎫 £3
plus/per person 🎫 £3
Ample space for coaches 🚌

Enclosures

Members Enclosure: viewing; betting
facilities; bar; restaurant and snack bar.
Tattersalls Enclosure: viewing; betting
facilities; bar and snack bar.
Course Enclosure: betting facilities; bar and
snacks.

Costs

Annual membership
Adult   🎫 £75
Members car park pass   🎫 £5

Day tickets
Members Enclosure   🎫 £10

Tattersalls Enclosure   🎫 £7
Under 16s   🚌

Course Enclosure   🎫 £3
Under 16s   🚌

Methods of payment: cash/cheque with valid
bankers card

PONTEFRACT

THE COURSE

The Racecourse
Pontefract Park
Pontefract
☎ 0977 703224

Racing was first recorded at Pontefract in
the 1640s. A left-handed, 2 mile 5 furlong,
oval course, it is the longest circuit in the
country and hosts 15 flat race days each
year.

MAJOR EVENTS

Pontefract's 15 race days fall between April
and October; it stages 2 two day meetings
in mid June and early August and 2 evening
meetings, in late May and late July.

✣ CALENDAR OF EVENTS ✣

April	9	Tuesday
	17	Wednesday
	29	Monday
May	24	Friday*
June	10	Monday
	11	Tuesday
July	1	Monday
	9	Tuesday
	26	Friday*
August	7	Wednesday
	8	Thursday
September	3	Tuesday
	23	Monday
October	7	Monday
	24	Thursday

GETTING THERE/GETTING IN

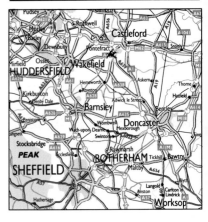

Rail: Pontefract B.R. station, 2 miles from
the course
Road: Off the M62, jct 32, access via the
A628 road to Pontefract
P 🚗 Ample space for cars and coaches

Enclosures

Club Enclosure: viewing; full betting
facilities; bars; Champagne Bar; Club
Restaurant and snack bars.
Paddock Enclosure: viewing; full betting
facilities; bars; Tattersalls Restaurant and
snack bars.
Silver Ring: betting facilities; bar and snack
bars.
Third Ring: betting facilities; picnic car
park; childrens playground and snack bar.

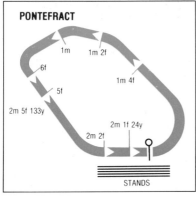

Costs

Annual membership
Adult	🎫	£75
Couple	🎫	£100

Day tickets
Club Enclosure	🎫	£10
Paddock Enclosure	🎫	£6
Silver Ring	🎫	£2.50

Third Ring
Car plus four occupants	🎫	£5
Per person (walking)	🎫	£1.50

Methods of payment: cash/cheque with valid
bankers card

REDCAR

THE COURSE

The Racecourse
Redcar
Cleveland
☎ 0642 484068

A left-handed, 1¾ mile, oval course, it was founded in 1871 and hosts 18 flat race days each year.

MAJOR EVENTS

Redcar's 18 race days are between May and October, they include 3 two day meetings and 2 evening meetings. The most important races staged at Redcar and the Zetland Gold Cup, the Sea Pigeon Handicap and the Racecall Gold Trophy.

May
The most popular meeting is the two day Whitsun Bank Holiday meeting during which the Zetland Gold Cup is run.

July
The Sea Pigeon Handicap is a "trial" for York's Ebor Handicap. In recent years the winner of this race has on four occasions gone on to win the York race. It is run in late July.

October
The Racecall Gold Trophy, an important new race is run during the last meeting of the year at the end of October.

✦ CALENDAR OF EVENTS ✦

May	2	Thursday
	27	Monday
	28	Tuesday
June	3	Monday
	21	Friday
	22	Saturday
July	10	Wednesday*
	23	Tuesday
	24	Wednesday*
August	6	Tuesday
	9	Friday
	10	Saturday
	28	Wednesday
September	27	Friday
	28	Saturday
October	8	Tuesday
	16	Wednesday
	29	Tuesday

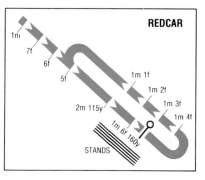

GETTING THERE/GETTING IN

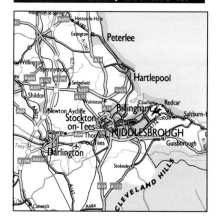

Rail: Darlington B.R. station, 18 miles from the course
Road: Off the A1085 and the A174, just south of Redcar town centre, signposted
P 🚌 Ample space for cars and coaches

Enclosures

Club Enclosure: viewing; betting facilities including Tote; bars; restaurant and snack bars.
Grandstand & Paddock Enclosure: viewing; betting facilities; bars; restaurant and snack bars.
Course Enclosure: betting facilities; bar and snack bars.
Other facilities: childrens playground.

Costs

Annual membership
Adult	🎫	£54
Couple	🎫	£85

Day tickets
Club Enclosure	🎫	£9
Grandstand & Paddock Enclosure	🎫	£5
Course Enclosure	🎫	£1.50

Methods of payment: cash/cheque with valid bankers card

RIPON

THE COURSE

The Racecourse
Boroughbridge Road
Ripon
North Yorkshire
☎ 0765 3696

Ripon is a right-handed, 1 mile 5 furlong, oval course, it hosts 13 flat race days each year.

MAJOR EVENTS

The most important races at Ripon are the Great St. Wilfrid Handicap, the Champion 2 Year Old Trophy and the Ripon Rowels.

August
The two day Bank Holiday meeting is the most popular in Ripon's calendar. The Great St. Wilfrid Handicap is run during another August meeting.

✼ CALENDAR OF EVENTS ✼

April	10	Wednesday
	11	Thursday
	27	Saturday
May	29	Wednesday*
June	19	Wednesday
	20	Thursday
July	8	Monday*
	20	Saturday
August	5	Monday
	17	Saturday
	26	Monday
	27	Tuesday
	31	Saturday

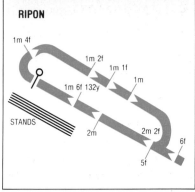

GETTING THERE/GETTING IN

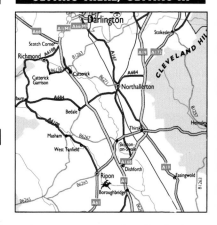

Rail: Harrogate B.R. station, 12 miles from the course
Road: Off the B6265, signposted
P 🅿 Ample space for cars and coaches

Enclosures

Club Enclosure: viewing; betting facilities; Members Bar; restaurant and snack bar.
Tattersalls Enclosure: viewing; betting facilities; bar; restaurant and snack bar.
Silver Ring: betting facilities; bar and snack bar.
Course Enclosure: betting facilities; bar and snack bar.
Other facilities: two childrens playgrounds on the course.

Costs
Annual membership
| Adult | 🎫 £55 |
| Couple | 🎫 £85 |

Day tickets
Club Enclosure	🎫 £10
Tattersalls Enclosure	🎫 £6
Silver Ring	🎫 £2.50
Course Enclosure	🎫 £1.50

Methods of payment: cash/cheque with valid bankers card

SALISBURY

THE COURSE

Salisbury Racecourse
Netherhampton
Salisbury
Wiltshire
☎ 0772 26461

Salisbury is one of the oldest racecourses in the country, Queen Elizabeth I reportedly attended a meeting at the course in 1588. A right-handed, loop course; it hosts 13 flat race days each year.

MAJOR EVENTS

Racing at Salisbury takes place from early May to the end of October. The most important race of Salisbury's calendar is the Veuve Cliquot Champagne Stakes.

June
The most popular meeting of the year is the two day meeting at the end of June which features the Veuve Cliquot Champagne Stakes.

⚞ CALENDAR OF EVENTS ⚟

May	2	Thursday
	7	Tuesday
	8	Wednesday
June	11	Tuesday
	26	Wednesday
	27	Thursday
July	13	Saturday
August	14	Wednesday
	15	Thursday
	22	Thursday*
September	5	Thursday
October	2	Wednesday
	29	Tuesday

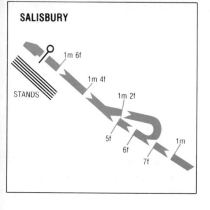

SALISBURY

GETTING THERE/GETTING IN

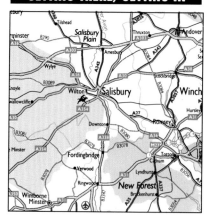

Rail: Salisbury B.R. station, 3 miles from the course
Road: Off the A3094, 3 miles west-south-west of Salisbury
P 🚗 Ample space for cars and coaches

Enclosures

Members Enclosure: viewing; betting facilities; Wessex Bar; Members Restaurant and snack bar.
Tattersalls Enclosure: viewing; betting facilities including betting shop; Pavilion Bar (summer months only) and snack bars.
Course Enclosure: betting facilities and snack bars.

Costs

Annual membership

Adult	🎫	£50

Day tickets

Members Enclosure	🎫	£8.50
Tattersalls Enclosure	🎫	£6
Course Enclosure	🎫	£2.50

Methods of payment: cash/cheque with valid bankers card

SANDOWN PARK

THE COURSE

The Racecourse
Esher
Surrey
☎ 0372 63072

A right-handed, 1 mile 5 furlong, oval course, it was founded in 1875 and hosts 1 mixed, 15 flat and 11 national hunt race days each year.

⚞ CALENDAR OF EVENTS ⚟

January	5	*Saturday*
February	2	*Saturday*
	14	*Thursday*
	15	*Friday*
March	8	*Friday*
	9	*Saturday*
	26	*Tuesday*
April	26	*Friday*
	27	Saturday
May	8	Wednesday*
	27	Monday
	28	Tuesday*
June	14	Friday
	15	Saturday
July	5	Friday
	6	Saturday
	17	Wednesday*
	18	Thursday
	24	Wednesday*
August	26	Monday
	30	Friday
	31	Saturday
September	17	Tuesday
	18	Wednesday
November	2	*Saturday*
	29	*Friday*
	30	*Saturday*

MAJOR EVENTS

Sandown Park is a fine example of a popular and well organised racecourse. It has the distinction of having been awarded "Racecourse of the Year" 7 times in the last 13 years. Its 27 race days include 10 two day meetings and as part of its calendar it hosts 4 popular evening meetings.

It hosts many important races, both national hunt and flat, these are the most important national hunt races.

January
The Mildmay Cazalet Memorial Handicap Chase run in early January.

February
The Agfa Chase run in early February.

March
The William Hill Imperial Cup run in mid March, a 2 mile race first contested in 1907.

April
The Whitbread Gold Cup which is run at the end of April as part of a flat meeting. This 3 mile 5 furlong 118 yard race was the first sponsored race in the UK when it was established in 1957.

November
The William Hill Handicap Hurdle at the end of November.

These are the most important flat races.

April
The Trusthouse Forte Mile run at the end of April.

May
The Sears Temple Stakes run at the end of the May Bank Holiday meeting and the Brigadier Gerard Stakes run at the same meeting.

July
The Coral Eclipse Stakes run in early July is a 1 mile 4 furlong race for 3 year olds which was first contested in 1886.

August
The Imry Solario Stakes run at the end of August.

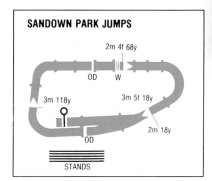

SANDOWN PARK

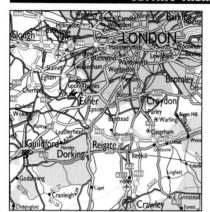

Rail: Esher B.R. station adjoins the course
Road: Off the A307 as you enter Esher from Kingston upon Thames
P 🅿 Ample car space at Portsmouth Road
Members car park 🎫 £2
Ample space for coaches 🚌

Enclosures

Club Enclosure: viewing; full betting facilities; bars; restaurants and snack bars.
Grandstand Enclosure: viewing; full betting facilities; bars; restaurants and snack bars.
Park Enclosure: in the centre of the course; betting facilities; bar and snack bar.
Sandown Park Leisure Complex
Golf Centre: in the centre of the course; 9-hole golf course; pitch and putt; driving range and bar with snacks.
Snooker Club: 8 tables; bar; opens half an hour after the last race on race days.
Ski School: 3 dry ski slopes.

Costs

Annual membership

Adult	🎫	£160
Junior adult (16–25)	🎫	£70

Day tickets

Enclosure	Whitbread Gold Cup & Coral Eclipse Stakes Meetings	Premium Days	All Other Days
Club	£20	£12	£10
Club junior (16–25)	£13	£9	£7
Grandstand	£12	£8	£6
Park	£4	£3	£3

Methods of payment: cash/cheque with valid bankers card/Visa/Access/Mastercard

SEDGEFIELD

THE COURSE

The Racecourse
Sedgefield
Stockton-on-Tees,
Cleveland
☎ 0740 20366

A left-handed, 1 mile 2 furlong, rectangular course, it was founded in 1867 and hosts 21 national hunt race days each year. Sedgefield is a small rural course, which has strong local support and rightly refers to itself as the "Friendly Racecourse".

MAJOR EVENTS

Northern trainers and jockeys use Sedgefield to put their horses through their paces. The most important race in Sedgefield's calendar is the Durham National Handicap Steeplechase.

March
The Durham National Handicap Steeplechase.

May
An evening meeting in early May incorporates a barbecue with the racing.

✦ CALENDAR OF EVENTS ✦

January	3	Thursday
	15	Tuesday
	23	Wednesday
	29	Tuesday
February	8	Friday
	19	Tuesday
March	5	Tuesday
	12	Tuesday
April	16	Tuesday
	30	Tuesday*
May	7	Tuesday*
	24	Friday
September	6	Friday
	17	Tuesday
October	2	Wednesday
	15	Tuesday
	30	Wednesday
November	12	Tuesday
	22	Friday
December	10	Tuesday
	26	Thursday

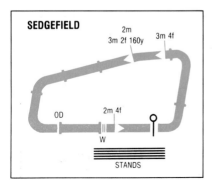

SEDGEFIELD

GETTING THERE/GETTING IN

Rail: Stockton B.R. station, 7 miles from the course or Darlington B.R. station, 8 miles from the course
Road: Off the A689 Bishop Auckland to Sedgefield road
P ⛽ 500 car spaces; ample coach space

Enclosures

Paddock Enclosure (Tattersalls): viewing; betting facilities; bars with snack food (including the famous Sedgefield pie and peas) and a restaurant.
Course Enclosure: betting facilities; bars; snack bars, including fresh fish and chips.

Costs

Day tickets
Paddock Enclosure (Tattersalls)
		£6
OAPs		£3
Course Enclosure		£2.50

Methods of payment: cash/cheque with valid bankers card

SOUTHWELL

THE COURSE

The Racecourse
Rolleston
Newark
Nottinghamshire
☎ 0636 814481

A left-handed, 1¼ mile, triangular course, it was founded in 1867 and hosts 40 flat racing days and 25 national hunt days.

MAJOR EVENTS

The new all weather track at Southwell has transformed racing at the course, adding 38 new race days each year. The AWT is used from the start of November to early March each year.

The old turf course is used from the end of March to the end of October including 8 evening meetings (2 in May, 1 in June, 4 in July, 1 in August) and a Three Day Festival in the middle of August.

There are Bank Holiday meetings on May Day and the August Bank Holiday.

☆ CALENDAR OF EVENTS ☆

Jan	2	W	May	6	M
	4	F		18	Sa*
	7	M		25	Sa*
	9	W	June	7	F
	11	F		14	F
	14	M		21	F*
	16	W	July	5	F
	18	F		13	Sa*
	21	M		20	Sa*
	23	W		27	Sa*
	25	F		31	W*
	28	M	Aug	10	Sa*
	30	W		14	W
Feb	1	F		15	Th
	4	M		16	F
	6	W		26	M
	8	F	Sept	7	Sa
	11	M		20	F
	13	W		25	W
	15	F	Oct	7	M
	18	M		12	Sa
	20	W		19	Sa
	22	F		24	Th
	25	M	Nov	12	Tu
	27	W		19	Tu
Mar	1	F		29	F
	4	M	Dec	4	W
	6	W		12	Th
	8	F		17	Tu
	16	Sa		28	Sa
	20	W			
	28	Th			
	30	Sa			
Apr	13	Sa			
	26	F			

GETTING THERE/GETTING IN

Rail: Rolleston B.R. station, 100 yards from the course
Road: Off the A612 Nottingham to Newark road, signposted from Southwell
P 2000 car spaces
Public 🚻
Members 🅿 £2
Picnic 🅿 £5
30 coach spaces 🚻

Enclosures

Members Enclosure: viewing; betting facilities; Members Bar; Nosebag Restaurant (try the homemade Nosebag Game Pie) and The White Lady Restaurant.
Paddock Enclosure (Tattersalls): viewing; betting hall; Saddle Bar; Tattersalls Bar, Course Bar and Champagne Bar; Pig Roast Restaurant and a fast food area.

Costs

Annual membership
Adult	🅿	£100
Couple	🅿	£170
Six-month winter membership	🅿	£60

Day tickets
Members Enclosure	🅿	£8

Paddock Enclosure (Tattersalls)
	🅿	£5
OAPs	🅿	£3

Methods of payment: cash/cheque with valid bankers card

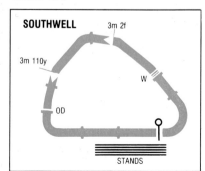

SOUTHWELL

STRATFORD-ON-AVON

THE COURSE

The Racecourse
Luddington Road
Stratford-on-Avon
Warwickshire
☎ 0789 67949

A left-handed, 1¼ mile, conical course, it was founded in 1880 and hosts 14 national hunt race days each year.

MAJOR EVENTS

Stratford-on-Avon's 14 race days run from early September to the start of June, although there is no racing in January. The most important race in Stratford's calendar is the Horse and Hounds Cup Final Champion Hunters Chase run during June.

✯ CALENDAR OF EVENTS ✯

February	2	Saturday
	23	Saturday
March	7	Thursday
April	20	Saturday
May	10	Friday*
	18	Saturday*
	31	Friday*
June	1	Saturday*
September	7	Saturday
	28	Saturday
October	19	Saturday
	31	Thursday
November	26	Tuesday
December	28	Saturday

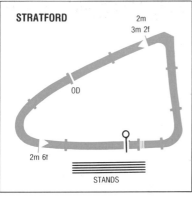

STRATFORD
2m
3m 2f
OD
2m 6f
STANDS

GETTING THERE/GETTING IN

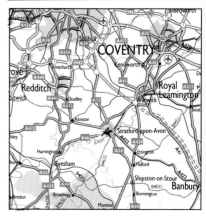

Rail: Stratford-on-Avon B.R. station, 1½ miles from the course
Road: Off the A439 Stratford to Evesham road
P 1000 car spaces 🏫 £2
Parking outside course 🏫
50 coach spaces 🏫

Enclosures

Club Enclosure: viewing; betting facilities; Members Bar, Bridge Bar, Champagne Bar, John Kenny Seafood Bar; Paddock Suite Dining Room and snack bars.
Tattersalls Enclosure: viewing; betting facilities; Chris Rookes Bar, Tattersalls Bar, Garrick Bar; use of Paddock Suite Dining Room; hot snacks in Tattersalls and Garrick Bars.
Course Enclosure: betting facilities; bar and snack bars.

Costs

Annual membership
Adult   🏫 £55

Day tickets
Club Enclosure   🏫 £9

Tattersalls Enclosure   🏫 £7

Course Enclosure   🏫 £3.50

Methods of payment: cash/cheque with valid bankers card

TAUNTON

THE COURSE

The Racecourse
Orchard Portman
Taunton
Somerset
☎ 0823 337172

A right-handed, 1¼ mile, oval course, it hosts 10 national hunt race days each year.

MAJOR EVENTS

Taunton's 10 race days spread from mid October to the middle of May. All the meetings are one day meetings except two evening meetings held at the end of April and the middle of May.

✹ CALENDAR OF EVENTS ✹

January	17	Thursday
February	14	Thursday
April	11	Thursday
	26	Friday*
May	10	Friday*
October	17	Thursday
November	14	Thursday
	28	Thursday
December	5	Thursday
	27	Friday

GETTING THERE/GETTING IN

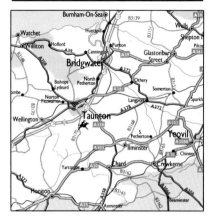

Rail: Taunton B.R. station, 2½ miles from the course
Road: Off the B3170, 2½ miles south of Taunton
P 🚌 Ample space for cars and coaches
Picnic cars, in centre of course 🎫 £2

Enclosures

Members Enclosure: viewing; betting facilities; bar and snack bar.
Paddock Enclosure: viewing; betting facilities including betting shop; bar; restaurant and snack bars.
Centre Course: betting facilities; bar and snack bar.

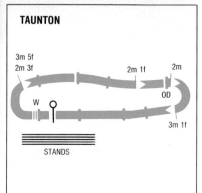

Costs

Annual membership
Adult	🎫	£55
Couple	🎫	£90

Day tickets
Members Enclosure	🎫	£9
Paddock Enclosure	🎫	£7
Centre Course	🎫	£3

Methods of payment: cash/cheque with valid bankers card

THIRSK

THE COURSE

The Racecourse
Station Road
Thirsk
North Yorkshire
☎ 0845 522276

A left-handed, 1 mile 2 furlong, oval course, it was founded in 1855 and hosts 12 flat race days each year.

MAJOR EVENTS

Thirsk hosts 12 race days from April to September each year including one evening meeting in August.

April
The Thirsk Classic Trial, an important 2000 Guineas Classic trial, is run on the Saturday of the April Meeting.

May
The Thirsk Hunt Cup is held in early May.

August
The Directors Trophy is run on the Saturday of the two day August meeting.

✲ CALENDAR OF EVENTS ✲

April	19	Friday
	20	Saturday
May	4	Saturday
	17	Friday
	18	Saturday
June	18	Tuesday
July	19	Friday
August	2	Friday
	3	Saturday
	12	Monday*
	30	Friday
September	7	Saturday

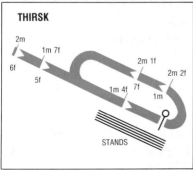

GETTING THERE/GETTING IN

Rail: Thirsk B.R. station, ¾ mile from the course
Road: On the A61 Thirsk to Ripon road
P ☒ 1500+ car spaces; 200+ coach spaces

Enclosures

Club Enclosure: access to Paddock and Parade Ring; full betting facilities including Tote; restaurant in the Hambleton Rooms; Cherry Tree Bar and Members Bar with self-service catering.
Tattersalls Enclosure: full betting facilities; Riders Bar and Saddle Room Buffet.
Silver Ring: full betting facilities; bar and cafeteria in the enclosure.
No 3 Ring: full betting facilities; bar and self service snacks.

Costs

Annual membership

Adult	🎟	£50
Couple	🎟	£85

Day tickets

Club Enclosure	🎟	£10
Tattersalls Enclosure	🎟	£6
Silver Ring	🎟	£2.50
No 3 Ring	🎟	£1.50

Methods of payment: cash/cheque with valid bankers card

TOWCESTER

THE COURSE

The Racecourse
Easton Neston
Towcester
Northamptonshire
☎ 0327 53414

A right-handed, 1¾ mile, square course, it was founded in 1880 and hosts 14 national hunt race days each year.

MAJOR EVENTS

Towcester's season runs from the middle of October to the end of May with one evening meeting which is held in the middle of May. The most popular meetings at Towcester are the Easter Monday meeting and the early May Spring Bank Holiday meeting.

✯ CALENDAR OF EVENTS ✯

January	18	Friday
	31	Thursday
February	12	Tuesday
March	21	Thursday
	30	Saturday
April	1	Monday
May	6	Monday
	14	Tuesday*
	24	Friday
October	9	Wednesday
November	14	Thursday
	23	Saturday
December	7	Saturday
	19	Thursday

GETTING THERE/GETTING IN

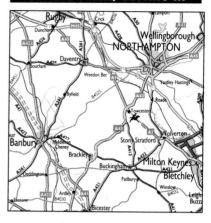

Rail: Northampton B.R. station, 9 miles from the course
Road: Off the A5, 1 mile south east of Towcester
P ☼ Ample space for cars and coaches

Enclosures

Members Enclosure: viewing; betting facilities; bar; restaurant and snack bar.
Tattersalls Enclosure: viewing; betting facilities; bars with snacks and snack bars.
Course Enclosure: betting facilities; snack bars and picnic area.

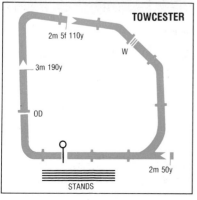

Costs

Annual membership
Adult	🎫	£45

Day tickets
Members Enclosure	🎫	£8
Tattersalls Enclosure	🎫	£6
Course Enclosure	🎫	£3
Per car	🎫	£10

Methods of payment: cash/cheque with valid bankers card

UTTOXETER

THE COURSE

The Racecourse
Wood Lane
Uttoxeter
Staffordshire
☎ 0889 562561

A left-handed, 1¼ mile, oval course, it was founded in 1907 and hosts 16 national hunt race days each year.

MAJOR EVENTS

Uttoxeter's 16 race days include 3 evening meetings, 2 in May and 1 in August, and two popular Bank Holiday meetings, Easter Monday and the late May Whitsun Holiday. The Midlands Grand National is the most important race in Uttoxeter's calendar.

April
The Midlands Grand National is staged in April.

✵ CALENDAR OF EVENTS ✵

February	9	Saturday
March	16	Saturday
April	1	Monday
	2	Tuesday
May	4	Saturday
	9	Thursday*
	27	Monday
	28	Tuesday*
August	8	Thursday*
September	19	Thursday
October	5	Saturday
	17	Thursday
November	7	Thursday
December	4	Wednesday
	20	Friday
	21	Saturday

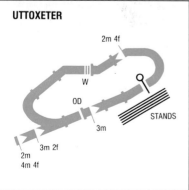

GETTING THERE/GETTING IN

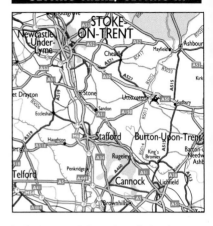

Rail: Uttoxeter B.R. station adjoins the course
Road: Off the A50 Stoke-on-Trent to Burton-upon-Trent road
P 🚻 Ample space for cars
200 coach spaces 🚻

Enclosures

Club Enclosure: viewing; betting facilities; bars; members restaurant in Paddock Suite and snack bars.
Tattersalls Enclosure: viewing; betting facilities; bars; restaurant and snack bars.
Silver Ring: betting facilities; bar and a snack bar.
Course Enclosure: betting facilities; snacks and picnic facilities.
Other facilities: fun fair on the course at Bank Holiday meetings.

Costs

Annual membership
Adult	🎫	£60
Couple	🎫	£95

Day tickets
Club Enclosure	🎫	£9
Tattersalls Enclosure	🎫	£6.50
Silver Ring	🎫	£4.50
Course Enclosure	🎫	£4.50

Methods of payment: cash/cheque with valid bankers card

WARWICK

THE COURSE

Warwick Racecourse
Hampton Street
Warwick
Warwickshire
☎ 0926 491553

A left-handed, 1¾ mile, oval course, it was founded in 1714 and hosts 13 flat and 12 national hunt race days each year.

MAJOR EVENTS

The national hunt season at Warwick runs from mid-October to May. The 12 race days include two evening meetings, both in mid-May. The most important national hunt race at Warwick is the Racephone National Handicap Chase run in mid-January.

The flat season includes 2 popular two day meetings, one starting on Easter Monday and the other in early October. 6 evening meetings are held between May and the end of July. The most important flat race at Warwick is the Warwick Oaks.

⚑ CALENDAR OF EVENTS ⚑

January	12	*Saturday*
	19	*Saturday*
February	5	*Tuesday*
	20	*Wednesday*
March	5	*Tuesday*
April	1	Monday
	2	Tuesday
	13	Saturday
May	6	Monday
	11	*Saturday**
	18	*Saturday**
	25	Saturday*
June	22	Saturday*
	29	Saturday*
July	3	Wednesday
	12	Friday
	27	Saturday*
August	26	Monday
October	7	Monday
	8	Tuesday
November	2	*Saturday*
	16	*Saturday*
	28	*Thursday*
December	9	*Monday*
	30	*Monday*

GETTING THERE/GETTING IN

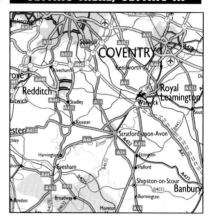

Rail: Warwick B.R. station, 1 mile from the course
Road: Signposted from the A41/A46 jct just west of Warwick
P Limited spaces for cars 🎫 £1
100 coach spaces 🚌

Enclosures

Club Enclosure: viewing; betting facilities; bar; restaurant and snack bars.
Grandstand & Paddock Enclosure: viewing; betting facilities; bars with snacks and snack bars.
Course Enclosure: betting facilities; bar; snack bars and childrens playground.

Costs

Annual membership
Adult 🎫 £75
plus £5 car park pass
Junior (10–20) 🎫 £37.50
National Hunt member only 🎫 £37.50

Day tickets
Club Enclosure 🎫 £9

Grandstand & Paddock
Enclosure 🎫 £6

Course Enclosure 🎫 £3

Methods of payment: cash/cheque with valid bankers card

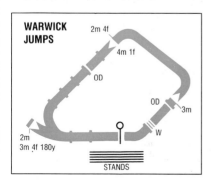

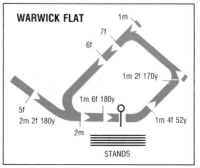

WETHERBY

THE COURSE

The Racecourse
York Road
Wetherby
North Yorkshire
☎ 0937 62035

A left-handed, 1½ mile, oval course, it was founded in 1867 and hosts 14 national hunt race days each year.

MAJOR EVENTS

Wetherby hosts 14 race days per year including 1 evening meeting in May. The two day meetings are the most popular and also include the most important races at Wetherby.

April
A two day meeting starts on Easter Monday and features the Wetherby Handicap Chase.

November
A two day meeting is held in early November during which the Charlie Hall Memorial Wetherby Pattern Chase is run.

December
The Rowland Meyrick Handicap Chase is run on Boxing Day and the Castleford Handicap Chase is run the day after during the popular Boxing Day meeting.

✯ CALENDAR OF EVENTS ✯

January	11	Friday
February	2	Saturday
	27	Wednesday
April	1	Monday
	2	Tuesday
May	8	Wednesday*
	27	Monday
October	16	Wednesday
November	1	Friday
	2	Saturday
	19	Tuesday
	30	Saturday
December	26	Thursday
	27	Friday

GETTING THERE/GETTING IN

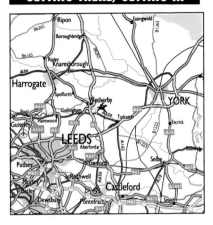

Rail: Leeds B.R. station, 12 miles from the course
Road: Off the B1224 road to York, east of Wetherby town centre
P 🚌 Ample space for cars and coaches

Enclosures

Club Enclosure: viewing; betting facilities; bars and restaurant.
Tattersalls Enclosure: viewing; full betting facilities; bars serving hot snacks and snack bars.
Course Enclosure: betting facilities; bar; snack bar and childrens playground.

Costs

Annual membership
Adult	🎟	£50
Couple	🎟	£80

Day tickets
Club Enclosure	🎟	£10
Tattersalls Enclosure	🎟	£5
Course Enclosure	🎟	£1.50

Methods of payment: cash/cheque with valid bankers card

WETHERBY

2m 4f 100y
W
OD
OD
3m 100y
2m 50y
STANDS

WINCANTON

THE COURSE

The Racecourse
Wincanton
Somerset
☎ 0963 32344

The current course was built in 1927, and is a right-handed, 1 mile 3 furlong, oval course. It hosts 13 national hunt race days each year.

MAJOR EVENTS

The Wincanton season lasts from October to April and includes one evening meeting, the last meeting of the season. The Bank Holiday meetings on Boxing Day and Easter Monday are the most popular.

The two most important races at Wincanton are the Kingwell Pattern Hurdle run in late February and the Badger Beer Chase which is run in November.

⚞ CALENDAR OF EVENTS ⚞

January	10	Thursday
	25	Friday
February	7	Thursday
	21	Thursday
March	7	Thursday
April	1	Monday
	12	Friday
	25	Thursday*
October	10	Thursday
	24	Thursday
November	7	Thursday
	21	Thursday
December	26	Thursday

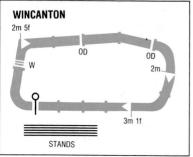

WINCANTON

GETTING THERE/GETTING IN

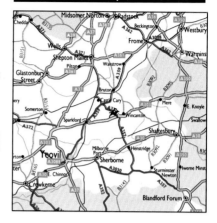

Rail: Gillingham B.R. station, 8 miles from the course
Road: On the B3081, off the A303, east of Wincanton
P 🅿 3500 car spaces
Picnic cars on course 🎫 £3
Ample space for coaches 🎫

Enclosures

Club Enclosure: viewing; betting facilities; Paddock Bar, Stalbridge Bar; Members Restaurant and snacks.
Tattersalls Enclosure: viewing; betting facilities including Tote; bars and snack bars.
Course Enclosure: betting facilities; snacks and picnic area.

Costs

Annual membership
Adult	🎫	£60

Day tickets
Club Enclosure	🎫	£9
Tattersalls Enclosure	🎫	£6

Course Enclosure
Per car	🎫	£3
Per adult	🎫	£3

Methods of payment: cash only

WINDSOR

THE COURSE

The Racecourse
Maidenhead Road
Windsor
Berkshire
☎ 0753 865234

A long, narrow, 1 mile 6 furlong, figure-of-eight course, it was founded in 1866 and hosts 8 national hunt and 13 flat race days including 11 evening meetings, the highest number in the country. Windsor takes full advantage of its lovely setting beside the River Thames, the regal tourist attractions of the town and its proximity to London.

MAJOR EVENTS

Windsor hosts 11 very popular evening flat race meetings between April and August.

It also runs a national hunt programme during the Winter, its most important race is the New Year's Day Hurdle.

☆ CALENDAR OF EVENTS ☆

January	1	*Tuesday*
	16	*Wednesday*
	30	*Wednesday*
February	16	*Saturday*
March	4	*Monday*
April	29	Monday*
May	13	Monday*
June	17	Monday*
	24	Monday*
July	1	Monday*
	8	Monday*
	15	Monday*
	22	Monday*
	29	Monday*
August	3	Saturday*
	12	Monday
	19	Monday
	24	Saturday*
November	9	*Saturday*
	18	*Monday*
December	5	*Thursday*

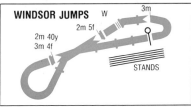

GETTING THERE/GETTING IN

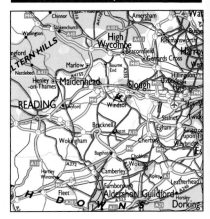

Rail: Windsor & Eton Riverside or Windsor & Eton Central B.R. stations, both are 2 miles from the course
Road: Off the A308 Windsor to Maidenhead road, north-west of Windsor
Water: The course is accessible by boat
P Cars 🅿 £1–£2
Picnic cars 🅿 £10
Coaches 🅿 £1

Enclosures

Club Enclosure: viewing including Paddock and Parade Ring; betting facilities; Cocktail Bar, Jamstick Bar; Seafood and Champagne Bar; Club Restaurant and buffet bar.
Tattersalls & Paddock Enclosure: viewing; betting facilities; Paddock Bar, Tattersalls Bar and snack food bar.
Silver Ring: betting facilities; bar and cafeteria.

Costs

Annual membership
Adult   🅿 £65
Couple   🅿 £110
Note: there is a 5 year waiting list for membership.

Day tickets
Club Enclosure   🅿 £10

Tattersalls & Paddock Enclosure
                             🅿 £6

Silver Ring   🅿 £3

Methods of payment: cash/cheque with valid bankers card

WINDSOR JUMPS
W
3m
2m 5f
2m 40y
3m 4f
STANDS

WINDSOR FLAT
1m 3f 150y
1m 2f 22y
1m 70y
5f
6f
STANDS

WOLVERHAMPTON

THE COURSE

The Racecourse
Gorsebrook Road
Wolverhampton
☎ 0902 24481

A left-handed, 1½ mile, triangular course, it hosts 15 flat and 11 national hunt race days each year.

MAJOR EVENTS

The national hunt season at Wolverhampton runs from early November to mid-March. The most popular meeting is the two day meeting starting on Boxing Day. The most important national hunt race at Wolverhampton is the Wolverhampton Champion Hurdle Trial run in February.

The flat season includes 5 evening meetings, between June and August, two 2 day meetings in early April and at the start of October, and a one day meeting on August Bank Holiday.

☆ CALENDAR OF EVENTS ☆

January	7	*Monday*
	23	*Wednesday*
February	4	*Monday*
	18	*Monday*
March	15	*Friday*
	18	*Monday*
April	8	Monday
	9	Tuesday
	29	Monday
May	13	Monday
	20	Monday
June	17	Monday*
July	1	Monday*
	15	Monday*
	29	Monday*
August	17	Saturday*
	26	Monday
September	9	Monday
	30	Monday
October	1	Tuesday
	16	Wednesday
November	4	*Monday*
	11	*Monday*
	25	*Monday*
December	26	*Thursday*
	27	*Friday*

GETTING THERE/GETTING IN

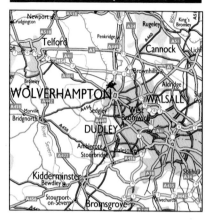

Rail: Wolverhampton B.R. station, 1 mile from the course
Road: Off the A449, 1 mile north of Wolverhampton
P Ample space for cars 🎫 £1
Ample space for coaches 🚍

Enclosures

Members Enclosure: viewing; betting facilities; bar; restaurant and snack bars.
Tattersalls Enclosure: viewing; betting facilities including betting shop; bars with snacks and snack bars.
Silver Ring: viewing (the Parade Ring is visible from all enclosures); betting facilities; bar; snack bars and childrens playground.

Costs

Annual membership
Adult 🎫 £85

Day tickets
Members Enclosure 🎫 £8

Tattersalls Enclosure 🎫 £6

Silver Ring 🎫 £3
OAPs 🎫 £2.20

Methods of payment: cash/cheque with valid bankers card

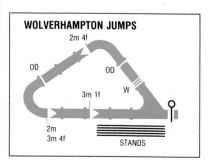

WOLVERHAMPTON JUMPS

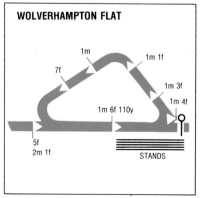

WOLVERHAMPTON FLAT

WORCESTER

THE COURSE

The Racecourse
Pitchcroft
Worcester
☎ 0905 25364

A left-handed, 1 mile 5 furlong, oval course,
it was founded in 1867 and hosts 20
national hunt race days each year.

MAJOR EVENTS

Worcester's national hunt season runs from
mid-August to mid-May. There is a two day
meeting in mid-September and 3 evening
meetings are held at the end of April, in
early May and mid-August, the August
meeting is the most popular at the course.

✦ CALENDAR OF EVENTS ✦

January	5	Saturday
February	13	Wednesday
	27	Wednesday
March	20	Wednesday
	27	Wednesday
April	3	Wednesday
	27	Saturday*
May	8	Wednesday*
	22	Wednesday
August	10	Saturday*
	12	Monday
	29	Thursday
September	13	Friday
	14	Saturday
	21	Saturday
October	12	Saturday
	26	Saturday
November	13	Wednesday
December	2	Monday
	11	Wednesday

GETTING THERE/GETTING IN

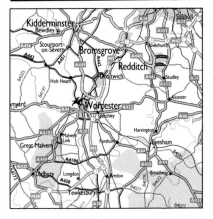

Rail: Worcester B.R. station, ½ mile from
the course
Road: Off the A443, north of Worcester city
centre
P ⛟ Ample space for cars and coaches

Enclosures

Members Enclosure: viewing; betting
facilities; bar; restaurant and snack bars.
Tattersalls Enclosure: viewing; betting
facilities; bar with snacks and snack bar.
Centre Course Enclosure: betting facilities;
bar and snack bars.

Costs

Annual membership   n/a

Day tickets
Members Enclosure   🎟 £9

Tattersalls Enclosure   🎟 £7

Centre Course Enclosure   🎟 £3.50

Methods of payment: cash only

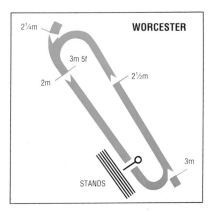

YARMOUTH

THE COURSE

The Racecourse
Jellicoe Road
Great Yarmouth
Norfolk
☎ 0493 843527

A left-handed, 1½ mile, oval course, it hosts 17 flat race days each year.

MAJOR EVENTS

Yarmouth's calendar runs from June to October and includes 3 two day meetings, one in June, one in July and one in August. The most popular and important meeting of the year is the three day Eastern Meeting held in mid–September.

This calendar obviously reflects Great Yarmouth's role as a major seaside holiday resort as does the encouragement of children at the course through the Family Enclosure and the adventure playground.

Yarmouth's proximity to Newmarket is often reflected in the quality of the 2 year old horses the trainers bring to the meetings to "trial".

✦ CALENDAR OF EVENTS ✦

June	4	Tuesday
	5	Wednesday
	25	Tuesday
July	3	Wednesday
	4	Thursday
	17	Wednesday*
	24	Wednesday
	25	Thursday
	26	Friday
August	1	Thursday
	13	Tuesday
	21	Wednesday
	22	Thursday
September	17	Tuesday
	18	Wednesday
	19	Thursday
October	30	Wednesday

GETTING THERE/GETTING IN

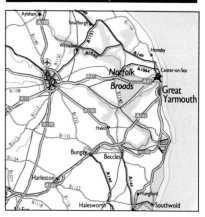

Rail: Great Yarmouth B.R. station, ½ mile from the course
Road: Off the A149, north of the town centre, well signposted
P 500 car spaces 🎫 £1
30 coach spaces 🎫

Enclosures

Members Enclosure: viewing; betting facilities; Champagne Bar; Oyster Bar; Members Restaurant and snack bar.
Tattersalls Enclosure: viewing; betting facilities; two bars and a snack bar.
Family and Course Enclosure: betting facilities; fast food and two bars.
Other facilities: childrens adventure playground.

YARMOUTH

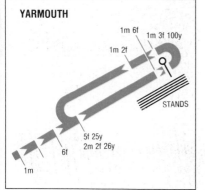

Costs

Annual membership

Adult	🎫	£80
Second (guest) membership	🎫	£50

Day tickets

Members Enclosure	🎫	£10
Tattersalls Enclosure	🎫	£7
Family and Course Enclosure	🎫	£3.50
Children	🎫	

Methods of payment: cash/cheque with valid bankers card

YORK

THE COURSE

The Racecourse
Knavesmire Road
York
☎ 0904 620911

The Knavesmire Course was founded in 1731 but formal, organised race meetings have been recorded in York since 1709 and the City Corporation were supporting races from 1530 onwards. A left-handed, 2 mile, open course, it hosts 15 flat race days each year. York is often described as the "Ascot of the North". The racecourse facilities are magnificent and the quality of the racing matches them.

✦ CALENDAR OF EVENTS ✦

May	14	Tuesday
	15	Wednesday
	16	Thursday
June	14	Friday
	15	Saturday
July	12	Friday
	13	Saturday
August	20	Tuesday
	21	Wednesday
	22	Thursday
September	4	Wednesday
	5	Thursday
October	9	Wednesday
	10	Thursday
	12	Saturday

MAJOR EVENTS

York's 15 race days are organised into a three day meeting in mid May, the May Festival, 2 two day meetings in mid June and in mid July, a three day meeting towards the end of August, the Ebor Meeting, a two day meeting in early September followed by a two day meeting and a one day meeting in mid October.

The two most important meetings are the Ebor Meeting and the May Festival and each of these hosts major races.

May
The May Festival, a three day meeting in mid May hosts the Kosset Yorkshire Cup, a 1 mile 6 furlong race for 4 year olds and upwards, the William Hill Dante Stakes, an important Derby trial, and the Tattersalls Musidora Stakes.

June
The William Hill Golden Spurs Trophy is run at the June meeting.

July
The John Smith's Magnet Cup Handicap is run at the July meeting.

August
The Ebor Meeting, a three day meeting during which the following races are staged. The Tote Ebor Handicap, a 1 mile 6 furlong race for 3 year olds first raced in 1843, the Juddmonte International Stakes, the Keeneland Nunthorpe Stakes, the Great Voltigeur Stakes, the Scottish Equitable Gimcrack Stakes, first run in 1846, the Aston Upthorpe Yorkshire Oaks, the Bradford and Bingley Handicap, and the Pacemaker Update Lowther Stakes.

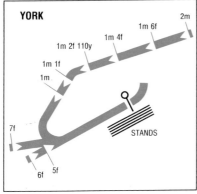

YORK

2m
1m 6f
1m 4f
1m 2f 110y
1m 1f
1m
7f
STANDS
6f 5f

YORK

GETTING THERE/GETTING IN

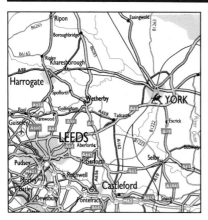

Rail: York B.R. station, 1 mile from the course
Road: Off the A64 Tadcaster Road, south-west of York city centre
P 🅿 10,000 car spaces
Limited members car park 🎫 £2
1000 coach spaces 🅿

Enclosures

County Stand: members enclosure; viewing including Paddock, Parade Ring and Winners Enclosure; full betting facilities; bars; Alcoves Bar; Champagne Pavilion; The Champagne and Seafood Restaurant and the Gimcrack Rooms (members dining room and bar). *Note:* There are no transfers from other Enclosures to the County Stand.
Grandstand & Paddock Enclosure (Tattersalls): viewing including Parade Ring; betting hall and other betting facilities; 5-tier Grandstand; bars; Father William's Tavern; The Zetland Restaurant and a Racing Museum on the 4th floor.
Silver Ring: full betting facilities; Stick & Willie Pub; bars; self-service restaurant and a fish and chip shop.
Course Enclosure: betting facilities; bar; snack and sandwich counters and a picnic space.

Costs
Annual membership
Adult 🎫 £75
Couple 🎫 £125

Day tickets

Enclosure	May Festival Meeting	Ebor Meeting (August)	All other race days
County Stand	£14	£25	£12
3-day badges	£35	£60	
Tattersalls	£7.50	£9.50	£7.50
3-day badges	£16	£20	
Silver Ring	£3	£3	£3
3-day badges	£6	£6	
OAPs	£1.50	£1.50	£1.50
Course	£1.50	£1.50	£1.50
3-day badges	£3	£3	
OAPs	80p	80p	80p

Methods of payment: cash/cheque with valid bankers card/Visa card/Access/Mastercard

ASCOT

Including Windsor

County: Berkshire
i Central Library, Town Square,
   Bracknell
☎ 0344 423149
i Central Station, Thames Street,
   Windsor
☎ 0753 852010
Early closing: Wednesday (Windsor)
Market day: Saturday (Windsor)
Population: 7500 (Ascot) 30,000 (Windsor)
Ascot, a small town surrounded by large
estates, hosts the most fashionable race
meeting of the year, the Royal Meeting in
June. Ascot provides a good centre for
drives and walks in the nearby Windsor
Great Park, over 4500 acres of dense
beechwood and formal gardens to enjoy.
The Great Park lies south of Windsor Castle,
founded by William the Conqueror, it has
been a royal residence since the reign of
Henry I and is the largest residential castle
in the world.

Across the Thames from Windsor is Eton
with its famous 15th century boys' college
and quaint high street. This beautiful
stretch of the Thames river valley provides
numerous attractive riverside villages, pubs
and hotels to visit by road or water. Among
the larger riverside towns, Henley-
on-Thames provides a most attractive
watering place. Henley held the first river
regatta in the world in 1830 and the Royal
Regatta is now held there every July, one of
the main events in both society's and the
rowing fraternity's calendar.

ADVENTURE

Multi-activity Centres

Spice (Thames Valley)
"An adventure group for ordinary people
who want to do extraordinary things" it
organises ballooning, assault courses,
abseiling, racing car driving.
38 Albany Road, Reading, Berkshire
☎ 0734 584632

AERIAL SPORTS

Gliding

Booker Gliding Club
Wycombe Air Park, Marlow
☎ 0494 442501

HEALTH

Leisure Centres

Windsor Leisure Pool
Wave pool, water slide, solarium, sauna,
fountain and poolside jacuzzis, gym, etc.
Nr the town centre
Stovell Road, Windsor
☎ 0753 850004

Magnet Leisure Centre
Pool, squash, special events.
Holmanleaze, Maidenhead
☎ 0628 33899

LOCAL FEATURES

Art Galleries

Stanley Spencer Gallery
King's Hall, High Street,
Cookham-on-Thames
☎ 0628 524580
Off the M4, exit 7

Arts and Crafts

Brass-Rubbing Centre
Windsor Parish Church
☎ 0753 852730 pm only

Festivals and Fairs

May
Royal Windsor Horse Show

June
Garter Ceremony, Windsor

July
Henley Royal Regatta
Royal Windsor Rose and Horticultural Show
Windsor Championship Dog Show
Swan Upping at Cookham

September
National Carriage Driving Championships,
Windsor

September/October
Windsor Festival

Food and Drink

Ascot Vineyard
Sunningwell Park, Ascot
☎ 0990 23563
P ⌖

Duffey's Old Bakery
Oldest coal-fired bread oven still in use in
Britain. Building reputed to be haunted.
Oxford Road, Windsor
☎ 0753 865545
🚗 ✗

ASCOT

Fun Parks

Thorpe Park
Landscaped theme park and lakes; maritime displays; boat, train and go-kart rides; sailing and water skiing schools.
Staines Lane, Chertsey
☎ 0932 62633
➟A A320

Gardens

Alexandra Gardens
Attractive riverside gardens. Sunday band concerts in the summer.
Windsor

Savill Gardens
Outstanding 35 acre garden.

Valley Gardens
400 acres of woodland.
Savill Gardens 1 mile away.

Guided Tours

Windsorian Coaches
Short tours in an open-topped bus depart from the public entrance to Windsor Castle.
☎ 0753 756841

Windsor Horsedrawn Carriages
Horse-drawn carriage tours. Hackney Carriage stand outside castle.
☎ 0753 865301
☎ 0784 35983

Windsor Tourist Information Centre
Leaflets detailing town trails supplied. Guided walking tours leave from the Tourist Information Centre.

Historic Buildings

Cliveden

A National Trust property set on cliffs 200 feet above the River Thames, 375 acres including formal gardens, woodland and riverside walks.
Taplow
☎ 06286 5069
Off the B476 north of Taplow
✕ ♿

Dorney Court
Enchanting Tudor manor house built about 1440 with period furniture and family portraits. Fruit picking in the summer.
Borney
☎ 0628 604638
On the B3026, 2 miles west of Eton
✕

Eton College and Museum of Eton Life
Britain's most famous school, founded in 1440, over 20 Prime Ministers educated here.
High Street, Eton
☎ 0753 86359
🚌

Windsor Castle
A royal residence at certain times of the year, Windsor Castle represents 900 years of history. The State Apartments, Royal Mausoleum, Queen Mary's Doll's House, Queen's carriages and Old Master Drawings are open to the public. St George's Chapel, within the grounds, is open when no service is in progress, it is the burial place of 10 sovereigns.
☎ 0753 831118

Museums

Household Cavalry Museum
Combermere Barracks, St Leonard Road, Windsor
☎ 0753 868222
Off the B3022
🎦

Royalty and Empire Exhibition

Restored GWR station built in 1897, with animated theatre show of Madame Tussaud's waxwork figures.
Windsor and Eton Central Station, Thames Street, Windsor
☎ 0753 857837
✕ ♿

ASCOT

Natural History

Courage Shire Horse Centre
Courage prize-winning shire horses;
farrier's workshop; small animal/bird area
and play area.
Cherry Garden Lane, Maidenhead Thicket,
Maidenhead
☎ 0628 824848
➔A A4
P 🚌 ✕ ♿ ♿

Parks

Home Park
Beautifully located beside the river and
beneath the castle, the public park is a
popular sport and recreation area.
Windsor

Runnymede
The riverside meadow where the Magna
Carta was signed in 1215 (National Trust).
A memorial to President J F Kennedy, and
another, to the men and women of the RAF
who died in World War II with 'no known
grave', stand on Cooper's Hill, nearby.
3 miles south-east of Windsor

Windsor Great Park
Over 4,500 acres of parkland and gardens,
this used to be part of the Great Royal
Hunting Forest. Crown Property, most of
the beechwoods and formal gardens
including Savill and Valley Gardens are now
open to the public.
☎ 0753 860222
P 🚌 ✕ ♿

Theatres

Theatre Royal
Thames Street, Windsor
☎ 0753 853888
✕

Wilde Theatre
Modern theatre with varied all-year-round
programme of arts events. Large and
enterprising arts centre with gallery spaces,
cinema, recital room and sculpture park.
South Hill Park Arts Centre, Bracknell
☎ 0344 484123
Off the A322 Bagshot road
P ✕

Zoos

Windsor Safari Park
Daily programme of shows including birds
of prey, performing parrots, African Queen
river boat ride, play area, elephants, lions,
dolphins and even a whale!
Winkfield Road, Windsor
☎ 0753 869841
Off the B3022
P ✕ ♿ ♿

Golf

Visitors welcome weekdays at:
Berkshire Golf Club ⛳
Swinley Road, Ascot
☎ 0990 21496

Royal Ascot Golf Club ⛳
Winkfield Road, Ascot
☎ 0990 25175

Sunningdale Golf Club ⛳
Ascot
☎ 0990 21681

Polo

Smith's Lawn
Windsor Great Park
i Fixture list from the Tourist Office.

Skiing/Ice Skating

John Nike Leisuresport Complex
Artificial dry-slope skiing.
John Nike Way, Bracknell
☎ 0344 860033
➔A A329
P ✕

Boat Hire

Rowing and motor boats to hire and at
Windsor and Marlow. Cruisers can be hired
from Maidenhead.

Boat Trips

French Brothers
The Runnymede Boathouse, Old Windsor
☎ 0753 851900

Salter Bros
A large range of passenger launch trips.
Folly Bridge, Oxford
☎ 0865 243421

Sailing/Water Skiing

Thorpe Park
see under Fun Parks

AYR

Region: Strathclyde
i 39 Sandgate, Ayr
☎ 0292 284196
Early closing: Wednesday
Market day: Indoor market "Petticoat Lane" in Dalblair Road, open 10am–5pm daily; Open air Sunday market, Ayr Racecourse
Population: 48,000
Ayr is situated on the west coast of Scotland. An attractive resort with excellent, safe beaches, it provides traditional seaside fun for the family. Away from the beach there are three golf courses, several beautiful parks and gardens, two theatres and an art gallery. Ayr has been immortalised in the lyrics of Robert Burns, Scotland's national bard.

ADVENTURE

Shooting and Stalking

Dalvennan Shooting Ground
Clay target shooting for all.
Kirkmichael, Maybole
☎ 0292 531134
✗

Gamesport (Ayr) Ltd
Specialists in guns and fishing tackle; local shooting information freely given.
60 Sandgate, Ayr
☎ 0292 263822

EQUESTRIAN

Riding and Pony Trekking

High Mains Pony Trekking
Ian Loch, Wallacetown, Maybole
☎ 046581 504

Little Turnberry Stables
Linda McFadzean,
Lands of Turnberry,
Maidens, Girvan
☎ 0655 31534

LOCAL FEATURES

Architecture

Wallace Tower
Neo-Gothic tower, 113 feet high, with statue of Sir William Wallace.
High Street, Ayr

Factory Visits

The Diamond Factory
Design studios and factory.
1st Floor, Queens Court Centre, Sandgate
☎ 0292 280476

John Walker & Sons Ltd
The world's largest Scotch whisky blending and bottling plant.
Hill Street, Kilmarnock
☎ 0563 23401
▱

Festivals and Fairs

April
Ayrshire Agricultural Show

June
Ayrshire Arts Festival and Burns Festival
Ayr Golf Week

July
Culzean Country Fair

August
Culzean Festival of Flowers and Music
Ayr Flower Show

Gardens

Belleisle Estate
Formal gardens, deer park, duck pond and aviaries.
South of Ayr
✗

Rozelle Estate
Gardens, shrubbery, walks and sculpture park.
Alloway, 1½ miles from the town centre

Historic Buildings

Bachelor's Club
A 17th century house where Burns, his brother and five others formed themselves into a debating society and Bachelors' Club in 1780. The club met in this building, now a National Trust property.
Tarbolton
☎ 0292 541424
▱

Burns Cottage and Museum
Robert Burns was born in 1759 in this two-roomed clay and thatched cottage. The museum contains his manuscripts and private possessions.
Alloway
☎ 0292 41215
▱ ♿

Burns Monument and Gardens
Sculptures of characters from Burns' poems, designed by Thomas Hamilton junior, and built in 1823.
Alloway
☎ 0292 41321
▱

92

AYR

Culzean Castle
18th century castle set in 560 acres of grounds, designed by Robert Adam and beautifully furnished; a fine collection of family portraits.
4 miles north of Kirkoswald
☎ 06556 274
⌂

Dunure Castle
On the coast south of Ayr are the attractive ruins of this prominent castle.
P

Souter Johnnie's Cottage
A thatched cottage, home of village cobbler 'Souter' John Davidson, the original Souter Johnnie of Burns' poem "Tam O'Shanter".
Kirkoswald
⌂

Museums

Tam O'Shanter Museum
A Burns museum housed where Tam O'Shanter's memorable ride commenced.
Ayr
☎ 0292 269794
⌂

Natural History

Enterkine Nature Trail
Natural woodland with badgers' setts, a pond and varied birdlife.
Scottish Wildlife Trust
On the B744 nr Tarbolton

Parks

Craigie Park
Riverside walks, gardens, boating.

Theatres

Gaiety Theatre
Carrick Street
☎ 0292 264639

Civic Theatre
Craigie Road
☎ 0292 263755

Cycling

The Cycle Shop
6 The Cross, Prestwick
☎ 0292 77360

Fishing

Game fishing on the River Ayr, River Doon and River Girvan for salmon, sea trout and brown trout. Loch fishing on nearby lochs and reservoirs.
i Contact the Tourist Information Centre for a detailed leaflet.
Gamesport (Ayr) Ltd
60 Sandgate, Ayr
☎ 0292 541674

Sea angling is good along Newton Shore, Ayr harbour mouth and from the rocky coastline at the Heads of Ayr. Boat fishing for cod, haddock, thornback, ray and flatfish can produce good catches.

Boat Hire
Ayr Sea Angling Centre
Tony Medina, 10 Britannia Place, Ayr
☎ 0292 285297

Ayr Marine Charters
59 Woodlands Crescent, Ayr
☎ 0292 281638

Brian Burns
Flat 2, 16 Bellevue Road, Ayr
☎ 0292 281648

Golf

There are many top golf courses along the Ayrshire coast. The most famous are:

Belleisle Golf Course
⛳ public course.
Belleisle Park, Ayr
☎ 0292 41258

Old Prestwick Golf Course
⛳ private course. Visitors must have a letter of introduction from their club.
2 Links Road, Prestwick
☎ 0292 77404

Royal Troon Golf Club
⛳ welcomes weekday visitors.
Old Course, Craigend Road, Troon
☎ 0292 311555

Turnberry, Ailsa & Arran Golf Course
⛳ Visitors must book in writing.
Turnberry Hotel, Turnberry
☎ 06553 202

Ice Skating

Ayr Ice Rink
Skate hire and disco music.
9 Limekiln Road, Ayr
☎ 0292 263024

Walking and Rambling

i Details of local walks available from the Tourist Information Centre.

Culzean Country Park
Four walks including a cliff walk.

The Park Centre
Off the A719, 12 miles south of Ayr
P ⌂ 🚌 |wc|

Boat Trips

P. S. Waverley, the last sea-going paddle steamer in the world, sails from Ayr to ports on the Clyde and to the islands during the summer months.
☎ 041 221 8152

BANGOR-ON-DEE

WHAT TO DO AND SEE

County: Clwyd, Wales
i Civic Centre, High Street, Whitchurch, Shropshire
☎ 0948 4577
i Memorial Hall, Bodhyfryd, Wrexham, Clwyd
☎ 0978 357845 summer;
☎ 0978 290444 rest of year
i Town Hall, Llangollen, Clwyd
☎ 0978 860828
Early closing: Thursday (Llangollen)
Market day: Tuesday (Llangollen)
Population: Wrexham 41,000
Bangor-on-Dee, with its peaceful riverside setting and beautiful 17th century bridge, lies on the Welsh border surrounded by richly contrasting scenery. The Ceiriog valley offers exciting walks and a river to fish. Nearby Llangollen is famous as the scene for the International Musical Eisteddfod, a competition of international standard for performers in music, dance and song. One of Wales' most important annual events, it is held in July. Llangollen also hosts national and international canoeing events and rallies. Wrexham, the industrial centre of North Wales, is within easy reach, as is Ellesmere and the ancient and well preserved walled city of Chester.

ADVENTURE

Clay Pigeon Shooting

Clay Target Club
Qualified instruction and shotguns available, non-members welcome.
Llandegla
☎ 0978 364158

Multi-activity Centres

Ashley Activity Holidays
Cycling, walking and fishing weeks in self-catering accommodation.
☎ 093922 224

AERIAL SPORTS

Parachuting

Sport Parachute Centre
Prees Heath, nr Whitchurch

EQUESTRIAN

Riding

The Golden Pheasant Riding Centre
Tal-y-Garth, Glyn Ceiriog, nr Llangollen
☎ 069172 408

Pengwern Mill Riding Stables
Llangollen
☎ 0978 860435

HEALTH

Leisure Centres

Plas Madoc Leisure Centre
Leisure pool, sun beds, sauna and gym; also hosts cabaret, entertainments and major sports events.
Acrefair, Wrexham
☎ 0978 821600
On the A539, 7 miles from Wrexham on the Llangollen road

LOCAL FEATURES

Arts and Crafts

Johnsons Basket Centre
Baskets made to specification.
Bangor-on-Dee
☎ 0978 780417
On the A525/B5069

Alf Strange
Demonstrations by practising blacksmith.
☎ 069171 2628
➔A A495

The Rocking Horse Workshop
Watch the traditional art of making wooden rocking horses, hand carved and painted in Georgian and Victorian styles.
Ashfield House, The Foxholes, Wem
☎ 0939 32335

Festivals and Fairs

May
Llangollen Jazz Festival

July
International Musical Eisteddfod

July and Aug
Sheepdog trials, Ceiriog Valley and Llangollen

Oct–Jan
Canoe Championships

Gardens

Cholmondeley Castle Gardens
Hillside gardens and 19th century castle; lakeside picnic areas.
Malpas
☎ 082922 383
➔A A49
P ✗ ♿

Dorothy Clive Gardens
Nr Woore
☎ 0782 680322

Hodnet Hall Gardens
Trees, lawns, lakes and ancient buildings.
Hodnet, nr Weston-under-Redcastle
☎ 063084 202

Oak Cottage Herb Garden
Nesscliff
☎ 074381 273

BANGOR-ON-DEE

WHAT TO DO AND SEE

Historic Buildings

Borfold Hall
Nantwich
☎ 0270 625245
→A A534
P 🚐

Erddig House
Late 17th century house; formal walled garden, extensive woods and parkland. Country walks. National Trust.
Nr Wrexham
☎ 0978 355314

Moreton Corbet Castle
A grand ruin, part Elizabethan mansion and part mediaeval castle.
Nr Shawbury

Plas Newydd
Home of the "Ladies of Llangollen".
Llangollen

Valle Crucis Abbey
Ruined Cistercian abbey.
Llangollen
☎ 0978 860326
On the B5103, west of Llangollen

Natural History

Bridgemere Wildlife and Heritage Centre
35 acre wildlife park and a craft centre.
Nr Woore
☎ 09365 223
Off the A51, 5 miles south-east of Nantwich
P ✕ ♿

Bradeley Green Waterfowl Sanctuary
Working farm; water gardens; waterfowl collection and farm nature trails.
Nr Whitchurch

Stapeley Water Gardens and Palms Tropical Oasis
Exotic birds, rare plants, sharks, piranhas, tropical and cold water fish.
London Road, Stapeley, nr Nantwich
☎ 0270 623868
On the A51, 1 mile south of Nantwich
P ✕ ♿

Parks

Marbury Country Park
200 acres of woodland, open spaces and picnic areas.
Comberbach, nr Whitchurch
☎ 0606 77741
→A A559
P ♿

Ty Mawr Country Park
Riverside walks, picnic areas, abundant wildlife and farm animals.
Cae Gwilym Lane, Cefn Mawr
☎ 0978 822780
🏛

Railways

Llangollen Railway Llangollen
Rides to the picturesque Horsheshoe Falls.
Llangollen Railway Society
☎ 0978 860951

OUTDOOR LEISURE

Birdwatching

Ellesmere Visitors Centre
Large mere noted for its wildfowl. Rowing boats, picnic area, fishing and playground.
The Mere
☎ 0691 3461
A495 Whitchurch to Oswestry road
P ✕ ♿

Cycling

Butlers
37 Scotland Street, Ellesmere
☎ 0691 2101

High Sports
Chapel Street, Llangollen
☎ 0978 861680

Fishing

There is good fishing in the area's pools, meres and rivers, such as the Tern and the Perry. The River Dee is a noted salmon river; there are also brown trout, sea trout and grayling. Permits available from:

The Newsagent
Chapel Street, Llangollen
☎ 0978 860155

Golf

Hawkestone Park ⛳18
Weston-under-Redcastle
☎ 093924 209

John Garner Golf School
☎ 0948 4232

Hill Valley Golf and Country Club ⛳18
Terrick Road, Whitchurch
☎ 0948 3584

Market Drayton ⛳9
Sutton Road, Market Drayton
☎ 0630 2266

Vale of Llangollen Golf Club ⛳18
☎ 0978 860040

Walking

Llangollen Ramblers
Les Potts
☎ 0978 861685
𝒊 Leaflets for walking are available at the Tourist Information Centre in Llangollen.

WATERSPORTS

Boat Trips

Horse-drawn barges cruise along the Shropshire Union Canal; at Llangollen they travel through unrivalled scenery.

Canoeing

Llangollen is a notable canoeing centre for events and rallies. Course tuition from:

Nomad Canoes
Mile End Mill, Llangollen
☎ 0978 861444

BATH

County: Avon
i Abbey Church Yard, Bath
☎ 0225 462831
Early closing: Monday and Thursday
Market day: Wednesday
Population: 84,000
Bath is one of Britain's oldest and most beautiful cities, famous since Roman times for its natural mineral springs. An important Roman settlement (Aquae Sulis, 'the waters of Sul', a Celtic goddess) the well preserved baths and adjoining museum offer an impressive record of Roman times.

It is the most complete and best-preserved Georgian city in Britain, largely the work of the architect, John Wood. The Pulteney Bridge, designed by Robert Adam, spans the Avon and fine Georgian streets such as the famous Royal Crescent abound.

Always popular, Bath became the meeting place of the 18th century's aristocratic and artistic worlds so establishing a cultural tradition that continues today.

EQUESTRIAN

Riding and Pony Trekking

Midford Valley Riding Stables
Midford Road
☎ 0225 837613

Mendip Riding Centre
Lyncombe Lodge, Churchill, nr Bristol
☎ 0934 852335

Montpelier Riding Centre
Weston Farm Lane, Weston
☎ 0225 23665

Wellow Trekking Centre
Little Horse Croft Farm, Wellow
☎ 0225 834376

HEALTH

Leisure Centres

Bath Sports and Leisure Centre
North Parade
☎ 0225 462563

LOCAL FEATURES

Art Galleries

Victoria Art Gallery
Collection includes European Old Masters and 18th–20th century British paintings.
Bridge Street
☎ 0225 461111
🖰

Festivals and Fairs

May
Badminton Horse Trials, 2–5 May

May–June
Bath International Festival of Music and the Arts, 24 May–9 June

Guided tours

Free guided walking tours
A detailed look at Bath's historic buildings, they leave from outside the Pump Room entrance in Abbey Church Yard. Mayor's Honorary Guides are all volunteers.

Ghost walks
Start at the Garrick's Head near the Theatre Royal.
☎ 0225 63618
☎ 0225 66541 for tickets

Car and coach tours
Private guides and open top bus tours are run at frequent intervals.
i Details from the Tourist Information Cent

Historic Buildings

Bath Abbey
Late 15th century abbey built on the site of an earlier Saxon and Norman building. Magnificent example of the perpendicular style of English Gothic architecture.

Dyrham Park
Richly furnished mansion built in Bath stone set in beautiful parkland with views across the Bristol Channel. Fallow deer roam the park. National Trust.
☎ 027 582 2501
On the A46, 8 miles north of Bath
✗

Museums

American Museum in Britain
Eighteen period furnished rooms and galleries all illustrating American life between the 17th and 19th centuries. Splendid views from the gardens.
Claverton Manor
☎ 0225 60503
Off the A36 Warminster road
🚍 ✗

BATH

WHAT TO DO AND SEE

Bath Postal Museum
History of the Post and its Bath connections – original letters from the 17th century, postcards, uniforms, working machinery. The building housed Bath's Post Office when the world's first postage stamp was used here on 2 May 1840.
Broad Street
☎ 0225 460333
➜A A4/A36

Roman Baths Museum
This Roman bathing establishment flourished between the 1st and 5th centuries. The waters can be tasted in the 18th century Pump Room.
☎ 0225 462831
🚌 ✕ ♿ ♿

Theatres

Theatre Royal
One of Britain's oldest and most beautiful theatres; a varied all-year programme; backstage tours.
Sawclose
☎ 0225 448844 Box Office
♿ ♿ wheelchair spaces available at half price, accompanied only
✕ Theatre Vaults Restaurant
☎ 0225 442265;
Chikako's, the only Japanese restaurant in a British theatre
☎ 0225 464125
🚌

Zoos

Longleat
The magnificent home of the Marquess of Bath and his famous lions.
Warminster, Wiltshire
☎ 09853 551
➜A A362

Farleigh Springs Trout Farm
Fresh trout for sale.
Farleigh, Hungerford
☎ 02214 62059

Golf

Bath Golf Club ⛳18
☎ 0225 63834
Close to Sham Castle

Entry Hill Golf Course
⛳9 municipal course.
☎ 0225 834248
1 mile from city centre

Kingsdown Golf Club
⛳18 overlooking the Box Valley.
☎ 0225 742530

Landsdown Golf Club ⛳18
☎ 0225 22138
3 miles north of the city alongside the racecourse

Tracy Park Golf and Country Club
Modern championship course with all the sporting facilities of a country club.
☎ 027 582 2251

Skiing

Avon Ski Centre
All equipment provided.
Lyncombe Lodge, Churchill, nr Bristol
☎ 0934 852828

Tennis

Hard courts at Royal Victoria Park, Sydney Gardens and Alice Park.
☎ 0225 423915

Grass court at the Recreation Ground.
☎ 0225 462563

OUTDOOR LEISURE

Cycling

Cycle path
Easy going, winding path along the Avon river valley using the flat, traffic-free route of a disused railway, it offers safe and peaceful cycling.

Avon Valley Cyclery
Underneath the Arches, Arch 37
☎ 0225 61880
Rear of Bath Spa Station

Fishing

Crudgington I.M. Ltd
37 Broad Street
☎ 0225 466325

Bath Trout Farm
Anglers' lake, and fresh trout for sale.
Old Cleveland Baths, Hampton Row, Bathwick
☎ 0225 60714

WATERSPORTS

Boat Hire

The Boathouse at Bath
Victorian boating station with wooden skiffs and punts to hire.
Forester Road
☎ 0225 466407
Less than a mile from the city centre

Avondale Guest House
Hire of canoes, punts and rowing boats.
London Road East, Bathford
☎ 0225 859847

Boat Trips

River boat trips available on passenger launches from Pulteney Bridge. Canal trips from Widcombe Top Lock.

John Rennie Cruising Restaurant
Sydney Wharf, Bathwick Hill
☎ 0225 447276

BEVERLEY

County: North Humberside
i The Guildhall, Register Square, Beverley
☎ 0482 867430
Early closing: Thursday
Market day: Saturday
Population: 19,400
Beverley, a picturesque market town with mediaeval streets is dominated by its magnificent Minster. An impressive, cathedral size Gothic church, the present building dates back to 1220. Surrounded by the rich farmland of the Yorkshire Wolds, Beverley provides access to the Humberside coast or the cities of Hull and York.

AERIAL SPORTS

Flying

Hull Aero Club
Full facilities for flying lessons and visiting aircraft.
Brough Airfield, Brough, nr Hull
☎ 0482 667985

Gliding

Wolds Gliding Club
A large gliding club with full facilities; 5-day courses available during the summer. One day membership with training flight.
The Airfield, Pocklington, York
☎ 0759 303579

EQUESTRIAN

Riding and Pony Trekking

Bleach Yard Stables
New Walk, Beverley
☎ 0482 882557

LOCAL FEATURES

Art Galleries

Ferens Art Gallery
Old Masters, marine paintings, 20th century and contemporary works.
Queen Victoria Square, Hull
☎ 0482 222750
→A M62/A63 (city centre)
🐾 🚐

Arts and Crafts

Withernwick Forest Crafts
Resin casting of animals, birds, oriental and fantasy chess sets.
Main Street, Withernwick
☎ 0964 527858

Festivals and Fairs

May
Early Music Festival, Beverley

June
Victorian Hayrie, Beverley

Fun Parks

Hornsea Pottery Leisure Park and Factory
Watch the complete manufacturing process from a gallery walk. Landscaped parkland attractions include butterfly world, adventure playground, mini bikes and a model village. A huge discount shopping area including discounted pottery.
Hornsea
☎ 0964 532161
On the B1242 on the outskirts of town
P ✕ ♿

Gardens

Burnby Hall Gardens
Extensive gardens with a fine display of water lilies, a rose garden, a selection of picnic areas and fishing spots.
The Balk, Pocklington
☎ 0759 302068
1 mile from the A1079
P 🚐 ✕ ♿

Historic Buildings

Beverley Minster
The present building dates from 1220 and is one of the finest Gothic churches of cathedral size in Europe.
☎ 0482 868540
→A A1079
🚐

Burton Constable Hall
Magnificent Elizabethan house set in grounds landscaped by Capability Brown.
Sproatley
☎ 0964 562400
On the B1238 east of Beverley
P 🚐 ✕ ♿

Skidby Windmill
One of the best remaining working windmills in Britain.
Skidby, Cottingham
☎ 0482 882255
→A A164
P 🚐 ✕

Skipsea Castle
Norman motte and bailey castle.
West of Skipsea village
🐾

Museums

Beverley Museum, Art Gallery and Heritage Centre
Champney Road, Beverley
☎ 0482 882255
→A A164 (town centre)
P 🐾

BEVERLEY

WHAT TO DO AND SEE

Museum of Army Transport
Acres of road, rail, sea and air exhibits
excitingly displayed.
Flemingate, Beverley
☎ 0482 860445
P ⇔ ✕ ♿

Streetlife – Hull Museum of Transport
Horse-drawn vehicles, motor vehicles
1890–1910, rare trams.
High Street, Hull
☎ 0482 222737
→A A63 (city centre)
🛈 ⇔ ♿

Town Docks Museum
Whaling, fishing and trawling exhibits.
Queen Victoria Square, Hull
☎ 0482 222737
→A A63 (city centre)
✕ ♿

Natural History

Cruckley Animal Farm
Working farm with modern and rare breeds
of animals; hatchery; waterfowl lake and
daily milking demonstration.
Foston-on-the-Wolds, nr Great Driffield
☎ 026288 337
Off the B1249
P ⇔ ✕

Northern Shire Horse Centre
Shire horses, harness, museum, forge,
country trail, horse-drawn vehicles; rare and
unusual breeds.
Flower Hill Farm, North Newbald
☎ 0430 827270
→A A1034
P ⇔ ✕ ♿

Parks

Humber Bridge Country Park
Woodland, meadows, play area, picnic areas.
Guided walks start from the restored mill
on Hessle foreshore. Trails for the blind.
☎ 0482 641989
Via Hull on the A63 (across Humber
Bridge)
P ⇔ ✕ ♿

Theatres

New Theatre
Kingston Square, Hull
☎ 0482 226655

Cycling

Star Bikes
204 Willerby Road, Hull
☎ 0482 564673

Fishing

Beverley Beck
A small canalised stream running from the
Forester's Arms to the River Hull; small-
sized road, perch, gudgeon, skimmers,
pike and eels.
🐟

Lakeminster Park Lakes
There are 2 ponds. Day permits allow
fishing for carp, tench, roach and bream.
Woodmansey Road
South of Beverley off the Beverley–Hull road

Golf

Beverley Golf Club ⛳18
Westwood
☎ 0482 867190

Ice Skating

Humberside Ice Arena
An Olympic sized arena.
Kingston Street, Hull
☎ 0482 25252
A63 next to Hull Marina
P ✕ ♿

Tennis

Hodgson's Recreation Ground
Courts to hire.

Walking

The Minster Way
51 mile route linking York and the Beverley
Minsters.

The Wolds Way
80 mile path along the Yorkshire Wolds
from the Humber to Filey.
ℹ The Tourist Information Centre can
provide details of these routes.

Bishop Burton College of Agriculture
Themed nature trails.
Bishop Burton
☎ 0964 550481

County Leisure and Tourism Rangers
ℹ The Tourist Information Centre can
provide details of dates and meeting points.

OUTDOOR LEISURE

Birdwatching

Hornsea Mere RSPB Reserve
A large natural freshwater lake with
adjoining reedbeds and woodland close to
the centre of Hornsea. Famous for little
gulls in summer and large numbers of
geese and ducks in winter.

Far Ings Nature Reserve
Barton-upon-Humber

WATERSPORTS

Barton Clay Pits
All year round recreation; watersports
(sailing and waterskiing for club members),
fishing and bird watching, walking with a
programme of guided walks.
Barton-upon-Humber
☎ 0652 33283
→A A1077/A15
P ⇔ ♿

BRIGHTON
Including Plumpton

County: East Sussex
i Tourist Office, Marlborough House,
54 Old Steine, Brighton
☎ 0273 23755
i Tourist Office, King Alfred
Leisure Centre, Kingsway, Hove
☎ 0273 720731
Early closing: Wednesday and Thursday
Population: 200,000

Brighton, one of England's first seaside resorts, was originally a small fishing hamlet, the preserved, narrow streets of which are now lined with excellent shops and called the Lanes.

Brighton's popularity during different periods has produced richly contrasting architectural styles, Regency terraces, late-Victorian villas and graceful Georgian streets providing the backdrop for the extravagant Royal Pavilion. Commissioned as a summer palace by the Prince of Wales (later George IV) the exterior was built in the style of an Indian palace and the interior decorated in rich Chinese style.

Contemporary Brighton remains an ever-popular resort, with its shingle beach, 3 miles of seafront promenade, pier and amusements, swimming pools, aquarium, vast yacht marina, theatres and cosmopolitan restaurants. Its position in an area of varied coastal and inland scenery with an array of interesting towns, stately homes and gardens ensures complete entertainment for the whole family.

EQUESTRIAN

Riding and Pony Trekking

Brendon Riding School
Haresdean Farm, Pyecombe
☎ 07918 2158

Gatewood Farm
Robin Post Lane, Wilmington, Polegate
☎ 03212 3709

Three Greys Riding School
2 School Lane, Pyecombe
☎ 07918 3536

HEALTH

Leisure Centres

King Alfred Leisure Centre
Tropical leisure pool with beach, island and waterchute; sauna, sun beds, ten-pin bowling centre, table tennis, etc.
Kingsway, Hove
☎ 0273 734422

LOCAL FEATURES

Aquariums

Brighton Aquarium and Dolphinarium
Dolphin shows, seals, sharks, marine, tropical and freshwater fish.
Marine Parade
☎ 0273 604233
→A A23/M23 (town centre)
✗

Festivals and Fairs

May
Brighton Festival

November
London–Brighton Veteran Car Rally

Food and Drink

Barkham Manor Vineyard
35 acre vineyard surrounding the manor house. Vinery gardens, Piltdown Manor memorial. Guided tours including tastings.
Piltdown, nr Uckfield
☎ 082572 2103
→A A272
P 🚌

Fun Parks

Pirates Deep
Indoor childrens adventure playground featuring ball crawls, slides, ropes, children's cocktail bar and video room.
Madeira Drive, Brighton
☎ 0273 674549
→A A23 (town centre)
✗

Gardens

Borde Hill Garden
Large garden and parkland.
Borde Hill, Haywards Heath
☎ 0444 450326
→A A272
P 🚌 ✗ ♿

Kidbrooke Park
Parkland laid out by Humphrey Repton.
Forest Row
☎ 034282 2275
B2110/A22
P ♿

BRIGHTON

WHAT TO DO AND SEE

Sheffield Park Garden
Large 18th century garden laid out by
Capability Brown, noted for its rare trees.
National Trust.
Danehill, nr Uckfield
☎ 0825 790655
P ✕ ♿

Historic Buildings

Alfriston Clergy House
Thatched, half-timbered 14th century
building with an exhibition on Wealden
house building and a cottage garden.
National Trust.
The Tye, Alfriston
☎ 0323 870001
Off the B2108

Firle Place
Tudor house with Georgian additions in
downland park; notable for its art, ceramics
and furniture.
Firle, nr Lewes
☎ 079159 335
➤A A27
P 🚌 ✕

Glynde Place
16th century Sussex brick and flint house
built around a courtyard; notable portrait
collection.
Glynde, nr Lewes
☎ 079159 337
➤A A27
P 🚌 ✕ ♿

Lewes Castle
Shell keep of a Norman stronghold.
Lewes
☎ 0273 474379
➤A A277 (town centre)

Preston Manor
Georgian manor house with Edwardian
interior and fine furnishings.
Preston Park, Brighton
☎ 0273 603005
➤A A23 (town centre)
P ✕ ♿

Royal Pavilion
Eastern style palace built by Holland and
Nash; original and contemporary interiors;
Chinese porcelain and a magnificent music
room.
Old Steine, Brighton
☎ 0273 603005
➤A A23 (town centre)
🚌 ✕

Museums

Brighton Museum and Art Gallery
Fine collection of ceramics, art deco, art
nouveau, archaeology and fine art.
Church Street, Brighton
☎ 0273 603005
➤A A23 (town centre)
🛗 ✕

Hove Museum and Art Gallery
Paintings, pottery, porcelain and silver.
19 New Church Road, Hove
☎ 0273 779410
➤A A259 (town centre)
P 🛗 🚌 ✕ ♿

Natural History

Ashdown Forest Farm
Small farm with rare breeds of livestock and
poultry; a spinning and weaving exhibition,
thatching demonstrations, shearing and
sheep dipping.
Wych Cross
☎ 082571 2040
➤A A22
P ✕

Bentley Wildfowl and Motor Museum
Private collection of over 1000 birds in
parkland with lakes. Motor museum.
Bentley, nr Halland
☎ 082584 573
➤A A26/A22
P 🚌 ✕ ♿

Railways

Lavender Line Steam Museum
Restored station buildings, vintage standard
gauge steam engines.
Isfield Station, Isfield, nr Uckfield
☎ 082575 515
➤A A26
P 🚌 ✕

Bluebell Railway Living Museum
Five miles of standard gauge track with a
large collection of steam locomotives.
Victorian stations and a museum.
Sheffield Park Station, Sheffield Park,
nr Uckfield
☎ 082572 2370
➤A A275
P 🚌 ✕ ♿

Theatres

Connaught Theatre
Union Place, Worthing

Theatre Royal
New Road, Brighton

Zoos

Drusillas Zoo Park
New style zoo with generous enclosures. A
farmyard, railway, adventure playground,
butterfly house, pottery and gardens.
Alfriston
☎ 0323 870234
➤A A27
P 🚌 ✕ ♿

OUTDOOR LEISURE

Cycling
Harman Hire
Surrey Street, Brighton
☎ 0273 207649

BRIGHTON

Bicycle Hire
4 Temple Gardens, Brighton
☎ 0273 737979

Preston Cycling Track
Preston Park, Brighton

Fishing

The Brighton Angler
Aquarium Colonnade, 1 Madeira Drive
☎ 0273 671398

Jack Ball Fishing Tackle
171 Edward Street
☎ 0273 671083

The Tackle Box
Brighton Marina
☎ 0273 696477

Charter boats for sea fishing trips:

Blue Bird Speedboats
☎ 0323 765559
☎ 0323 29016

Brighton Marina Breakwaters
Brighton Marina
☎ 0273 693636

Golf

There are two municipal courses:

Hollingbury Park
Ditchling Road, Brighton
☎ 0273 500086

Waterhall Course ⛳18
Devil's Dyke Road, Brighton
☎ 0273 508658

Private clubs include:

Brighton and Hove Golf Club ⛳9
Dyke Road, Brighton
☎ 0273 556482

Dyke Golf Club
Dyke Road, Brighton
☎ 079156 296

East Brighton Golf Club ⛳18
Roedean Road, Brighton
☎ 0273 604838

West Hove Golf Club ⛳18
Oled Shoreham Road, Hove
☎ 0273 419738

Ice Skating

Sussex Ice Rink
Queen's Square, Brighton
☎ 0273 24677

Dry Slope Skiing

Stanley Deason Leisure Centre
Wilson Avenue, Brighton
☎ 0273 694281

Borowski Centre
New Road, Newhaven
☎ 515402

Tennis

Numerous options exist for hire of courts.

Walking

Heaven Farm Country Tours and Museum
A prize-winning nature trail that crosses the
Greenwich Meridian Line.
Furners Green, nr Uckfield
☎ 0825 790226
→A A275
P 🚐 ✕ ♿

Sailing

Brighton Marina
Brighton Marina has 1700 berths; bistros,
bars, restaurants and speciality shopping.
Yacht and fishing charter are available.
☎ 0273 693636
→A A259

Dinghies and catamarans:

Sunsports
185 King's Road Arches, Brighton
☎ 0273 28584

Hove Lagoon
Kingsway, Hove
☎ 0273 430100

CARLISLE

WHAT TO DO AND SEE

County: Cumbria
i Tourist Office, Old Town Hall,
  Green Market
☎ 0228 512444
Population: 73,000

Carlisle, Cumbria's great Border city, was frequently raided by the Scots during the centuries of Border wars. Its castle, built in 1092, was used as both a fortress and a prison, with Mary Queen of Scots its most famous inmate. The beautiful cathedral, set on the city walls, is one of the smallest in the country. The city boasts the award-winning Lanes shopping centre as well as an attractive Victorian covered market.

Carlisle, a major agricultural centre of northern England, is surrounded by unspoilt Border farmland and large stretches of forestry. The Lake District, to the south, is also within easy access.

ADVENTURE

Multi-activity Centres

Cumbria Outdoors
Three residential centres (two near Keswick, one at Caldbeck), providing full board and tuition courses in sailing, windsurfing, canoeing, caving, climbing and general adventure. For families, individuals and groups, including the disabled.
Cumbria Education Dept, 5 Portland Square, Carlisle
☎ 0228 23456 ext 2565

Clay pigeon Shooting

Greenquarries Shooting Ground
Sporting clay pigeon shooting; gun hire, tuition.
Off the B5299, 9 miles south-west of Carlisle
☎ 06996 392

EQUESTRIAN

Riding

Blackdyke Farm
Blackford, Carlisle
☎ 022874 633

Townhead Farm Stables
Newbiggin, Heads Nook, Carlisle
☎ 076886 208

HEALTH

Leisure Centres

Sands Leisure Centre
Entertainment centre featuring a varied programme of opera, pop and choral music as well as comedy, ballet and children's shows. Sports facilities include roller skating, squash, badminton and a climbing wall.
☎ 0228 25222

LOCAL FEATURES

Festivals and Fairs

July
Cumberland Show, July 19

August
Carlisle Great Fair, August 25

Guided Tours

Coach tours
To Hadrian's Wall and the Lake District.
i Information from the Tourist Office.

Walking tours
Daily, May–Sep
i Cumbria and Border Heritage Guides, The Old Town Hall (Tourist Office).

Heritage

Hadrian's Wall
Built by the Romans between AD122 and AD128 to mark the northern boundary of the Roman Empire in Britain. The wall was originally 15ft high and 40ft thick with forts and mile castles dotted along its length to keep out the marauding Picts. Abandoned in the 4th century, the wall is still well preserved particularly at Banks (south of the minor road east of Banks village) and Birdoswald (2 miles west of Greenhead on a minor road off the B6318).

Historic Buildings

Carlisle Castle
Impressive remains of the mediaeval castle that has watched over the Anglo-Scottish border since 1092. English Heritage.
On the north side of the city, beyond the cathedral
☎ 0228 31777
🚌 ♿

Carlisle Cathedral
Built in the 12th century; it features a fine 13th century stained glass east window.
Castle Street
🚌

Lanercost Priory
Well preserved despite being repeatedly damaged by the Scots between 1296 and 1346. Evensong services by candlelight. English Heritage.
☎ 06977 3030
2 miles north-east of Brampton, off a minor road south of Lanercost
P ♿

Naworth Castle
Home of the Earls of Carlisle.
Brampton
☎ 06977 2692
On the A69, 11 miles from Carlisle and 2 miles from Brampton

103

CARLISLE

Museums

Guildhall Museum
Carlisle's only mediaeval town house now displaying guild, civic and local history.
Greenmarket
☎ 0228 34781

Roman Army Museum
The museum is housed in one of the highest standing wall sections on the central sector of Hadrian's Wall next to Walltown Crags, and provides an educational insight into the life and times of the Roman soldier.
Carvoran, Greenhead
☎ 06972 485
P ✕ &

Parks

Talkin Tarn Country Park
Over 180 acres of farmland, woodland and water; facilities for rowing, watersports, coarse fishing and picnics.
Brampton
☎ 06977 3129

Railways

Leeds–Settle–Carlisle Line
A spectacular 70 mile railway route, from Carlisle to Settle, through the Yorkshire Dales, over the Pennines and through the Eden Valley.
British Rail station, Carlisle
☎ 0228 44711

OUTDOOR LEISURE

Golf

Brampton Golf Club ⚑₁₈
Talkin Tarn, Brampton
☎ 06977 2255

Carlisle Driving Range
The Racecourse, Durdar
☎ 0228 49583

Carlisle Golf Club ⚑₁₈
No visitors on Saturdays
Aglionby
☎ 0228 513303

Carlisle Municipal Golf Course ⚑₁₈
Stoneyholme
☎ 0228 34856

Solway Village Golf Centre
⚑₉ driving range set on Cumbrian coast, plus nearby championship course. All inclusive tuition holidays for groups and individuals from beginner to scratch golfer.
Skinburness Drive, Silloth-on-Solway
☎ 06973 31236

Skiing

Carlisle Ski Club
Dry ski slope, rope tow, equipment hire and classes; membership required.
Edenside Cricket Ground, Carlisle
☎ 0228 61634

Walking

Fortify the Spirit
Guided walking holidays led by experienced guides, based at hotels.
The Barn, Wellrash, Boltongate, Wigton
☎ 09657 522

Town and countryside walks
i Programme of walks throughout the year available from the Tourist Office.

CARTMEL

WHAT TO DO AND SEE

County: Cumbria
i Tourist Office, Victoria Hall,
  Main Street, Grange-over-Sands
☎ 04484 4026
i Tourist Office, Town Hall,
  Highgate, Kendal
☎ 0539 25758
i Tourist Office, Victoria Street,
  Windermere
☎ 09662 6499
Early closing: Thursday (Grange-over-Sands)
Population: 4000 (Grange-over-Sands)
Cartmel, a cathedral city in miniature, grew up around its famous 12th century priory. One of Lakeland's oldest and most attractive villages, its ancient winding streets and humpbacked bridges lead on to the various galleries and shops that exhibit the work of local artists.

   Cartmel provides a good base for exploring Lake Windermere, Coniston Water and the entire Lake District; the Kent and Lune valleys and the Yorkshire Dales are also nearby. The seaside is only minutes away, Morecambe Bay with its numerous species of wildfowl and shore birds is accessible via the pleasant seaside town of Grange-over-Sands.

ADVENTURE

Multi-activity Centres

YMCA National Centre
Outdoor adventure; activity skills training.
Lakeside, Ulverston, Cumbria
☎ 05395 31758

Summitreks
Outdoor activity courses and instruction.
14 Yewdale Road, Coniston, Cumbria
☎ 05394 41212

Bigland Hall Sporting Estates
Fishing, riding, trekking, clay pigeon shooting and archery. Novices welcome.
Backbarrow, nr Ulverston, Cumbria
☎ 05395 31728

EQUESTRIAN

Riding and Pony Trekking

Bigland Hall
Blackbarrow, Newby Bridge
☎ 05395 31728

Claife and Grizedale Riding Centre
Sawrey Knotts Estate, Hawkshead
☎ 09662 2105

HEALTH

Leisure Centre

Flook's Leisure Centre
Multi-gym, sauna, sunbed, squash and badminton. Day visitors welcome.
Main Street, Grange-over-Sands
☎ 05395 32455
✗

South Lakeland Leisure Centre
Multi-purpose sports hall, swimming, squash, sauna and fitness unit.
Burton Road, Kendal
☎ 0539 29777

LOCAL FEATURES

Arts and Crafts

Art Crystal
Watch master craftsman at work.
Clock Tower Works, Low Wood, Haverthwaite, Newby Bridge
☎ 05395 31796

Cumbria Crystal Ltd
See lead crystal blown. Factory shop.
The Auction Mart, Lightburn Road, Ulverston
☎ 0229 54400
&

Falconry

Leighton Hall
Watch eagles fly at this beautifully sited country house. Courses available.
Carnforth
☎ 0524 734474
Off the M6, exit 35, signposted

Festivals and Fairs

August
Hot Air Balloon Rally, Aug 5
Sheepdog Trials
Windermere, Aug 9 Grasmere, Aug 16
Patterdale, Aug 25 Kendal, Aug 27

Gardens

Graythwaite Hall Gardens
Newby Bridge
☎ 05395 31248
→A A590

Historic Buildings

Dove Cottage
The home of the poet, William Wordsworth, during his most creative years.
Grasmere
☎ 09665 544
Off the A591, just south of Grasmere village
🚍

Holker Hall
Former home of the Dukes of Devonshire, known for its fine wood carvings and impressive gardens. A Craft and Countryside Museum and the Lakeland Motor Museum are also situated here – over 100 cars, motor cycles and tractors to fascinate the enthusiast. Adventure playground. Other events throughout the year include a hot air balloon rally, carriage driving trials and historic vehicle rally.
Cark-in-Cartmel
☎ 044853 328
On the B5278 from Newby Bridge via A590
🚍 ✗ &

CARTMEL

WHAT TO DO AND SEE

Levens Hall
Finely furnished Elizabethan house and
magnificent ancient topiary gardens;
working steam collection.
Kendal
☎ 05395 60321
On the A6, 5 miles south of Kendal
✗

Rydal Mount
Wordsworth's home
Ambleside
☎ 0966 33002
Off the A591, 1½ miles from Grasmere
🚐

Sizergh Castle
14th century, Elizabethan carvings,
panelling, furniture and portraits. 18th
century gardens. National Trust.
Nr Kendal
☎ 05395 60070
3 miles south of Kendal
P 🚐 ✗

Museums

Laurel and Hardy Museum
Old photographs and personal mementoes
of the Laurel and Hardy comedy duo plus a
small cinema.
7 King Street, Ulverston
☎ 0229 52292

Museum of Lakeland Life and Industry
Reconstructions of workshops, farmhouse
rooms, agriculture exhibits; also the Lake
District Art Gallery and Museum.
Abbot Hall, Kendal
☎ 0539 22464
Nr Kendal Parish Church
P 🚐 ♿

Parks

Bardsea Country Park
Coastal park, woodland and picnic areas.
Bardsea, nr Ulverston
➔A A5087

Fell Foot Country Park
18 acre lakeside park; bathing, fishing, an
adventure playground and boat hire.
National Trust.
Newby Bridge
☎ 05395 31273
At the extreme south end of Windermere
P ✗ ♿

Lake District National Park
Visitors Centre exhibitions "Living
Lakeland", slide shows, films, shop, gardens,
lakeside walk.
Brockhole, Windermere
☎ 09662 6601
➔A A591
P ✗ ♿

Railways

Lakeside and Haverthwaite Railway
Steam locomotive trips.
Nr Newby Bridge
☎ 05395 31594

Theatres

Theatre in the Forest
Classical and folk music, natural history
lectures, films and dramas.
Grizedale, Ambleside
☎ 0229 84291
P 🚐 ♿

OUTDOOR LEISURE

Birdwatching

Leighton Moss Reserve
RSPB-managed, 321 acre reserve.
Carnforth, north-east of Morecambe Bay

South Walney Nature Reserve
Europe's largest gullery; eider colony.
Walney Island, Barrow-in-Furness
☎ 0229 41066
➔A A590
🚐

Cycling

Cumbria Cycle Way
Circular 280 mile (450km) waymarked
route following quiet roads.
i Route available from Tourist Offices.

Fishing

Trout fishing
On the River Eea, south of Cartmel. Permit
required from the North West Water
Authority.

Golf

Grange-over-Sands Golf Club
Meathop Road, Grange-over-Sands
☎ 05395 33180

Grange Fell Golf Club
Grange Fell Road, Grange-over-Sands
☎ 05395 32536

Ulverston Golf Course
Bardsea, Ulverston
☎ 0229 52824

Walking

Grizedale Forest (Visitors Centre)
Marked forest trails, picnic areas, cycle
trails and fishing areas.
Grizedale, Ambleside
☎ 0229 84373

Guided Walks
i Enquire at the Kendal Tourist Office.

WATERSPORTS

Sailing

Lake Windermere Facilities
Permanent and holiday moorings,
launching, recovery, boat registration,
pump-out, winter storage and water supply.
Ferry Nab, Bowness-on-Windermere
☎ 09662 2753

CATTERICK

County: North Yorkshire
i Richmond Tourist Office,
 Friary Gardens, Victoria Road,
 Richmond
☎ 0748 850252
i Leyburn Tourist Office,
 Thornborough Hall, Leyburn
☎ 0969 23069 summer only
Early closing: Wednesday
Market day: Saturday (Richmond), Friday
(Leyburn)
Population: 8000 (Richmond)
Catterick lies in the heart of the Yorkshire
Dales, an area of great natural beauty and
historical interest, ideal walking and hiking
country. Richmond, one of Yorkshire's most
attractive towns, lies on the River Swale and
is dominated by the ruins of its 11th
century castle which has magnificent views
across the dales into the Vale of York. The
old town surrounding the rounded market
place has retained its cobblestones and
character, a rich contrast to the Georgian
elegance found elsewhere in the town.
Shops, restaurants, hotels and guest houses
abound offering the visitor a perfect base
from which to tour the Dales.

AERIAL SPORTS

Ballooning
Pennine Balloon School
The Barn, Caldeburgh, Leyburn
☎ 0969 40674

EQUESTRIAN

Riding and Pony Trekking
Brookleigh Riding Centre
Eppleby
☎ 0325 718286
North of Richmond

New Close Farm
Gammersgill, Coverdale
☎ 0969 40668
South of Leyburn

HEALTH

Leisure Centres
Richmondshire Sports Centre and
Swimming Pool
Pool and sun beds.
☎ 0748 4581

LOCAL FEATURES

Arts and Crafts
Crakehall Water Mill
Little Crakehall, Bedale
☎ 0677 23240
On the A684 Bedale to Leyburn road

Maurice Stafford
Blacksmith producing wrought-iron work.
High Street, Gilling West
☎ 0748 4373
On the B6274, 2 miles outside Richmond

Outhwaite and Son
Traditional ropemaking.
Town Foot, Hawes
☎ 0969 7487

Old School Arts Workshop
Demonstrations and weekend courses.
Middleham, nr Leyburn
☎ 0969 23056

Swineside Pottery
Leyburn
☎ 0969 23839
On Leyburn's small industrial estate.

White Rose Candles
Watch traditional and modern methods of
candle making and decorating.
Wensley, nr Leyburn
☎ 0969 23544

Festivals and Fairs
August
Sheepdog trials and demonstrations
i Enquire at Tourist Office for dates and
venues

Historic Buildings
Bolton Castle
Well-preserved mediaeval castle.
Nr Leyburn
☎ 0969 23981
➤A A684
🚌 ✗

Easby Abbey
Extensive ruins on banks of River Swale.
1 mile south-east of Richmond off the
B6271
P

Kiplin Hall
Jacobean house with large grounds,
ancestral home of Lord Baltimore, the
founder of Maryland.
Scorton
☎ 0748 818178
Off the B6271, 6 miles south-east of
Richmond
P 🚌

Mount Grace Priory
Fine 14th century Carthusian ruin.
Osmotherley, Northallerton
☎ 0609 83249
On the A19 nr Ingleby Arncliffe
P

Richmond Castle
One of the most imposing Norman ruins in
England; 11th century walls intact.
Richmond
☎ 0748 2493
➤A A6108 (town centre)
P

CATTERICK

Museums

Museum of Badges and Battledress
The Green, Crakehall, Bedale
☎ 0677 23301
🚐

Green Howards Regimental Museum
Trinity Church Square, Richmond
☎ 0748 2133
➤A A6108 (town centre)
P 🚐

Richmondshire Museum
Local history plus the BBC TV series set for the 'Herriot' vets' surgery (*All Creatures Great and Small*).
Ryder's Wynd, Richmond
☎ 0748 5611
➤A A6108 (town centre)
🚐

Swaledale Folk Museum
History and traditions of the dale.
Reeth Green, Reeth
☎ 0748 84517
Off the B6270
P ♿

Upper Dales Folk Museum
Farming implements and tools of related country trades.
Station Yard, Hawes
☎ 09697 494
On the A684 Leyburn–Kendal road

Yorkshire Museum of Carriages and Horse-Drawn Vehicles
Aysgarth Falls
☎ 0748 3275
A684 between Leyburn and Hawes
P 🚐 ✕ ♿

Theatres

Georgian Theatre Royal and Theatre Museum
Museum and original 1788 theatre still staging productions.
Victoria Road, Richmond
☎ 0748 3021
🚐

Cycling

Swaledale Cycling Club
Meets every Sunday in the Market Place, Richmond for cycle tours and family rides.

Fishing

The River Swale is one of the country's best mixed rivers.

For permits and local information contact:

Metcalfe's Sports Shop
Market Place, Richmond
☎ 0748 2108

Sargent's Sports Shop
14 Finkle Street, Richmond
☎ 0748 5376

Reeth Post Office
☎ 0748 84201

Gilson Sports Shop
2 High Street, Leyburn
☎ 0969 23942

Thornton Steward Reservoir
Day ticket fishing for brown and rainbow trout (Mar–Oct). Permits sold at:

Bedale Post Office
Nr Bedale, south-east of Leyburn

Golf

Richmond (Yorkshire) Golf Club ⚑18
Bend Hagg, Richmond
☎ 0748 2457

Catterick Garrison Golf Club ⚑18
Leyburn Road, Catterick Garrison
☎ 0748 833268

Akebar Park Golf Club ⚑9
Akebar Park, nr Leyburn
☎ 0677 50201

Motoring

The Herriot Trail
i The Tourist Office can provide leaflet itineraries from which to follow the "Herriot Trail", a circular drive from Richmond through the Dales where the TV series *All Creatures Great and Small* was filmed.

The Turner Trail
Follow the route of Britain's greatest watercolourist J.M.W. Turner (1775–1851).

Walking

The Pennine Way and the Coast to Coast long-distance walks run through the district; there are numerous short, scenic walks. Special interest guided walks are organised throughout the year.
i Further information is available from the National Park Visitor Centres and the Tourist Offices.

Yorkshire Dales National Park Visitor Centres:

Station Road, Hawes
☎ 0969 7450
Aysgarth Falls
☎ 0969 3424

CHELTENHAM

County: Gloucestershire
i Tourist Office, 77 Promenade
☎ 0242 522878
Early closing: Wednesday
Population: 85,000
Cheltenham, a gracious Regency spa town at the edge of the Cotswold Hills, is a fashionable educational, artistic, musical and commercial centre. An impressive town with wide spacious tree-lined avenues, beautiful gardens and elegant buildings, it affords easy access to the many inviting villages of the nearby Cotswolds.

AERIAL SPORTS

Ballooning

Ballooning in the Cotswolds
36 Cheltenham Road, Rendcomb,
nr Cirencester
☎ 028583 515

Cheryl Gillott
Stroud
☎ 0453 873529

Jon Langley & Co.
Stroud
☎ 045382 5447

EQUESTRIAN

Riding and Pony Trekking

Badgworth Riding Centre
Cold Pool Lane, Up Hatherley, Cheltenham
☎ 0452 713818

Cheltenham Horse Riding Centre
Noverton Farm, Noverton Lane, Prestbury
☎ 0242 570824

Southam Riding School
Southam, Cheltenham
☎ 0242 242194
☎ 0242 244527

HEALTH

Leisure Centres

Cheltenham Recreation Centre
Pool, sauna, spa pool and sunbeds.
Tommy Taylors Lane, Cheltenham
☎ 0242 528764

Stratford Park Leisure Centre
Stratford Park, Stroud
☎ 0453 766771

Gloucester Leisure Centre
Bruton Way, Gloucester
0452 306498

Cotswolds Sports Centre
Cirencester
☎ 0285 654057

LOCAL FEATURES

Art

Nature in Art
(The International Centre for Wildlife Art)
Georgian mansion housing a unique collection of wildlife painting; outside sculptures and nature garden.
Wallsworth Hall, Sandhurst, nr Gloucester
☎ 0452 731422
Entrance is on the A38
P 🚌 ✗ ♿

Falconry

Cotswold Falconry
Displays of birds in flight.

Batsford Park
Moreton–in–Marsh
☎ 0386 701043

Birds of Prey Trust and Falconry Centre
Trained hawks, falcons and eagles.
Newent
☎ 0531 820286
Off the B4215
P ✗

Festivals and Fairs

March
Gold Cup Week

July
Festival of Music

August
County Cricket Festival

October
Cheltenham Literature Festival

Gardens

Barnsley House Garden
Garden begun in 1770, Gothic summerhouse and classic temple.
Barnsley, nr Cirencester
☎ 0285 74281

Batsford Arboretum
50 acres with over 1000 species of trees.
Moreton-in-Marsh
☎ 0608 50722
➡A A44
✗

Hidcote Manor Gardens
One of England's most beautiful gardens; many rare plants. National Trust.
Hidcote Bartrim, nr Chipping Campden
☎ 038677 333
➡A A46
P ✗ ♿

Historic Buildings

Berkeley Castle
Perfectly preserved castle, over 800 years old and the scene of the murder of Edward II. Ornamental gardens.
Berkeley, Gloucester
☎ 0453 810332
➡A A38
P 🚌 ✗

CHELTENHAM

Gloucester Docks
Spectacular collection of beautifully restored Victorian warehouses. Attractions include Waterways Museum, Robert Opie Collection and antique centre.
Southgate Street, Gloucester
→A A38

Hailes Abbey
Ruins of mediaeval abbey built in 1246.
Hailes, nr Winchcombe
☎ 0242 602398
→A A46

Pittville Pump Rooms

Regency building within its own park; spa waters are available. Also houses the Gallery of Fashion; costume, jewellery and fashion accessories on display.
Pittville Park
☎ 0242 512740
→A A435
P 🚌

Snowshill Manor
National Trust property with interesting collection of musical instruments, clocks, toys and bicycles within typical Cotswold manor house.
Nr Broadway
☎ 0386 852410
3 miles south-west of Broadway, 4 miles west of the A44/A424
P 🚌

Sudeley Castle
Home and burial place of Katherine Parr, last wife of Henry VIII. Art collection, craft centre, gardens and falconry displays. Open-air theatre (late June). Adventure playground.
Winchcombe
☎ 0242 602308
On the A46, 6 miles north of Cheltenham
P ✗

Tewkesbury Abbey
Superb Norman abbey with 14th century vaulting and windows; it has the tallest Norman towers in England and was formerly a Benedictine monastery.
Church Street, Tewkesbury
☎ 0684 850959
A38 Tewkesbury to Gloucester road
P 🚌 &

Museums

Cheltenham Museum and Art Gallery
Fine Dutch paintings, collections of ceramics and porcelain from China and the Far East with a section devoted to Edward Wilson, (one of Cheltenham's most famous sons) who perished with Captain Scott on the ill-fated Antarctic Expedition of 1910.
Clarence Street
☎ 0242 237431
→A A40
🎨 ✗ &

Cotswold Countryside Collection
Collection of agricultural history housed in former house of correction.
Fosse Way, Northleach
☎ 0451 60715
Jct A40 and Fosse Way A429
P ✗ &

Gustav Holst Birthplace Museum
4 Clarence Road
☎ 0242 524846
→A A435
🚌 &

Natural History

Newent Butterfly and Natural World Centre
Tropical butterflies, snakes, insects and pet animal zoo.
Birches Lane, Newent
☎ 0531 821800
Off the B4215

Railways

The Gloucestershire–Warwickshire Railway
A working steam railway with 1904 period buildings at Toddington and a Victorian station at Winchcombe; a 6 mile round trip.
Toddington Station, Toddington
☎ 0242 69405

Theatres

Everyman Theatre
Professional repertory theatre producing a mixed programme of drama, musicals, comedies and classics.
Regent Street, Cheltenham
☎ 0242 572573

Playhouse Theatre
Base for amateur theatre companies.
Bath Road, Cheltenham
☎ 0242 522852

Zoos

Cotswold Farm Park
Set high on the Cotswold Hills; a collection of rare breeds of British farm animals; pets corner and picnic areas.
Guiting Power
☎ 04515 307
On the B4068
P 🚌 ✗ &

CHELTENHAM

WHAT TO DO AND SEE

Cotswold Wildlife Park
Set in 200 acres of lawns and gardens, the animals in this park range from the white rhino to reptiles. Picnic areas and an adventure playground.
Outskirts of Burford
☎ 099382 3006

OUTDOOR LEISURE

Birdwatching

Slimbridge Wildfowl Trust
Trust set up by Sir Peter Scott, this is the world's largest and most varied collection of wildfowl – over 2300 birds of 180 different species. Winter viewing of birds.
Slimbridge
☎ 045389 333
Signposted from the M5, jcts 13 and 14
🚌 ✕ ♿

Cycling

Crabtrees
50 Winchcombe Street, Cheltenham
☎ 0242 515291

Fishing

Pittville Lake
Situated in the Pittville Park in the town centre. Permits required.
Ian Coley Ltd
442/444 High Street, Cheltenham
☎ 0242 522443

Golf

Cleeve Hill Municipal Golf Course 🏌18
Cleeve Hill
☎ 0242 629592

Players welcome with handicap certificate:
Cotswolds Hills Golf Club 🏌18
Ullenwood, nr Cheltenham
☎ 0242 515264

Lilleybrook Golf Club 🏌18
Cirencester Road, Charlton Kings, Cheltenham
☎ 0242 525201

Outside Cheltenham:
Gloucester Country Club 🏌18
Must pre-book.
Robinswood Hill, Matson Lane, Gloucester
☎ 0452 411331

Painswick Golf Club 🏌18
Welcomes casual visitors Mon–Sat (accompanied by member Sun).
Painswick Beacon, Glocester
☎ 0452 812180

Tewkesbury Park Golf Club 🏌18
Driving range.
Lincoln Lane, Tewkesbury
☎ 0684 294892

Motoring Trail

Cotswold Clue Trail
Devised by the Tourist Office, this is a mystery motoring trail which lasts a day and consists of a number of cryptic clues leading to numerous places of interest.
i Map and clues £2.50 from the Tourist Office.

Skiing

Gloucester Ski Centre
Robinswood Hill, Gloucester
☎ 0452 414300
P ✕

Tennis

Hard courts can be hired (Apr–Oct) in both Pittville Park and Montpelier Gardens.

WATERSPORTS

Boat Hire

Pittville Park Boating Lake
Rowing boats and canoes for hire, a smaller children's lake, pitch and putt and a playground.

Boat Trips

Gloucester Docks
On the canal by the Waterways Museum.

Windsurfing

Cotswold Water Park
1500 acres of lakes developed for a wide range of activities; angling, birdwatching, sailing, windsurfing, jet skiing and water skiing too; walking, cycling and horse riding routes too.
Ashton Keynes, nr Cirencester
☎ 0285 861459
5 miles south of Cirencester, 20 miles from Cheltenham

111

CHEPSTOW

WHAT TO DO AND SEE

County: Gwent
i Chepstow Tourist Office,
   The Gatehouse, High Street
☎ 02912 3772 summer only
i Tintern Tourist Office, Tintern Abbey
☎ 0291 689431 summer only
Population: 10,000
Chepstow is a small, historic, Welsh border town with mediaeval streets and the impressive ruins of its Norman castle which overlooks the beautiful Wye river valley. The surrounding countryside includes the unspoilt Vale of Usk, the Royal Forest of Dean, Wentwood Forest and the Brecon Beacons, all areas of outstanding natural beauty waiting to be explored. Walkers can follow the Saxon pathway that begins in Chepstow and follows Offa's Dyke, whilst the nearby towns of Monmouth, Usk and Abergavenny provide historical insight into the turbulent past of this Border country.

EQUESTRIAN

Riding and Pony Trekking

Beacon Stables
Monmouth
☎ 0600 860404

HEALTH

Leisure Centres

Chepstow Leisure Centre
Pool, fitness room, sauna and solarium.
Crossways Green
☎ 02912 3832

LOCAL FEATURES

Arts and Crafts

Stuart Crystal Craft Centre
Factory tours include demonstrations
Bridge Street (town centre)
☎ 02912 70135
P &

Festivals and Fairs

August
Chepstow Agricultural Show

Historic Buildings

Caldicot Castle and Country Park
Built during the 12th to 14th centuries, the fortress was restored in the 19th century and contains local history, craft and furniture displays. Mediaeval banquets.
Nr Newport
☎ 0291 421425
A48 Chepstow/Newport road, signposted

Chepstow Castle
Overlooking the River Wye, the ruins dominate the town.
Town centre

Tintern Abbey
The abbey was built on a bend in the River Wye, by the Cistercian order in 1311. It is one of the most beautiful and architecturally important ruins in Britain.

Museums

Clearwell Caves Mining Museum
Ancient iron mines. Guided tours and caving trips available.
Coleford
☎ 0594 32535
East of Monmouth

Railways

Dean Forest Railway
Static display with steam train rides. Riverside walk and picnic areas.
Norchard Steam Centre, Lydney
☎ 0594 843423
B4234 off the A48 at Lydney
P

OUTDOOR LEISURE

Fishing

Local tackle shops can advise on fishing available in the Wye and Usk rivers, the Wentwood Reservoir, Llandegfedd Reservoir and the Monmouthshire/Brecon Canal.

Golf

St Pierre Golf and Country Club
⊩₁₈ parkland courses. Visitors welcome.
☎ 02912 5261
On the A48, 1 mile from Chepstow

Skiing

Gwent Grass Ski Centre
Usk

Walking

Offa's Dyke
Chepstow is the starting point for long-distance walkers following the path along the Saxon Offa's Dyke, on the English side of the River Wye. The path (168 miles/270 km) follows the English Welsh border from Chepstow to Prestatyn.

Wye Valley Walk
A waymarked path, it begins at Chepstow Castle.

Dean Heritage Museum Trust
Heritage information centre; reconstructed cottage and mine; archaeology and woodcraft exhibits; nature and picnic area and an adventure playground.
On the B4227, nr Cinderford
☎ 0594 22170

The Forestry Commission
Marked trails in the woods above the River Wye, in both the Forest of Dean and the Wentwood Forest; superb scenic viewpoints.

CHESTER

WHAT TO DO AND SEE

County: Cheshire
ℹ Chester Visitor Centre, Vicars Lane
☎ 0244 351609
Town Hall
☎ 0244 324324
Early closing: Wednesday
Market day: daily
Population: 120,000

Chester, an ancient walled city, was the site of a major Roman camp. It has most of the original Roman walls remaining, a fine collection of Roman remains and an amphitheatre that testifies to its importance as a frontier outpost of the Roman Empire.

Chester thrived as a mediaeval city; a major port until the River Dee silted up, it has many fine half-timbered buildings including the famous and unique, two-tiered, galleried shops known as The Rows.

A 14th century cathedral, fine Georgian buildings, the River Dee with its riverside walks and pleasure boat trips, and pedestrianised shopping combine to make Chester an attractive and varied city. Its proximity to the Welsh border provides access to some very inviting countryside.

ADVENTURE

Clay Pigeon Shooting

Teal Sporting Clays
Experienced instructors for individual or group tuition. Beginners and ladies welcome, all equipment provided.
Chester
☎ 0244 383219
☎ 0244 880553

Karting

Deeside Indoor Karting Centre
Race and leisure karts with speeds of up to 40 mph. Expert tuition, race suits, huge indoor circuit and children's track.
Engineers Park, Sandycroft, Deeside, Clwyd
☎ 0244 531652
➡A A55
✗

Motor Safari

Teal All Terrain Driving
Off-road training and adventure driving four-wheel drive vehicles under full instruction.
Cholmondeley
☎ 0244 383219
☎ 0244 42492

Shooting

North Wales Shooting School
Sealand Manor, Sealand
☎ 0244 812219

EQUESTRIAN

Riding and Pony Trekking

Upton Riding School
Heath Road
☎ 0244 380709

Waverton Riding and Livery Centre
Christleton Road
☎ 0244 335202

Wirral Riding and Saddlery Centre
Haddon Lane, Ness, Wirral
☎ 051 336 3638

HEALTH

Leisure Centres

Northgate Arena
Wide range of indoor sport facilities plus a leisure pool, sauna, sunbeds and gym.
Victoria Road
☎ 0244 380444
P ✗ ♿

LOCAL FEATURES

Art

Lady Lever Art Gallery
English paintings and sculpture; Wedgwood pottery and Chinese porcelain.
Port Sunlight Village
☎ 051 645 3623
P

Arts and Crafts

Cheshire Workshops
The Candle Makers, Burwardsley
☎ 0829 70401
10 miles south-east of Chester, signposted
✗ ♿

Trithy Craft and Needlework Centre
Colony of craft workshops.
Coed Talon, nr Mold
☎ 0352 771359
Off the A5104, Chester to Corwen road, signposted
✗

Festivals and Fairs

May
Rowing Regatta, 26–28 May
June
Cheshire County Show, Tatton Park
July
River Carnival and Raft Race, 8 July

Food and Drink

Ruthin Castle
Mediaeval banquets. Book through the Tourist Office.
23 miles from Chester

CHESTER

Worsley Old Hall
Mediaeval banquets. Book through the
Tourist Office.
30 miles from Chester

Gardens

Cholmondeley Castle Gardens
Hillside gardens capped by 19th century
castle; water, rose and temple gardens;
lakeside picnic areas.
Malpas
☎ 082922 383
➤A A49
P ✕ ⅋

Ness Gardens
50-acre hillside site overlooking Dee estuary
with rose, herb and water gardens.
University of Liverpool Botanic Gardens,
Neston
☎ 051 336 2135
P ⇛ ✕ ⅋

Tirley Garth
Gardens designed in the 20th century;
cartwheels, rectangles, crescents, terraces
and woodland garden.
Nr Kelsall
☎ 08293 2301

Guided tours

Walking Tours
2 hour tours taking in the principal sites of
the town. Depart Chester Visitor Centre.

Ghost Walks
Night-time walks with a ghostly theme
leave from the Town Hall.

Guided bus tours
Operate within the city; also day excursions
to places of interest in the Chester area.
ⅈ Details and tickets from the Tourist
Office.

Historic Buildings

Beeston Castle
Ruins of 13th century castle in magnificent
clifftop setting on Peckforton Hills.
Beeston, Tarporley
☎ 0829 260464
Off the A49, 11 miles south-east of Chester
P

Chester Cathedral
Originally the 11th century abbey of St
Werburgh, this building has been the
Cathedral of Chester since 1541 and reflects
all the Gothic architectural styles.
St Werburgh Street
☎ 0244 324756
➤A A51 (city centre)
⇛ ✕ ⅋

Stretton Mill
Small working water mill set in beautiful
countryside; grinding demonstrations.
Nr Farndon
☎ 0606 41331
Off the A534 between Farndon and Broxton
P ⇛

Museums

Boat Museum
Museum with over 50 historic craft, largest
floating collection in the world; steam
engines, boat trips, and indoor exhibitions.
Ellesmere Port
☎ 051 355 5017
Off the M53, jct 9
P ⇛ ✕ ⅋

Grosvenor Museum
Roman finds, natural history and paintings.
Grosvenor Street
☎ 0244 321616
➤A A55 (city centre)

Mouldsworth Motor Museum
Cars, motorcycles, models and a replica
1920s garage; old toys and pedal cars for
children to use.
Smithy Lane, Mouldsworth
☎ 0928 31781
On the B5393, 6 miles east of Chester
P

Port Sunlight Heritage Centre
Creation and planning of Port Sunlight.
Greendale Road, Port Sunlight
☎ 051 644 6466
Off the A41 to M53, jct 4

Salt Museum
The story of salt-making in Cheshire from
Roman times to the present day.
London Road, Northwich
☎ 0606 41331
Signposted from the A556
P ⇛

Toy and Doll Museum
Over 1000 antique toys.
42 Bridge Street Row
☎ 0244 316251

Parks

Grosvenor Park
Landscaped parkland bordering the river in
the heart of the city. Scented garden for the
blind.

Theatres

Gateway Theatre
Modern drama productions and the classics.
The Forum, Hamilton Place
☎ 0244 340392/3
✕

Theatre Clwyd
Mold
☎ 352 55114
12 miles from Chester

Zoos

Chester Zoo
All the traditional attractions of a zoo in
extensive landscaped grounds.
Upton-by-Chester
☎ 0244 380105 recorded message
☎ 0244 380280
Just off the A41, 2 miles north of Chester
P ⇛ ✕ ⅋

CHESTER

WHAT TO DO AND SEE

OUTDOOR LEISURE

Birdwatching

Hilbre Island Local Nature Reserve
Important high-tide roost for wading birds during winter. Access on foot is restricted by tides which surround the islands twice daily for up to 6 hours. Admission is free but permits are required in advance.
Off West Kirby, at the north-west tip of the Wirral peninsula

Cycling

Budget-Rent-a-Car (cycle hire)
Lower Bridge Street
☎ 0244 325064

Fishing

Coarse fishing/salmon and migratory trout on the Dee and Clywd rivers and their tributaries. Licences available from:

Welsh Water Authority
Shire Hall, Mold, Clywd
☎ 0352 2121

Day licences available from fishing tackle shops.

Golf

Westminster Park
⛳ municipal course
Hough Green, Chester
☎ 0244 673071

Chester Golf Club ⛳18
Curzon Park
☎ 0244 675130

Eaton Golf Club ⛳18
Eaton Park, Eccleston
☎ 0244 674385

Upton-by-Chester ⛳18
Upton Lane, Upton
☎ 0244 23638

Vicar's Cross ⛳18
Tarvin Road, Littleton
☎ 0244 335174

Tarran Way ⛳18
Moreton on the Wirral
☎ 051 677 6606

Ice Skating

Deeside Leisure Centre
Queensferry
☎ 0244 812311

Dry-skiing

North-East Wales Institute
Kelsterton College, Connah's Quay, Deeside
☎ 0244 82215

Oval Sports Centre
Old Chester Road, Bebington
☎ 051 645 0596

Tennis

Water Tower Gardens
Alexandra Park, Hoole

Wealstone Playing Fields
Upton

Walking

Short Walks
ℹ The Tourist Office can supply information on walks under 5 miles in the area (often theme walks).

Delamere Forest
Extensive network of waymarked walks in the forest which is administered by the Forestry Commission; 4000 acres of woodland and lake.
☎ 0606 2167
Signposted from the A556, 6 miles west of Northwich

Wirral Country Park (Visitor Centre)
12 miles of transformed railway line from Hooton to West Kirby on Wirral peninsula. Separate bridle paths throughout the park. Main visitor centre is at Thurstaston with other car parks and picnic areas at Caldy, Heswall, Parkgate, Neston and Willaston. Thustaston
☎ 051 648 4371
Off the A540

WATERSPORTS

Boat trips

River cruises on the Dee and trips by horse-drawn canal barges. Cruises go to Eccleston Ferry and Ironbridge, sailing through the Eaton Estate, home of the Duke of Westminster. Narrowboats depart from Tower Wharf or Cow Lane Bridge.

Windsurfing

West Kirby
A mile long promenade, beach and marine lake where visitors can sail, windsurf or water-ski.

DEVON AND EXETER

WHAT TO DO AND SEE

County: Devon
i Civic Centre, Paris Street, Exeter
☎ 0392 37581
Market day: Monday and Friday
Population: 900,000
Exeter, a cathedral and university town, is one of Britain's oldest towns; it retains a major portion of the city walls built by the Romans. A flourishing port until removed from tidal reach, Exeter's Ship Inn was frequented by the famous seafarers Drake and Raleigh. Exeter's magnificent cathedral has a beautifully carved west front, Norman towers and an astronomical clock. The surrounding countryside offers the West country's rich farmland and rolling hills, the Devon coast and the mysteries of Dartmoor to explore.

EQUESTRIAN

Riding and Pony Trekking
Bellevue Valley Equestrian Centre
Argyll Road, Pennsylvania
☎ 0392 216928

HEALTH

Leisure Centres
The Plaza
Wave pool and water chute, health club, roller skating and sports areas.
Cowick Street, Exeter
☎ 0392 221771
B3212/A30
P ✕ ♿

LOCAL FEATURES

Art Galleries
City Gallery

Arts and Crafts
The Devon Guild of Craftsmen
Museum and demonstrations; continuous series of changing craft exhibitions.
Riverside Mill, Bovey Tracey
☎ 0626 832223
On the A382, 15 miles west of Exeter
P ✕

Quayside Crafts
Exhibition and sale of work by over 50 West Country craftsmen. Scenic model railway.
Exeter
☎ 0392 214332

Festivals and Fairs
May
Devon County Show, Exeter

May/June
Exeter Festival

September/October
Autumn Festival, Exeter

October
Exeter Carnival

Gardens
Bicton Park
60 acres of gardens including an Italian garden laid out in 1735.
East Budleigh, Budleigh Salterton
☎ 0395 68465
P ✕

Northernhay Gardens
First landscaped in 1612; present design dates from the 1920s.
New North Road and Queen Street, Exeter

Rougemont Gardens
Gardens laid out in the 18th century in the outer bailey of the castle.
Castle Street, Exeter

Guided Tours
Walking Tours
i The Tourist Information Centre can provide details of free walking tours operating within the city.

Historic Buildings
A La Ronde
Unique 16-sided house built in 1795 with parkland walks; sea and estuary views.
Summer Lane, Exmouth
☎ 0395 265514
➜A A376
P 🚌 ✕ ♿

Castle Drogo
20th century granite 'castle' designed by Sir Edwin Lutyens. Gardens. National Trust.
Drewsteignton
☎ 06473 3306
4 miles south of A30 via Crockernwell
P ♿

Cathedral

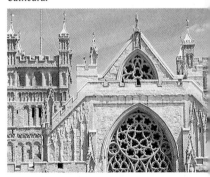

The Cathedral Church of St Peter dates from the 12th century, it has Norman transept towers, Gothic vaulting and a notable 14th century west front.
Cathedral Close, Exeter
☎ 0392 74779
➜A A30 (city centre)
🚌 ♿

DEVON AND EXETER

WHAT TO DO AND SEE

Guildhall
Oldest municipal building in the country with a mediaeval main hall and Tudor frontage; paintings and civic silver are displayed.
Exeter (town centre)
☎ 0392 56724

Killerton House
18th century house built for the Acland family; collection of costumes; hillside gardens. National Trust.
Broadclyst
☎ 0392 881345
On the B3185, 8 miles north of Exeter
P &

Powderham Castle
Home of the Courtenays, Earls of Devon, since 1390 and still inhabited by them; fine furnishings and family portraits.
Kenton
☎ 0626 890243
P ✗ &

Ugbrooke House and Park
Ancestral home of the Lords Clifford of Chudleigh with fine furniture and paintings, and a park landscaped by Capability Brown.
Chudleigh
☎ 0626 852179
→A A38
P ➡ ✗ &

Underground Passages
Tour the mediaeval system of water supply extending beneath the city centre.
Exeter
☎ 0392 56724

Museums

Country Life Museum
Working machines; farmyard animals, deer and llamas; crafts and playground.
Sandy Bay, Exmouth
☎ 0395 274533
→A A376
P &

Maritime Museum
Over 140 veteran sail and steam vessels from all over the world exhibited both outdoors on the canal and in the old warehouses. Playground. Boat rides.
The Haven, Exeter
☎ 0392 58075
→A A30
P

Royal Albert Memorial Museum and Art Gallery
Victorian building in Venetian Gothic style housing natural and local history collections.
Queen Street, Exeter
☎ 0392 265858
→A A377

Theatres

Barnfield Theatre
Small theatre offering professional and amateur productions.
Barnfield Road, Exeter
☎ 0392 71808

Northcott Theatre
Major professional theatre presenting a wide range of entertainment.
Stocker Road, Exeter
☎ 0392 54853

OUTDOOR LEISURE

Birdwatching and Wildlife

Dawlish Warren Nature Reserve
An important wildfowl habitat comprising 500 acres of mixed dune, saltmarsh and sandy shores.

Fishing

Squabmoor Reservoirs
4 acres holding carp, roach, rudd, tench and bream.
Towards Budleigh Salterton

Hogsbrook Lake
2½ acre lake stocked with carp, tench, roach and bream.
Woodbury Salterton

Upham Farm
Six ponds covering 2 acres; carp and tench.
Farrindon

River Exe
i The Tourist Information Centre can provide details of the several stretches of the River Exe which are open to day visitors and can be fished for roach, dace, perch and eels. All-year fishing is also possible on the Exeter Ship Canal, along the whole 6 mile length from the Basin to the Turf Locks, from both banks.

Golf

Exeter Golf and Country Club
↑18 parkland course.
Countess Wear
☎ 0392 874139

Municipal Course ↑18
Topsham Road

Dry-slope Skiing

Clifton Hill Sports Centre
Belmont Road
☎ 0392 265888

Walking

Dartmoor National Park (Headquarters)
Conducted walks for the family, a perfect introduction to Dartmoor.
Bovey Tracey

Stoke Woods
Walks through mixed woodland.

DONCASTER

County: South Yorkshire
i Tourist Office, Central Library,
Waterdale
☎ 0302 734309
Early closing: Thursday
Market day: Tuesday, Friday and Saturday
(antiques and curios on Wednesday)
Population: 75,000
Doncaster, called Danum by the Romans
and, historically, an important crossing
point on the River Don, is now a busy
industrial town. Mansion House and the
shops and houses of Hallgate and South
Parade provide some attractive Georgian
architecture. The Corn Exchange, a listed
building in Market Square, houses part of
the general market. Doncaster is well
known for its extensive markets.

AERIAL SPORTS

Parachuting and Microlighting

Doncaster Airport
Parachuting, microlight and light aircraft.
Bawtry Road
☎ 0302 532636

HEALTH

Leisure Centres

The Dome
Modern sports and recreation complex;
leisure pools, skating rink, squash and
snooker.
Bawtry Road
☎ 0302 370888
Adjacent to the racecourse
✗

Adwick Leisure Centre
Welfare Road, Woodlands East
☎ 0302 721447

Armthorpe Sports Centre
Mere Lane
☎ 0302 834268

EQUESTRIAN

Riding

Finningley School of Equitation
Finningley
☎ 0302 770259

LOCAL FEATURES

Festivals and Fairs

August
Horse of the Year Show

September
Finningley Air Display
St Leger week, 2nd week

Historic Buildings

Carlton Towers
Victorian Gothic house, and Yorkshire home
of the Duke of Norfolk.
Off the A1041, 15 miles north of Doncaster
✗

Conisbrough Castle
Dramatically set above the River Don; the
ruined white circular keep is one of the
oldest surviving in the country.
Conisbrough, nr Doncaster
☎ 0709 863329
Off the A630, 4½ miles south-west of
Doncaster

Monk Bretton Priory
Remains of Cluniac priory founded 1154.
Abbey Lane, Barnsley
☎ 0226 204089
→A A633

Nostell Priory
National Trust owned Palladian house built
in 1733; state rooms designed by Robert
Adam; adventure playground, picnic area.
On the A638 Doncaster to Wakefield road

Roche Abbey
12th century monastery ruin set in a
secluded valley.
☎ 0709 812739
Off the A634, 1½ miles south of Maltby

Museums

Cusworth Hall Museum of South Yorkshire Life
Georgian mansion in landscaped park; the
museum illustrates the area's history,
industries, agriculture and social life.
Cusworth Hall, Cusworth Lane
☎ 0302 782342
→A A638
P 🚌

Doncaster Art Gallery and Museum
Collections of Roman finds, costumes and
natural history displays.
Chequer Road
☎ 0302 734287
→A A638
🚌 ♿

Sandtoft Transport Museum
Restored working collection of trolley buses.
Belton Road, Sandtoft
☎ 0724 711391
P 🚌 ✗

Parks

Campsall Country Park
90 acre park with lake and picnic areas near
Askern.

Cusworth Hall Country Park
Gardens, terraces and lakes landscaped
around the Hall which contains the
museum of South Yorkshire life.

118

DONCASTER

WHAT TO DO AND SEE

Howell Wood Country Park
140 acres of woods, streams and ponds surrounding colliery villages.

Theatres

Civic Theatre
Amateur and professional theatre.
Waterdale
☎ 0302 342349
✗

OUTDOOR LEISURE

Birdwatching and Wildlife

Denaby Ings Nature Reserve
Wet pasture and marshland.
Off Pasture Road

Potteric Carr Nature Reserve
Fenlands with nature trail and footpaths through woods and waterside.
Permit required from Yorkshire Wildlife Trust
☎ 0904 59570
Via Carr Hill and Balby on the A6182

Sandall Beat Wood Nature Reserve
Oak, birch and sweet chestnut wood.

Thorpe Marsh Nature Reserve
Meadow land and lake, footpaths, nature trail and field centre.
Permit required from Yorkshire Wildlife Trust
☎ 0904 59570

Fishing

Nostell Priory
Fishing in three lakes.
Contact Fisheries Manager
☎ 0302 863562

Also at Arksey Fishing Pond, Askern Lake, Cusworth Hall Park, Hatfield Marina, River Don and Stainforth/Keadby Canal.

Golf

Doncaster Golf Club
☎ 0302 868404

Hickleton Golf Club 🏌18
Hickleton, nr Doncaster
☎ 0709 892496

Thorne Golf Club 🏌18
Thorne, nr Doncaster
☎ 0405 812084

Town Moor Golf Club 🏌18
☎ 0904 535286

Wheatley Golf Club 🏌18
Armthorpe Road, Doncaster
☎ 0302 831655

Crookhill Park Golf Course
🏌18 municipal course.
Carr Lane, Conisbrough
☎ 0709 862979

Tennis

Doncaster Tennis Club
☎ 0302 536134

Walking

Short Walks
i The Tourist Office can provide leaflets detailing town walks.

The Ramblers' Association
Meet regularly for group walks at Clock Corner, Frenchgate.
Contact Ken Gibson
☎ 0302 788689

WATERSPORTS

Sailing

Hatfield Marina
Boating, sailing, sailboarding, canoeing, rowing, sub-aqua, trout and coarse fishing.
☎ 0302 841572
Off the M18, north of Doncaster
✗ &

Hexthorpe Flatts
Water bus cruises between Doncaster, Spotbrough, Conisbrough and Mexborough

Seven Lakes Leisure Park
All watersports catered for; seven lakes available for fishing, windsurfing, water skiing, sailing. Children's boating lake.
Ealand, Crowle, nr Scunthorpe
☎ 0724 710245
➔A A161
P ✗ &

DOWNPATRICK

County: Down
i Tourist Officer, Down District Council,
24 Strangford Road, Downpatrick
☎ 0396 614331
Population: 8245
Early closing: Wednesday (Downpatrick)
Thursday (Ardglass and Crossgar)
Market days: Downpatrick, Tuesday,
Saturday (fruit/veg/variety), Thursday–
Saturday (Livestock)
Downpatrick is situated in County Down in
the south-eastern corner of Northern
Ireland. Down has many connections with
St. Patrick, who is buried near the Down
Cathedral in Downpatrick, a block of
Mourne granite marks the grave. The
Mourne Mountains are visible from the
cathedral.

EQUESTRIAN

Riding and Pony Trekking
Ballynahinch Riding Centre,
13 Ballycreen Road, Ballynahinch
☎ 0238 562883

HEALTH

Leisure Centres
Down Leisure Centre
Swimming, squash, handball and sauna.
114 Market Street, Downpatrick
☎ 0396 613426

LOCAL FEATURES

Heritage
Inch Abbey
Ruins of a Cistercian monastery founded in
the 1180's.
→A A7

Mound of Down
Manmade egg-shaped earthwork on which a
Norman castle was once situated.
→A A25

Ballynoe Stone Circle
Neolithic or Early Bronze Age circle of
closely spaced stones.
Access from footpath off the Downpatrick–
Rathmullan road

Clough Castle
Anglo-Norman motte and bailey castle
topped by a stone tower.
Jct of A24/A25

Jordan's Castle
15th century tower-house.
Ardglass

St. John's Point Church
Remains of a 10th century church.
Nr. Ardglass

Struell Wells
Group of healing wells and bath houses in a
secluded rocky valley.
Downpatrick

Museums
Down County Museum
Stone Age artifacts and Bronze Age gold are
displayed in this former jail.
English Street, Downpatrick
☎ 0396 615218

Parks
Quoile Pondage National Nature Reserve
16th century Quoile Castle ruins nearby.
→A A25

Railways
Downpatrick & Ardglass Railway Company
Downpatrick Railway Station
☎ 0396 615779

OUTDOOR LEISURE

Fishing
Rock Fishing
Conger eel, wrasse, dogfish, codling,
pollack, coalfish and mackerel at Killard
Point, near Ardglass and around the
harbour.

Sea Fishing
Turbot, cod, whiting, flatfish, rays and
dogfish at Ardglass Bank and Gun's Island.

Coarse Fishing
Pike, perch, rudd, eels and brown trout at
Lough Money and Quoile Basin, 100 acres.

Tackle shops:
Charles Mulhall
1 Quay Street, Ardglass
☎ 0396 841301

Angus Cochrane
The Harbour, Ardglass
☎ 0396 841255
☎ 0396 841278

Golf
Ardglass Golf Club ⛳₁₈
Castle Place, Ardglass
☎ 0396 841219

Bright Castle Golf Club ⛳₁₈
14 Coniamstown Road, Bright, Downpatrick
☎ 0396 841319

Downpatrick Golf Club ⛳₁₈
43 Saul Road, Downpatrick
☎ 0396 612152

Walking
Quoile Pondage National Nature Reserve
Guided walks and trails.
→A Off the A25

The Ulster Way
Route details available from:

Sports Council for NI
House of Sport, Upper Malone Road, Belfast
☎ 0232 381222

DOWN ROYAL

WHAT TO DO AND SEE

County: Down
i Northern Ireland Tourist Board,
River House, 48 High Street, Belfast
☎ 0232 246609
Early closing: Wednesday (Lisburn) Monday
(Hillsborough)
Market day: Tuesday
Lisburn, situated in the centre of the Lagan
Valley, is not far from Belfast, the busy
capital of Northern Ireland. The original
town, created in 1609, was known as
Lisnagarvey, in 1662 for no clear reason the
town name was changed to Lisburn. In
1707, Lisburn was ravaged by a fire which
destroyed most of the buildings. A tablet
built into the north wall of the Ulster
buildings in Market Square marks the first
building erected after the fire. The visitor
can enjoy Lisburn's many antique shops and
collectors' corners.

EQUESTRIAN

Riding and Pony Trekking

Ballynock Riding School
Miss Jennifer Howes, 38 Ballynock Road,
☎ 0846 692144

Yvette Linton's Riding School
23 Lurganure Road
☎ 0846 621523

HEALTH

Lisburn Leisure Centre
Squash, snooker, trampolining, yoga, judo,
aerobics, archery, sauna and sunbed.
Warren Park, Lisburn
☎ 0846 672121

Lisburn Swimming Pool
Market Place, Lisburn
☎ 0846 662306

LOCAL FEATURES

Art Galleries

Lisburn Museum
Assembly Rooms, Market Square, Lisburn
☎ 0846 672624

Arts and Crafts

Harmony Hill Arts Centre
54 Harmony Hill, Magheralave, Lisburn
☎ 0846 678219

Festivals and Fairs

July
Orangemen's Day, 12th July

Gardens

Wallace Fountain Castle Gardens
Lisburn

Heritage

Hillsborough Fort
A fort built in 1650.

Dromore Mound
Anglo-Norman motte and bailey castle.

Museums

Lisburn Museum
Assembly Rooms, Market Square, Lisburn
☎ 0846 672624

Music, Dance and Drama

Lisburn Arts Advisory Council
Dramatic and orchestral concerts, art
exhibitions.
Honorary Secretary, Borough Offices, The
Square, Hillsborough
☎ 0846 682477

Parks

Wallace Park
Lisburn

Moira Demesne
44 acres just outside Moira.

Duncan's Park
Off the A3, 7 miles from Moira

Lagan Valley Regional Park
4140 acres of parkland.

OUTDOOR LEISURE

Cycling

106 mile round trip; Belfast to the Mournes.
i Route details from tourist information
centre.

Fishing

Game fishing for brown trout and rainbow
trout is available during the season at
Hillsborough Lake, 40 acres; Stoneyford
Reservoir, 160 acres; Leathamstown
Reservoir, 28 acres and in the River Lagan.

Lisburn Sports Centre
1/9 Smithfield Square, Lisburn

McBrides Sport Shop
Haslem's Lane, Lisburn

W J Mairs
Cash Stores, Stoneyford

Golf

Lisburn Golf Club ⛳18
68 Eglantine Road, Lisburn
☎ 0846 677216

Aberdelghy Golf Course ⛳9
Bells Lane, Lambeg, Lisburn
☎ 0238 08462

Walking and Rambling

Hillsborough Forest Park
Lakeside paths and forest walks.

WATERSPORTS

Water Skiing

Lough Aughrey Ski Club
Contact Rodney Watson
18 Cuan Beach, Killyleagh

EDINBURGH

Region: Lothian
i Waverley Market, Princes Street
☎ 031 557 1700

Edinburgh, a beautiful city and Scotland's capital since 1437, is built on a series of hills overlooking the Firth of Forth. Edinburgh Castle dominates the city, its oldest part dating from 1100 it has been the scene of many historic episodes and affords sweeping and spectacular views over the city below it. The castle now provides the setting for the famous Military Tattoo. It is linked to the Queen's official Scottish residence, Holyroodhouse, by the Royal Mile – the ancient streets where many of the city's oldest buildings can be found. New Town provides a sharp contrast, built in the 18th century it has wide streets, crescents and elegant squares of Georgian buildings.

Edinburgh is famed for its International Festival, three weeks of concerts, theatre, opera and 'fringe' events. A city of great variety, Edinburgh also has excellent sporting facilities including Murrayfield, the venue for international rugby matches, Meadowbank Stadium, the venue for international athletics, the Royal Commonwealth Pool, built for the 1970 Commonwealth Games, as well as numerous excellent golf courses.

AERIAL SPORTS

Ballooning
Balloon Ecosse Flying Club
☎ 031 551 3059

EQUESTRIAN

Riding and Pony Trekking
Edinburgh and Lasswade Riding Centre
Mr J. N. Beck, Kevock Road, Lasswade
☎ 031 663 7676

Tower Farm Riding Stables
Mrs J. Forrest, 85 Liberton Drive, Edinburgh
☎ 031 664 3375

Weftmuir Riding Centre
Totley Wells Grange, nr South Queensferry

HEALTH

Leisure Centres
Ainslie Park Leisure Centre
International standard competition pool, flumes, spa pool, toddler's pool, fountain and water cannon as well as fitness room and indoor sports facilities.
92 Pilton Drive, Edinburgh
☎ 031 551 2400

Meadowbank Sports Centre
The main Commonwealth Games Stadium.
London Road
☎ 031 661 5351

Royal Commonwealth Pool
Fitness centre, sauna, sunbeds, flumes and other sports facilities.
Dalkeith Road
☎ 031 667 7211

LOCAL FEATURES

Art Galleries
City Art Centre
Displays from the city's art collection, temporary exhibitions of fine and applied arts, open space exhibitions by local arts groups.
2 Market Street
☎ 031 225 2424 ext 6650
🎫 ♿

National Gallery of Scotland
Works by many famous artists as well as the Scottish Masters and temporary exhibitions.
The Mound
☎ 031 556 8921
🎫 ♿

National Portrait Gallery
Queen Street
☎ 031 556 8921
🎫 ♿

Scottish National Gallery of Modern Art
Belford Road
☎ 031 556 8921
🎫 ♿

Arts and Crafts
The Adam Pottery
Pottery studio producing hand-thrown stoneware.
76 Henderson Row, Stockbridge
☎ 031 557 3978
🎫 🚌

Brass Rubbing Centre
Mediaeval brasses and Scottish stone carvings.
Trinity Apse, Chalmers Close, High Street
☎ 031 556 4364

Scottish Craft Centre
Acheson House in the Royal Mile; a showcase for over 300 craftsmen and women.
140 Canongate, Royal Mile
☎ 031 556 8136
☎ 031 556 7370
🎫

Factory Visits
Edinburgh Crystal Visitor's Centre
Guided factory tours available.
Penicuik
☎ 0968 75128
➜A A701
🏠 🚌 ✗

EDINBURGH

Festivals and Fairs

March
Folk Festival

June
Royal Highland Show, Ingliston

August
Edinburgh International Festival
Fringe
Military Tattoo
Edinburgh International Film Festival
Jazz Festival

Food and Drink

Royal Mile Banquets
Mediaeval entertainment and feasting.
9 Victoria Street
☎ 031 220 1708

Scotch Whisky Heritage Centre
358 Castlehill, The Royal Mile
☎ 031 220 0441
🏠 ♿ ♿

Gardens

Royal Botanic Garden
Unique collection of unusual plants.
Inverleith Row
☎ 031 552 7171 ext 260
🚫 ♿

Guided Tours

Caddies Walking Tours of Edinburgh
The Early Witchery Walk; Mr Clapperton's
Ghosts and Gore etc. Tours by day and
night leave from the Witchery Restaurant.
Castle Hill, Royal Mile
☎ 031 225 6745

Guide Friday
City tours by double decker bus with guide.
Tours start from the Waverley Bridge.
☎ 031 556 2244

In City Guides
City and country tours in a 4/6 seater.
☎ 031 332 0727

Off the Beaten Track
Personally conducted tours through
Lowland Scotland.
Margaret Kinnear
☎ 031 667 4473

Robin's Tours
Tours of the old town start at the fountain
over Waverley Market, Princes Street.
Robin Sinton, 66 Willowbrae Road
☎ 031 661 0125

Heritage

Clan Tartan Centre
Where to track down your clan and tartan.
In the James Pringle Woollen Mill,
70/74 Bangor Road, Leith
☎ 031 553 5100
☎ 031 553 5161
P ✕

Historic Buildings

Craigmillar Castle
Mediaeval ruined castle associated with
Mary Queen of Scots.
Craigmillar
☎ 031 661 4445
On the A68 Edinburgh–Dalkeith Road
🏠

Dalmeny House
Period mansion house and grounds with a
notable art collection, French furniture,
porcelain and tapestries.
South Queensferry
☎ 031 331 1888
🏠

Edinburgh Castle
A famous historic stronghold, and home of
the Scottish National War Memorial, the
Scottish Crown Jewels, the Scottish United
Services and the Royal Scots Regimental
Museums.
☎ 031 225 9846
P 🏠 🚌

Hopetoun House
Scotland's biggest Robert Adam mansion set
in 100 acres of parkland, with sumptuous
rooms and state apartments, paintings by
Rubens, Titian and Canaletto, a walled
garden centre, nature trail and deer park.
South Queensferry
☎ 031 331 2451
🏠

Lauriston Castle
Mansion house with a fine furniture
collection and an outstanding display of
"Blue John" ware.
2 Cramond Road South
☎ 031 336 2060

Palace of Holyroodhouse
Official Scottish residence of H.M. The
Queen; an outstanding picture gallery and
state apartments.
Canongate
☎ 031 556 7371
🏠

Museums

Huntly House
Canongate
☎ 031 225 2424
🚫

John Knox House
High Street
☎ 031 556 2647
🚫

Lady Stair's House
A museum dedicated to the great Scottish
writers, Burns, Scott and Stevenson.
Lawnmarket
☎ 031 225 2424 ext 6593
🚫

EDINBURGH

Museum of Childhood
Historic toys, dolls, hobby items and costumes.
High Street
☎ 031 225 2424 ext 6646

Royal Museum of Scotland
Decorative art and science.
Chambers Street
☎ 031 225 7534

Royal Museum of Scotland
Queen Street
☎ 031 225 7534

Music, Dance and Drama

Usher Hall
Lothian Road
☎ 031 228 1155

The Queen's Hall
Clerk Street
☎ 031 668 3456

Natural History

Edinburgh Butterfly and Insect World
Dobbie's Garden Centre, Dalkeith
☎ 031 663 4932

Theatres

Kings Theatre
Leven Street
☎ 031 229 1201

Royal Lyceum Theatre
Grindlay Street
☎ 031 229 9697

The Playhouse Theatre
Greenside Place
☎ 031 557 2590

The Churchill Theatre
Morningside Road
☎ 031 447 7597

Zoos

The Scottish National Zoological Park
Corstorphine Road
☎ 031 334 9171

Birdwatching and Wildlife

Duddingston Loch
A bird sanctuary since 1923, the loch has many rare birds. Permission available from:
The Scottish Wildlife Trust
☎ 031 226 4602

Cycling

i Cycle touring routes available from the Tourist Office.

Fishing

Fishing is good in the rivers, lochs, and reservoirs around Edinburgh. Local tackle shops will supply information and permits.

Golf

Braids Hill Golf Course ⛳
Braids Hill
☎ 031 447 6666

Carrick Knowe Golf Course ⛳
Off Balgreen Road
☎ 031 337 1096

Craigentinny Golf Course ⛳
Lochend
☎ 031 554 7501

Portobello Golf Course ⛳
Stanley Street
☎ 031 669 4361

Silverknowes Golf Course ⛳
Silverknowes Parkway
☎ 031 336 3843

Ice Skating

Murrayfield Ice Rink
Riversdale Crescent
☎ 031 337 6933

Skiing

Hillend Ski Centre
Europe's largest artificial ski slope.
Biggar Road, Pentland Hills
☎ 031 445 4433

Walking

Mercat Walking Tours
☎ 031 441 3460
☎ 031 661 4541

Guided Walks
New Town
☎ 031 557 5222

Guided Walks around Holyrood Park
Scottish Wildlife Trust
☎ 031 226 4602

Union Canal Guided Walks
☎ 0506 856624

Boat Trips

Maid of Forth
Regular sailings from South Queensferry.
☎ 031 331 1454

The Edinburgh Canal Centre
Boat trips, cruises and boat hire.
Bridge Inn, Ratho
☎ 031 333 1320

Dinghy Sailing

Port Edgar Sailing Centre
Sailing, boat hire and courses available.
South Queensferry Yacht Club,
533 Queensferry Road
☎ 031 331 3330

EPSOM
Including Kempton Park, Lingfield Park and Sandown Park

County: Surrey

i Town Hall, New Zealand Avenue,
Walton-on-Thames

☎ 0932 228844

i The Civic Hall, London Road, Guildford

☎ 0483 575857

Epsom, famous in the 18th century for its medicinal spring and now for its racecourse, is situated in the attractive and varied Surrey countryside. The surrounding gentle, rolling, green downs provide ideal riding and walking country well supplied with footpaths and bridleways that lead the traveller to spectacular views southwards towards the Ashdown Forest. Villages with pubs and village greens abound as do historic towns such as Guildford; there are zoos, stately homes, museums, theme parks, cruises down the River Wey, theatres, cinemas, and a comprehensive range of sporting pursuits in the area.

AERIAL SPORTS

Ballooning

Flying Picture Balloons
Champagne flights.
Chobham

☎ 0276 855111 ext 125

Independent Balloon Co Ltd
Champagne flights.
74 North Street, Guildford

☎ 0483 300054

EQUESTRIAN

Riding and Pony Trekking

Bushy Park
The Green, Hampton Court

☎ 081 979 1748

HEALTH

Leisure Centres

Elmbridge Leisure Centre and Walton Pool
Pool, aerobics, weights room, sauna, sunbed, super shuttle slide and many sports activities.
Kings Close, Walton-on-Thames

☎ 0932 222984

Guildford Sports Centre
Pool with water chute, gym, sauna, hydrobath and sports hall.
Bedford Road, Guildford

☎ 0483 444777

LOCAL FEATURES

Art Galleries

Gomshall Mill and Gallery
Ancient watermill with art gallery, craft shops and antiques.
Gomshall

☎ 048641 2433

➔A A25

P &

Gardens

Claremont Landscape Garden
The earliest surviving English landscape garden begun in the early 1700s.
Portsmouth Road, Esher

☎ 0372 53401

P 🎍 🚌 ✕ & &

Painshill Park
18th century landscaped park.
Portsmouth Road, Cobham

☎ 0932 64674

P 🎍 🚌 ✕ &

Wisley Gardens
Home of the Royal Horticultural Society.
Guildford

☎ 0483 224234

A3 between Ripley and Cobham

P 🎍 ✕ & &

Historic Buildings

Albury Park
Large Victorian mansion by Pugin, famous for the ornate brickwork of the chimneys.
Albury, nr Guildford

☎ 048641 2964

➔A A248

P 🎍 🚌

Chilworth Manor
House open to visitors when the garden is open under the National Gardens Scheme.
Chilworth, nr Guildford

☎ 0483 61414

➔A A248

P 🎍 🚌 ✕ &

Clandon Park
Outstanding 18th century country house with fine marble hall and Gubbay collection of furniture, pictures and porcelain.
West Clandon, nr Guildford

☎ 0483 222482

➔A A3

P 🎍 🚌 ✕ & &

Greated Manor
Fine Victorian manor house.
Ford Manor Road, Dormansland, Lingfield

☎ 0342 832577

Off the B2028

P 🎍 🚌

125

EPSOM

Hatchlands
Handsome red brick house built in 1758, notable for its early interiors by Robert Adam and fine collection of keyboard instruments. Garden.
East Clandon, nr Guildford
☎ 0483 222787
→A A246
P 🏠 ✕ ♿

Polesden Lacey
Originally a Regency villa, remodelled after 1906; fine paintings, tapestries and silver with extensive grounds.
Great Bookham, nr Dorking
☎ 0372 58203
→A A246
P 🏠 ✕ ♿ ♿

Loseley Park
Elizabethan country house with many works of art; garden terrace, moat walk, childrens play area, farm trailer rides, dairy farm and rare breeds unit. Farm shop.
Guildford
☎ 0483 571881
→A A3100
P 🏠 🚌 ✕ ♿ ♿

Hampton Court Palace
Magnificent Tudor Palace with later Baroque additions; famous maze and gardens.
East Molesey
☎ 081 977 8441
🏠 ✕ ♿ ♿

Runnymede
The memorial marks the spot on which the Magna Carta was sealed in 1215.
Nr Egham
→A A30
🚗

Guildford Cathedral
The only modern cathedral in the south of England.
Stag Hill
☎ 0483 65287
P 🚌 ✕ ♿ ♿

Museums

Bourne Hall Museum
Spring Street, Ewell
☎ 081 393 9573
P ♿ ♿

Chertsey Museum
The history and archaeology of Runnymede and a collection of 18th and 19th century costume.
The Cedars, 33 Windsor Street
☎ 0932 565764
🚗 🚌 ♿

Weybridge Museum
Collections covering local, natural and social history, archaeology and costume; changing exhibitions.
Church Street, Weybridge
☎ 0932 843573
♿

Music, Dance and Drama

Civic Hall
Home of the Guildford Philharmonic Orchestra.
London Road, Guildford
☎ 0483 444555

Natural History

Chapel Farm Trail
Working farm set in magnificent countryside.
Westhumble, Dorking
☎ 0306 882865
🏠 ♿ ♿

Horton Park Farm
Childrens farm with lots of young animals.
Horton Lane, Epsom
☎ 03727 43984
🏠 ✕ ♿ ♿

Parks

Thorpe Park
Family leisure park with 400 acres of lakes and parkland; many attractions and rides.
Staines Road, Chertsey
☎ 0932 562633
🏠 ✕

Railways

Great Cockcrow Railway
Miniature steam railway with unique signalling system.
Hardwick Lane, Lyne, Chertsey
☎ 0932 228950
🏠 ✕ ♿ ♿

Theatres

Yvonne Arnaud Theatre
Millbrook, Guildford
☎ 0483 60191

Epsom Playhouse
Ashley Avenue, Epsom
☎ 03727 42555

Harlequin Theatre
Warwick Quadrant, Redhill
☎ 0737 773721

Zoos

Chessington World of Adventures
Large zoo, human circus, spectacular rides in a theme area, skyway monorail.
Leatherhead Road, Chessington
☎ 0372 727227
🏠 ✕ ♿

Birdwatching and Wildlife

Laporte Earths' Conservation Lake
Bird sanctuary, lake with paths and viewing platforms.
Nutfield Marsh Road, Nutfield
☎ 0737 765050
♿

EPSOM

WHAT TO DO AND SEE

Fishing

Weybridge Guns and Tackle Ltd
137 Oatlands Drive, Weybridge
☎ 0932 842675

Winslo Tackle
102 Gilders Road, Chessington
☎ 081 391 1777

Tillingbourne Trout
Anglers' lake, fly fishing, tackle shop,
fresh trout.
Albury Mill, Albury
☎ 048641 2567

Golf

Major golf clubs in the area include RAC
Club Epsom, Sunningdale, Walton Health
and Wentworth; venues for spectator events.
However, play is more likely at one of the
following:

Drift ⚑₁₈
☎ 04865 4641

Farnham Park ⚑₁₈
☎ 0252 715216

Foxhills ⚑₁₈
☎ 093287 2050

Hoebridge ⚑₁₈
☎ 04862 22611

Sandown Park ⚑₁₈
☎ 0372 63072

Horton Country Club ⚑₁₈
☎ 081 394 2626

Tennis

There are public courts at Cobham, Esher,
Oatlands, Molesey, Walton-on-Thames and
Weybridge. For bookings:

The Council Offices
☎ 0372 62111 ext 4024

Walking

There are some lovely walks in the Surrey
countryside and the many parks and
commons. Booklets of self-guided walks are
available from the Tourist Offices or at local
libraries. Surrey County Council has walk
leaders who can take you on fascinating
rambles. For further information:
☎ 081 541 9453

WATERSPORTS

Boat Hire

Guildford Boat House
River trips, holiday narrow boats, rowing
boats and canoes for hire.
Milbrook
☎ 0483 504494

Maidboats Ltd
Cruiser hire on the Thames, holiday
membership of rowing and sailing clubs,
trips in passenger boats.
Ferry Yacht Station, Ferry Road, Thames
Ditton, Surrey
☎ 081 398 0271/2

Sailing/Water Skiing

See Thorpe Park.

FAKENHAM

WHAT TO DO AND SEE

County: Norfolk
i Red Lion House, Market Place,
Fakenham
☎ 0328 851981
Early closing: Wednesday
Market days: Thursday and Saturday
Population: 37,323
Fakenham is a pleasant market town with a partly 15th century church, its tower dominates the town, and two Georgian inns that add their appeal to the marketplace. Weekly auctions, where bargains may still be found, are held on Thursdays. The north Norfolk coast with its notable bird sanctuaries, nature reserves, walks and good fishing is within easy reach. Holkham Hall, the early 18th century Palladian home of the Earl of Leicester is just one of the spectacular country houses to be found in this area.

EQUESTRIAN

Riding and Pony Trekking

North Norfolk Riding Centre
Old Wells Road, Little Walsingham
☎ 0328 72377

LOCAL FEATURES

Antiques and Collecting

Fakenham Flea Market and Auctions
Thursday mornings.
Hugh Beck Auctions
☎ 0328 51557

Architecture

Castle Acre Priory
Impressive ruins of a Cluniac Priory dated about 1090.
Stocks Green, Castle Acre, Kings Lynn
☎ 07605 294
➔A A1065
P 🏠

Creake Abbey
Remains of a 13th century abbey church.
Burnham Market
P 🏠

Walsingham Abbey
Remains of an Augustinian Priory with woodland and riverside walks.
Little Walsingham
☎ 0328 820259
On the B1105
Narrow gauge railway from Wells
P 🏠 🚌 👥 👥

Art and Crafts

Handworkers' Market
Embroidery and needlecraft specialists.
18 Chapel Yard, Holt
☎ 0263 711251

Made in Cley
Pottery in stoneware and porcelain.
High Street, Cley-next-the-Sea
☎ 0263 740134

Festivals and Fairs

June
Fakenham Carnival

July
Norwich Union Carriage Driving Trials
Kings Lynn Festival
Sandringham Flower Show

August
Wells Carnival
Cromer Carnival

Gardens

Mannington Gardens and Countryside
Gardens with outstanding collection of roses; a rose festival; country trails.
Mannington Hall, Saxthorpe
☎ 026387 4175
Off the B1149/B1354
P 🏠 🚌 👥 👥 👥

Norfolk Lavender Ltd
Lavender herb and rose gardens; tea room and shop.
Caley Mill, Heacham
☎ 0485 70384
➔A A149

Historic Buildings

Baconsthorpe Castle
A 15th century moated semi-fortified house.
Baconsthorpe, nr Holt
☎ 0223 455532 (area custodian)
➔A A148/B1149
P 🏠

Cley Mill
Well-preserved tower mill.
Cley-next-the-Sea
☎ 0263 740209
➔A A149
P 🏠 🚌

Holkham Hall
Beautiful 18th century Palladian manor by William Kent; fine paintings and tapestries.
Wells-next-the-Sea
☎ 0328 710733
➔A A149
P 🏠 👥 👥

Houghton Hall
Early 18th century house with superb state rooms, a collection of 20,000 model soldiers and stables with heavy horses.
Houghton
☎ 048522 569
➔A A148
P 🏠 🚌 👥 👥 👥

Letheringsett Watermill
Historic working watermill.
Riverside Road, Lethingsett, Holt
☎ 0263 713153
➔A A148
P 🏠 🚌

128

FAKENHAM

Sandringham House
Country home of H.M. the Queen; grounds, museum and country park.
King's Lynn, Norfolk
➔A A149

Museums

Bygones at Holkham
Unique collection of carriages, tools, engines, domestic, dairy and farming implements.
Holkham Park, Wells-next-the-Sea
☎ 0328 710806
➔A A149
P 🕭 ✗ ♿

Cockthorpe Hall Toy Museum
Over 2,500 toys displayed in seven rooms of a lovely 16th century manor house.
Cockthorpe, nr Stiffkey
☎ 032875 293
➔A A149
P 🕭 🚐 ✗

Forge Museum
A working forge.
North Creake, nr Fakenham
☎ 0328 738910
On the B1355, nr Burnham Market
🕭

Norfolk Rural Life Museum
A former workhouse illustrating rural life over the past 200 years.
Gressenhall
☎ 0362 860563
Off the B1110, nr Dereham
🕭

Shirehall Museum
Georgian courtroom.
Little Walsingham
☎ 0328 820510
🕭

Thursford Collection
Steam locomotives, showman's traction, mechanical organs, ploughing and traction engines. Live concerts on the Wurlitzer.
☎ 0328 477
Off the A148, nr Fakenham
P 🕭 ✗

Natural History

Dinosaur Natural History Park
Woodland walk to view dinosaurs, terrain adventure rides, wooded maze, picnic and play area and bygones museum.
Weston House, Weston Longville, Norwich
☎ 0603 870245
➔A A1067 nr Norwich

Sea Life Centre
Ocean tunnel, rock pools, sealife creatures in natural settings.
Southern Promenade, Hunstanton
☎ 04853 33576
➔A A149

Parks

Pensthorpe Waterfowl Park
Nature trails, adventure playground and wildlife exhibitions.
☎ 0328 51465
Off the A1067, nr Fakenham

Zoos

Norfolk Wildlife Park
European mammals and birds, rare trees and shrubs in 40 acres of beautiful parkland; small gauge steam railway; commando play areas, and tame domestic animals.
Great Witchingham.
☎ 0603 872274
On the A1067, nr Norwich

Birdwatching and Wildlife

Blakeney Point
Shingle spit; sand dunes with hides to see seals and birds. Shop and display in the Lifeboat House. National Trust.
Access by boat from Morston Quay.

Cley Marshes
Fresh water and salt marshes with a large number of rare migrants each year. Norfolk Naturalists' Trust. Cley Visitor Centre gives permits for the Reserve.

Holkham
Sand and mud flats, salt marshes and sand dunes; Canada Geese and wildfowl roosts.
Nature Conservancy Council.
Permits for birdwatching:
Estate Office, Holkham Hall
☎ 0328 710227

Scolt Head Island
Island reserve with salt marshes and sand dunes. Access by boat from Brancaster Staithe. Nature Conservancy Council.

Titchwell
Reed beds, salt marshes and sandy shores; waders and wintering wildfowl. Royal Society for the Protection of Birds.
Warden: Three Horseshoes Cottage, Titchwell.

Fishing

i A detailed leaflet is available from the local Tourist Office.

Golf

Fakenham Golf Club 🏌
Hempton Road, Fakenham
☎ 0328 3534

Walking

Excellent local walks and coastal paths, many with particular wildlife interest.
i The Tourist Office has free leaflets with details of walks.

FOLKESTONE

County: Kent
i Tourist Office, Harbour Street
☎ 0303 58594
Early closing: Wednesday
Market days: Thursday and Sunday
Population: 43,000

Folkestone, one of Britain's classic seaside resorts, combines the picturesque, old working harbour of winding, cobbled streets, and fisherman's cottages with more modern seaside attractions. Wide spacious streets, tree-lined avenues and the mile-long, beautifully laid-out clifftop promenade, The Leas, from which it is possible to see the coast of France on a clear day, add to its attraction. Formal floral displays, a bandstand with a summer concert programme, cross-channel ferries and fishing vessels, the Rotunda fairground and amusement centre, the Martello Tower surrounded by bowling greens and tennis courts provide a great variety of entertainment and activity.

The surrounding countryside offers the quiet, solitary countryside of the Romney Marshes, a marsh covered with winding dykes and populated by various species of flora and fauna unique to the area, and the charms of many historic market and seaside towns such as the Cinque Port of Hythe.

EQUESTRIAN

Riding

Broome Park Riding Stables
Broome Park, Barham, nr Canterbury
☎ 0227 831373

Valley Farm
Woodlands, Lyminge
☎ 0303 862888

Little Pett Bottom
Maxted Street, Stelling Minnis, Canterbury
☎ 023375 308

Saltwood Riding Stables
Hayne Barn, Saltwood
☎ 0303 260338

Limes Farm
Pay Street, Hawkinge
☎ 030389 2335

HEALTH

Leisure Centres

Folkestone Sports Centre
Modern centre: table tennis, dry ski run, swimming, 9-hole golf course, climbing wall, roller skating, sauna, solarium and sports equipment hire. Temporary membership available.
Radnor Park Avenue
☎ 0303 850222

Festivals and Fairs

February
Performing Arts Festival

April
Yehudi Menuhin International Violin
    Competition (every two years)

June
International Folklore Festival

August
Folkestone Carnival

October
Kent Literature Festival
European and All England Sea Angling
    Championships

Food and Drink

Biddenden Vineyards
Little Whatmans, Biddenden
☎ 0580 291726
➔A A262
P 🚐

Gardens

Chilham Castle Gardens
Terraces, rose garden and lakeside walk and displays of birds of prey.
☎ 0227 730319
➔A A252
P 🏠

Historic Buildings

Canterbury Cathedral
The Mother Church of Anglican Communion founded in 597; it was the site of Becket's martyrdom; noted for its beautiful stained glass.
☎ 0227 762862
➔A A2 (city centre)
🚐 ♿

Dover Castle
Imposing mediaeval fortress.
☎ 0304 201628
➔A A258
P 🚐 ✕

Dymchurch Martello
One of 74 Martello Towers built along the coast as a defence chain against Napoleon.
High Street, Dymchurch
☎ 0303 873684
➔A A259
P

Godinton House and Garden
Jacobean house containing fine furnishings and paintings; formal 18th century gardens including a topiary.
Godinton Park, nr Ashford
☎ 0233 620733
➔A A20
P 🚐

FOLKESTONE

WHAT TO DO AND SEE

Lamb House
Early Georgian house and walled garden; home of American writer Henry James and later the author, E. F. Benson.
National Trust.
West Street, Rye
☎ 0797 223763
➔A A2668/A259

Museums

Brenzett Aeronautical Museum
Display of World War II and Battle of Britain aircraft engines.
Ivychurch Road, Brenzett
➔A A259/A257
P ᚛

Eurotunnel Exhibition Centre
A fixed link between Britain and France and one of the biggest engineering projects of this century. Videos; full-size mock-up section of a tunnel train; viewing tower.
Cheriton High Street, Folkestone
☎ 0303 270111
M20, jct 12, then signposted
P ✕ ᚛

Folkestone Museum and Art Gallery
Local, natural and social history; changing art exhibitions.
2 Grace Hill, Folkestone
☎ 0303 850123
➔A A20
P ⌕

Kent Battle of Britain Museum
Hawkinge Airfield, Hawkinge
☎ 0303 893140
➔A A260
P

Music, Dance and Drama

Metropole Arts Centre
Art exhibitions; music, drama, children's shows, jazz, literature and dance.
The Leas, Folkestone
☎ 0303 55070
➔A A259 (town centre)
P ✕

Parks

Brockhill Country Park
54 acres of parkland overlooking the sea.

Railways

Kent and East Sussex Steam Railway
Full size steam railway; refurbished Edwardian station.
Tenterden
☎ 05806 5155
➔A A28
P ✕

Romney, Hythe and Dymchurch Railway
World's only main line in miniature, steam locomotives, sheds and exhibition.
New Romney
☎ 0679 62353
➔A A259
P

Zoos

Port Lympne Zoo Park
300 acre zoo park breeding rare animals; safari trailer journeys through animal paddocks; historic house, art gallery and gardens.
Lympne, nr Hythe
☎ 0303 264646
A20/M20, exit 11, signposted
P ✕ ᚛

OUTDOOR LEISURE

Cycling

i The Tourist Information office can provide leaflets of recommended routes; a perfect area for a cycling break.
Renham Cycle Centres
11 Cheriton High Street
☎ 0303 78537

Fishing

Folkestone Tackle Centre
57 The Old High Street
☎ 0303 59555

Garry's
12 Tontine Street
☎ 0303 53881

Golf

Broome Park Golf and Country Club ⛳18
Championship course.
Broome Park Estate, Barham
☎ 0227 831701

Sene Valley ⛳18
Sene
☎ 0303 68514

Skiing

Folkestone Sports Centre
Radnor Park Avenue
☎ 0303 850333

Walking

North Downs Way
141 mile path (227 km) starts at Farnham, Surrey and winds its way to Folkestone and Dover, following parts of the Pilgrims' Way route.

Romney Marshes
i The current calendar suitable for all the family with details of times and meeting places is available from the Tourist Office. Details of short circular walks produced by the Countryside Commission are also available.

WATERSPORTS

Water Skiing

Folkestone Activity Holiday Centre
Marine Crescent
☎ 0303 55651

GOODWOOD
Including Fontwell Park

County: West Sussex
ℹ Chichester Tourist Information Centre,
St Peter's Market, West Street,
Chichester, West Sussex
☎ 0243 775888
Early closing: Thursday
Market days: Wednesday, Saturday
Population: 26,500
Chichester with its famous cathedral is the
county town of west Sussex and still retains
its Roman town plan and long stretches of
the original Roman wall. Its rich history is
visible in its Georgian houses, ancient
churches, and mediaeval hospital; a
flourishing market town, its four main
streets meet at a 15th century market cross.
It also has a well known modern Arts
Festival theatre. Its location between the
wooded and varied countryside of the South
Downs to the north, Chicester Harbour and
the Sussex coast with its boating and
seaside attractions to the south, ensure that
there is much to interest everyone in the
area.

AERIAL SPORTS

Ballooning

Golf Centres Balloons Ltd
Balloon Booking Clerk, Cray Valley Golf
Club.
Sandy Lane, St Paul's Cray, Orpington,
Kent
☎ 0689 74388

Parachuting

Flying Tigers Skydiving Centre
Goodwood Airfield, nr Chichester
☎ 0243 780333

Flying

Goodwood Flying School
Goodwood Airfield
☎ 0243 774656

EQUESTRIAN

Riding and Pony Trekking

Escorted Rides
☎ 0243 527035
☎ 0243 527431

HEALTH

Leisure Centres

Westgate
Sports hall, swimming pools, creche, squash
courts, conditioning room, keep fit, bar and
terrace.
Avenue de Chartres, Chichester
☎ 0243 785651
🏠 ✕

LOCAL FEATURES

Festivals and Fairs

June
Petworth Festival

July
Chichester Festivities

August
Arundel Festival

Food and Drink

Arundel Vineyards
Church Lane, Lyminster
☎ 0903 883393
➔A A27
P 🏠 🚌 ✕ ♿

Chilsdown Vineyard
The Old Station House, Singleton,
Chichester
☎ 0243 63 398
➔A A286
P 🏠 🚌 ✕

Gardens

Apuldram Roses
Specialist rose nursery, mature rose garden.
Apuldram Lane, Dell Quay, Chichester
☎ 0243 785769
🏠

Denmans Garden
Garden, plant centre, shop and tea shop.
Clock House, Denmans, Fontwell
☎ 0243 542808
➔A A27
P 🏠 🚌 ✕ ♿

West Dean Gardens
35 acres of lawns, borders, specimen trees,
old roses, wild garden and pergola.
West Dean, nr Chichester
☎ 0243 63 303
P 🏠 ✕ ♿ ♿

Guided Tours

Mary Godby
Town walks, coach tours, visits, specialising
in West Sussex.
Stable House, Amberley, Arundel
☎ 0798 831614

Heritage

Fishbourne Roman Palace and Museum
Remains of a 1st century Roman palace.
Salthill Road, Fishbourne, Chichester
☎ 0243 785859
➔A A27
P 🏠 🚌 ♿ ♿

Historic Buildings

Arundel Castle
Ancestral home of the Dukes of Norfolk;
art treasures, paintings and furniture.
☎ 0903 883136
➔A A27
P 🏠 🚌 ✕ ♿

GOODWOOD

WHAT TO DO AND SEE

Chichester Cathedral
Beautiful cathedral in the heart of the city with works of art from Romanesque stone carvings to famous modern paintings, sculpture and tapestries.
The Royal Chantry, Cathedral Cloisters
☎ 0243 782595
→A A27
🏠 🚌 ✕ ♿ ♿

Goodwood House
Treasure house of the Dukes of Richmond with paintings including some fine Canalettos and Sevres porcelain.
☎ 0243 774107
✕ ♿

Parham House and Gardens
Elizabethan House situated in a deer park at the foot of the South Downs; important collection or portraits, fine furniture, tapestries and rare needlework.
Parham Park, Pulborough
☎ 09066 2021
→A A283
P 🏠 🚌 ✕ ♿

Petworth House and Park
Magnificent late 17th century house in a beautiful deer park with an important collection of paintings.
☎ 0798 42207
→A A272
P 🏠 ✕ ♿ ♿

Stansted Park
A Neo-Wren house; ancient chapel, walled gardens, theatre, museum and the longest beech avenue in the south of England.
Rowlands Castle
☎ 0705 412265
Off the B2148
P 🏠 ✕ ♿ ♿

Museums

Arundel Toy and Military Museum
23 High Street, Arundel
☎ 0903 883101
🏠 ♿

Chichester District Museum
Geology, archaeology and social history.
29 Little London, Chichester
☎ 0243 784683
🏠 ♿

Guildhall Museum
In the 13th century Greyfriars Church.
Priory Park, Chichester
☎ 0243 784683
🏠 ♿

Pallant House
Queen Anne town house with art gallery and garden.
9 North Pallant, Chichester
☎ 0243 774557
P ✕ 🚌 ♿

Tangmere Military Aviation Museum
Chichester
☎ 0243 775223

The Museum of D-Day Aviation
Manor Farm, Apuldram, Chichester
→A A259
P 🏠 🚌 ♿ ♿

Weald and Downland Open Air Museum
Collection of rescued historic buildings.
Singleton, Chichester
☎ 0243 63 348
→A A286
P 🏠 🚌 ♿ ♿

Natural History

The Wildfowl and Wetlands Centre
Mill Road, Arundel
☎ 0903 883355
→A A27
P 🏠 🚌 ✕ ♿ ♿

Theatre

Chichester Festival Theatre
Oaklands Park
☎ 0243 781312

OUTDOOR LEISURE

Cycling
i The Tourist Board publishes a useful leaflet: *Cycling Round West Sussex.*

Fishing
Chichester Canal
4½ miles of canal linking the city with the harbour. Angling and boat hire.

Golf
Goodwood
Goodwood, nr Chichester
☎ 0243 785012

Walking
i Details of suggested walks are available from the Tourist Office.

WATERSPORTS

Boat Hire
Chichester Harbour Water Tours
Peter Adams, 9 Cawley Road, Chichester
☎ 0243 786418

Canoeing
Chichester Canoe Club
Secretary, 7 Redmoor, Main Road, Birdham
☎ 0243 512144

Windsurfing
Southern Leisure Centre
Windsurfing and water skiing.
Vinnetrow Road, Chichester
☎ 0243 774678

Yacht Charter
Chichester Sailing Centre Inc
Chichester Marina
☎ 0243 512557

133

HAMILTON PARK

Region: Strathclyde
_i_ Hamilton Tourist Information Services, Road Chef Services, M74 Northbound, Hamilton
☎ 0555 61661
Early closing: Wednesday
Population: 50,000
Hamilton, known as Cadzow before being renamed after a local landowning family in 1445 has a rich and vivid history. It is the hereditary seat of the Dukes of Hamilton, although the palace has been demolished and the Low Parks transformed into a multi-purpose recreational centre, Strathclyde Park. The remarkable mausoleum planned and built by the 10th Duke of Hamilton betweeen 1840 and 1855 can still be seen as can the Chatelherault Lodge, a ducal hunting lodge designed by William Adam, and the ruins of the 12th century Cadzow castle.

East Kilbride, one of Scotland's impressive new towns and the home of the first Olympic-size pool to be opened in Britain, is 5 miles west of Hamilton.

EQUESTRIAN

Riding and Pony Trekking
Dalzell Riding School
Mase Road, Dalzell Estate, Motherwell
☎ 0698 68771

Woodfoot Equestrian Centre
Millheugh, Larkhall
☎ 0698 881608

HEALTH

Leisure Centres
Motherwell Leisure Centre
Major leisure, ice and pool complex featuring tyre ride and flume, wild water channel, ice tunnel and health suite.
☎ 0698 76464

LOCAL FEATURES

Gardens
Viewpark Nursery
Ornamental gardens and greenhouses.
Uddingston
☎ 0698 818269

Heritage
Tinto Hill
Highest hill in the Clyde Valley nr Biggar, it is capped by one of the largest bronze-age cairns in the country; well-defined but steep path to the summit (2,320 feet); allow three hours for the climb.

Historic Buildings
Bothwell Castle
An imposing red sandstone castle on the banks of the River Clyde, once the home of the Black Douglases, regarded as the finest surviving 13th century castle in Scotland.
☎ 0698 816894

Chatelherault Country Park
Beautifully restored 18th century hunting lodge of the Dukes of Hamilton designed by William Adam; the surrounding park has nature walks, Cadzow Castle, an ancient breed of white cattle and an adventure playground.
Ferniegair, nr Hamilton
☎ 0698 426213

Craignethan Castle
Built in the 15th century with later additions, this is an outstanding example of military fortification.
☎ 055586 364

Hallbar Tower
15th century fortified tower.
Braidwood, Carluke
→A B7056
_i_ Contact Tourist Information Service

Hamilton Mausoleum
Huge, remarkable monument built in the 18th century as a chapel and crypt for the Dukes of Hamilton; famous for its 15 second echo, the longest echo of any building in Europe.
The Director, Strathclyde Country Park, 366 Hamilton Road, Motherwell
☎ 0698 66155
West of the M74
🚍 booking essential.

Museums
Cameronian Museum, Hamilton
Museum housed in the Duke of Hamilton's former riding school.
☎ 0698 285382

Hamilton District Museum
Local history museum with a transport section, housed in a 17th century coaching inn.
☎ 0698 283981

David Livingstone Centre, Blantyre
☎ 0698 823140

Natural History
New Lanark and Falls of Clyde
An industrial village established in 1785; the site of Robert Owen's radical social and educational experiements, now a World Heritage Site. Twenty minutes walk from the village are the spectacular Falls of Clyde.
☎ 0555 65262

HAMILTON PARK

WHAT TO DO AND SEE

Parks

Dalzell Country Park and Baronshaugh Reserve
Pleasant woodland walks, secluded picnic spots, adjacent marsh meadow forms a RSPB reserve noted for its wildfowl and woodland birds.
☎ 031 556 5624, Reserve Manager

Strathclyde Country Park
Watersports, nature trails, visitor centre, fun fair, play and picnic areas, camping and caravan site.
☎ 0698 66155

Lanark Moor Country Park and Loch
Country park with playing fields, equestrian centre, boating, fishing, picnic spots, putting and pitch and putt.
☎ 0555 61853

Theatres

Puppet Theatre
Complete Victorian theatre in miniature; puppet plays, guided tours and exhibitions.
☎ 0899 20631
P ☕ ✕

Zoos

Glasgow Zoo
Uddingston
☎ 041 771 1185

OUTDOOR LEISURE

Birdwatching and Wildlife

Strathclyde Country Park
Over 150 species of birds have been recorded in the park since it was opened. Countryside rangers provide guided walks.
☎ 0698 66155

Baron's Haugh Nature Reserve
Owned by the RSPB and open all year. Excellent viewing of dabbling ducks and waders.
☎ 031 556 5624

Chatelherault Country Park
☎ 0698 426213

Falls of Clyde Nature Reserve
Scottish Wildlife Trust Reserve; believed to be the breeding ground of rare Willow Tits in Scotland.
☎ 0555 65262

Fishing

Strathclyde Country Park
Fishing on the River Clyde and on Strathclyde Loch.
Permits from The Director, Watersports Centre, 366 Hamilton Road, Motherwell
☎ 0698 66155

River Avon
Fishing for brown trout and grayling.
Avon Angling Club,
Mr Peter Brooks, 3 The Neuk, Stonehouse

Kype Reservoir
Fishing for brown trout and rainbow trout.
Kype Angling Club,
8 Townshead Street, Stonehouse
☎ 0698 791970

Newmill Trout Fisheries
Fishing for brown trout.
Newmill Trout and Deer Farm
☎ 0555 870730

Golf

Lanark Golf Club ⛳18
The Moor, Lanark
☎ 0555 2349

Strathclyde Park Golf Course ⛳9
Mote Hill, Hamilton
☎ 0698 66155

Strathclyde Park Golf Range
Mote Hill, Hamilton
☎ 0698 286505

Leadhills Golf Club ⛳9
Leadhills, nr Biggar
☎ 065974 222

Ice Skating

Lanarkshire Ice Rink
Mote Hill, off Muir Street, Hamilton
☎ 0698 282448

WATERSPORTS

Strathclyde Country Park
Windsurfing, rowing, canoeing and waterskiing.
☎ 0698 66155

HEREFORD

County: Hereford & Worcester
i Town Hall Annexe, St Owens Street
☎ 0432 268430
Infoline ☎ 0432 277000
Early closing: Thursday
Market day: Wednesday
Population: 48,400

Hereford is set on the banks of the majestic River Wye. This lovely old cathedral town has a turbulent history of sieges, raids and battles, dating back to Saxon times. Today it is a touring centre for mid-Wales and the lovely Wye Valley, a centre for the cider industry and home of the red and white Hereford cattle that graze in the surrounding countryside.

ADVENTURE

Caving

Hereford Caving Club
P.E. Hartwright, Whistlewood, Lyonshall
☎ 0544 8301

Shooting

Hereford Gun Club
M. Double, Hereford Rebore, Harrow Road, Plough Lane, Hereford
☎ 0432 267571

EQUESTRIAN

Riding and Pony Trekking

The Marches Equestrian College
P.A. Bacon, Harewood End, Herefordshire
☎ 098 987 234

HEALTH

Leisure Centres

Hereford Leisure Centre
Multi-purpose hall equipped for most sports, athletics track, nine-hole golf course, squash courts and modern fitness unit.
Holmer Road, Hereford
☎ 0432 278178
☎ 0432 271959

Swimming Baths Complex
Pools, squash, sauna, sunbed, table tennis.
St Martin's Avenue, Hereford
☎ 0432 272512

LOCAL FEATURES

Archaeology

City of Hereford Archaeology Committee
Excavations conducted in and around the City throughout the year. To visit sites contact Director of Excavations.
Mr Ron Shoesmith, Town Hall
☎ 0432 268121

Architecture

Hereford Cathedral

The See of Hereford is one of the oldest in England. The Cathedral is substantially Norman with a 13th century Lady Chapel. The Crypt houses the Diocesan Treasury including the Mappa Mundi. The famous Chained Library contains over 1400 chained books and 227 manuscripts.

City Walls
13th century walls remain in Victoria Street and West Street.

Wye Bridge
Stone bridge with six arches dating from 1490.

Art Galleries

Hereford City Art Gallery
Collections of 19th century watercolours and works by local artists. Exhibitions change monthly.
Broad Street, Hereford
☎ 0432 268121 ext 207

Festivals and Fairs

May
May Fair, Regatta and River Wye Raft Race
July
City Carnival
August
Three Choirs Festival and Fringe, held every three years, next in 1991
October
Antiques Fair

Food and Drink

Bulmers Cider Mill
The Cider Mills, Plough Lane
☎ 0432 352000
🚌

HEREFORD

Gardens

Abbey Dore Court
Walled and river garden with shrubs and herbaceous plants.
☎ 0981 240419
➔A A465
P 🏠 ✕ ♿

Churchill Gardens
Ornamental Park at Aylestone Hill.
🏠 ♿

Guided Tours

Guides are on duty during the summer to show visitors around the ancient City, meet at the Shire Hall forecourt.

Heritage

Dinedor Camp
Fine Iron Age Fort with superb views.
☎ 0432 268121 ext 249 for leaflet

Historic Houses

The Old House
Built in 1621, a fine example of Jacobean domestic architecture.
High Town, Hereford
☎ 0432 268121 ext 207 or 255
🏠

Museums

Hereford City Museum
Naturday history, archaeology, local history and an art gallery.
Broad Street, Hereford
☎ 0432 268121 ext 207

Churchill Gardens Museum
Fine furniture, costumes and paintings of the late 18th and 19th centuries.
Venns Lane, Hereford
☎ 0432 267409
➔A A465
P 🏠 🚐 ♿

The Broomy Hill Engines
Herefordshire Waterworks Museum with working exhibits.
44 Tower Road, Hereford
☎ 0432 273635
P 🏠

St John Mediaeval Museum
A 13th century building restored as a hospice with a history of the Ancient Order of St John.
Widemarsh Street
☎ 0432 272837
P 🏠

Parks

King George's Playing Fields
Tennis courts, putting green, paddling pool and playground.
St Martin's Street, Hereford

Railways

The Bulmer Railway Centre
Standard gauge steam railway museum, includes the famous GWR locomotive "King George V".
Whitecross Road
☎ 0272 834430

Theatre

New Hereford Theatre
Theatre, cinema and arts centre.
Edgar Street, Hereford
☎ 0432 59252

Cycling

Coombes Cycles
94 Widemarsh Street, Hereford
☎ 0432 354373

Fishing

i Detailed leaflet available from the Tourist Information Office.

Hereford Angling Association
The Lindens, Bishopstone, Hereford

Hattons
64 St Owen Street, Hereford
☎ 0432 272317

Golf

Belmont House Golf Course ⛳18
Belmont, Hereford
☎ 0432 352666

Municipal Golf Course ⛳9
Holmer Road, Hereford
☎ 0432 263310

Hereford Golf Driving Range ⛳9
Roman Road
☎ 0432 263310

Walking

Leaflets on local walks from the Tourist Office.

Hereford Ramblers
Mrs J. Parry, Jobey's Cottage, Coddington, Ledbury
☎ 0531 86640

Fishing

The river Wye is one of the premier salmon rivers in the country. The local river system is also good for trout and freshwater fish such as dace, grayling, roach, pike and club.

Licences from:
Wye division, Welsh Water Development Authority, St Nicholas House, Hereford
☎ 0432 57411

Hattons
64 St Owen Street, Hereford
☎ 0432 272317

HEXHAM

County: Northumberland
i Manor Office, Hallgate, Hexham
☎ 0434 605225
Early closing: Thursday
Market day: Tuesday
Population: 10,000
Hexham is an attractive market town perched on a hilltop overlooking the River Tyne and surrounded by varied and beautiful countryside rich in wildlife and inviting walks. Hadrian's Wall is easily accessible to explore and the town itself has a 7th century abbey and many other historic stone buildings.

AERIAL SPORTS

Ballooning
Ballooning Adventures Ltd
Mike Forster, 2 Richmond Lodge, Moor Road South, Gosforth
☎ 091 285 9343

Helicopters
Eagle Helicopters
1 Main Street, Ponteland, Northumberland
☎ 00661 71237

EQUESTRIAN

Riding and Pony Trekking
Plover Hill Riding School and Trekking Centre
By Dipton Mill Inn, Hexham
☎ 0434 607196

HEALTH

Leisure Centres
Hexham Swimming Pool
25 metre pool, weights room, sunbeds.
Gilesgate, Hexham
☎ 0434 694903
→A A695
🏠 ⅃ ⅃

Waterworld
Front Street, Prudhoe
☎ 0661 33144
→A A695

LOCAL FEATURES

Art Galleries
Moot Hall Exhibition Gallery
Private exhibitions.
Market Place, Hexham
☎ 0434 604011

Queen's Hall Art Centre
Exhibits of paintings and prints.
Beaumont Street, Hexham
☎ 0434 606787

Arts and Crafts
The Hand Made Shop
Pictures, woodwork, glass, pottery, knitwear and toys.
Colmans Arcade, St Mary's Chare, Hexham
☎ 0434 605623

Northumbria Painting Holidays
2 Westfield Terrace, Hexham
☎ 0434 605144
☎ 0434 602434

Thornton Pottery
Northumberland pottery and Roman Wall souvenirs.
Humshaugh, nr Hexham
☎ 0434●81406 406

Stoneware Pottery
Handthrown domestic stoneware pottery.
Caroline Westgate, 9 Quatre Bras, Hexham
☎ 0434 604747

Festivals and Fairs
May
Abbey Fair
Northumberland County Show

June–July
Abbey Festival
Ovington Goose Festival

Guided Tours
Hexham Town Trail
A walk around the special conservation area of the town centre.
i Leaflet with map and description of the sights from the Tourist Information Centre.

Heritage
Hadrian's Wall
2000 years ago the Wall marked the boundary between the civilised world and the barbarians. Visitor centres, museums, forts, milecastles, temples and turrets can be found along its entire length.
i The Tourist Information Centre publish a detailed leaflet and map to all the locations on the Wall. Most major sites are on or near the B6318.

Roman Wall sites near Hexham include: Cawfields to Winshields, Milecastle and Wall; Steel Rig to Housesteads; Vindolanda Fort and Museum, Chesterholm; Housesteads Fort, Vercovicium; Sewingshields Milecastle; Carrawburgh, Brocolitia; Black Carts Turret; Chesters Roman Fort and Museum, Cilurnum; Brunton Turret; and Corbridge Roman Town and Museum, Corstopitum.

Historic Buildings
Aydon Castle
A small castle built as a manor house in the late 13th century.
Corbridge, Northumberland
☎ 043471 2450
→A A68
P 🏠

HEXHAM

WHAT TO DO AND SEE

Hexham Abbey
Saxon Crypt, 15th century paintings,
misericords and Saxon chalice.
Beaumont Street, Hexham
☎ 0434 602031
➔A A69, A695

Prudhoe Castle
A ruined castle on a wooded hillside
overlooking the River Tyne. The 12th
century keep and gatehouse are the oldest
in the country.
Prudhoe, Northumberland
☎ 0661 33459
➔A A695
P

Wallington House and Walled Garden
Built in 1688 on the site of a mediaeval
castle, set in 100 acres of lakes and
woodlands; fine plasterwork and porcelain,
paintings, dolls' houses and coaches.
Cambo, Morpeth
☎ 067074 283
Off the B6343
P

Museums

Berwick Birthplace Museum
Cottage birthplace of the famous wood
engraver and naturalist; printing press,
farmyard and orchard walk.
Cherryburn, Micklay, nr Stocksfield
☎ 0661 843276
On the A695, 10 miles east of Hexham
P

Middle March Museum of Border History
Housed in a 14th century building, once the
town gaol.
Manor Office, Hexham
☎ 0434 604011 ext 245
A695 just off Market Place

Music, Dance and Drama

Queen's Hall Arts Centre
Theatre, music, special events, poetry and
exhibitions.
Beaumont Street, Hexham
☎ 0434 607272

Natural History

Greenhaugh Childrens Farm
Greenhaugh, Tarset, Hexham
☎ 0660 40300
5 miles north west of Bellingham

Parks

Allen Banks
200 acres of hill and river scenery; mature
woodland, many miles of paths. National
Trust. Guided walks with the warden.
☎ 04984 218
Off the A69, nr Bardon Mill
P

Bolam Lake Country Park
Lakes and woodland; boating, picnicing,
fishing and walking.
Belsay
☎ 0661 81234
➔A A696
P

Tyne Riverside Country Park
Linear country park; footpaths, cycle and
horse riding routes.
Station Road, Prudhoe
☎ 0661 34135
P

OUTDOOR LEISURE

Cycling

Heatherlea Cycle Hire
Mr and Mrs J. P. Shield
Allendale
☎ 0434 683236

Keilder Village Bike Hire
Avia Garage, Keilder
☎ Bellingham 240419

Fishing

i The Tourist Information Centre have a
detailed free leaflet on fishing in this area
The River Tyne has excellent fishing and
there are a number of lakes and reservoirs.
Licenses available from the Tourist
Information Centre, or:

Cresswell (Tackle shop)
38 Priestpopple, Hexham
☎ 0434 603823

Golf

Hexham Golf Club Ltd
Spital Park
☎ 0434 604904
On the B6531, 1 mile west of town
P

Tynedale Golf Club
Visitors welcome but must book on
weekends.
Tyne Green Road, Hexham
☎ 0434 604011
South side of the Tyne Bridge

Tennis

Public courts in the Seal.

Walking

In this wonderful walking country there are
endless possibilities for short, long or
themed walks.
i Free leaflets from the Tourist
Information Centre.

Discovery Walks
A full programme of themed walks.
National park and Countryside Office
☎ 0434 605555

HUNTINGDON

County: Cambridgeshire
i The Library, Princes Street
☎ 0480 425831
☎ 0480 425801
Early closing: Wednesday
Market day: Saturday
Population: 14,500

Huntingdon, formerly a county town, is famous as the birthplace of Oliver Cromwell and for its association with Samuel Pepys, both attended the same Huntingdon school. Several fine Georgian buildings remain in some unspoilt corners of the town and there are several coaching inns including The George Hotel where Shakespeare's plays are performed in the courtyard in the summer. Huntingdon is linked to Godmanchester, an important Roman settlement and one of the earliest boroughs (it received its charter in 1213), by a beautiful 13th century road bridge.

EQUESTRIAN

Riding and Pony Trekking

Beaconsfield Equine Centre
London Street, Godmanchester
☎ 0480 830688

HEALTH

Leisure Centres

St Ivo Recreation Centre
Swimming pool, sports hall, squash courts, weight training, solarium and tennis courts.
Westwood Road, St Ives
☎ 0480 64601

LOCAL FEATURES

Architecture

Peterborough Cathedral
Norman cathedral, 13th century painted nave ceiling; former grave of Mary Queen of Scots; grave of Katherine of Aragon.
Peterborough
☎ 0733 433342

Festivals and Fairs

March
Shire Horse Show, Peterborough

May
Truckfest, Peterborough
Cheese rolling, Stilton

June
Huntingdon Carnival

July
East of England Show, Peterborough

Guided Tours

East Anglian Tourist Guides Association
Guided tours around all the main centres.
Mrs Sheila Allen, 24 High Street, Brampton
☎ 0480 54087

Two Tours of Fenland
i Leaflet available from the Tourist Information Office.

Heritage

Flag Fen
Bronze age excavations.
Flag Fen Excavations, Fourth Drove, Fengate, Peterborough
☎ 0733 313414
Exit 7 from Peterborough ring road
P 🏛

Historic Buildings

Elton Hall
Elton, nr Peterborough
➔A A605
☎ 08324 468
☎ 08324 223

Hinchingbrooke House
The ancestral home of the Cromwells and Earls of Sandwich.
Huntingdon
☎ 0480 51121
Brampton Road, ½ mile west of Huntingdon
🏛 🚌 ✕ ♿

Houghton Mill
Believed to be the oldest remaining watermill on the Ouse, a massive timbered structure built in the 17th century.
Mill House, Mill Street, Houghton
☎ 0480 301494
Off the A1132, 3 miles south-east of Huntingdon
P 🏛

Island Hall
Built in the 1740s this elegant house takes its name from the island that forms part of the pleasure gardens.
Godmanchester
☎ 0480 459676
In the centre of Godmanchester
P 🏛 🚌 ✕

Museums

Cromwell Museum
Formerly the Grammar School where both Oliver Cromwell and Samuel Pepys were educated, the museum relates specifically to Oliver Cromwell.
Grammar School Walk, Huntingdon
☎ 0480 425830
Town centre
🎦 🚌 ♿

Norris Museum
☎ 0480 65101
🎦 🚌 ♿

HUNTINGDON

Ramsey Rural Museum
Items of local historical and agricultural interest displayed in a recently-restored barn.
Ramsey
☎ 0487 813223
☎ 0487 812016

Sacrewell Farm and Country Centre
Working water mill, bygones, farm, nature trail and gardens.
Sacrewell, Thornhaugh, Peterborough
☎ 0780 782222
Access off the A47
P ⛷ 🚐 ✕ & &

Natural History

Wood Green Animal Shelter
50 acre shelter with over 1000 animals.
Godmanchester
➔A A14
☎ 0480 830014

Parks

Hinchingbrooke Country Park
The park, once the grounds of Hinchingbrooke House, covers 156 acres of woodland, meadows, lakes and ponds and is open to the public for walking, picnics, riding and fishing.
Brampton Road, Huntingdon
☎ 0480 51568
➔A A141
P 🚐 & &

Railways

Nene Valley Railway
A preserved steam railway running on $7\frac{1}{2}$ miles of track between Wansford Station and Peterborough; over 25 steam and diesel locomotives.
Wansford Station, Stibbington, Peterborough
☎ 0780 782854
☎ 0780 782921 talking timetable
P ⛷ 🚐 ✕ & &

Zoos

Hamerton Wildlife Centre
Unique bird collection with rare species from around the world; lemurs, marmosets, meerkats, wallabies and a childrens farm.
➔A A1/A604
☎ 08323 604

Birdwatching and Wildlife

Little Paxton
Gravel pit lakes attracting migratory birds; walks.
Diddington
➔A A1

Cycling

Solec
Ermine Street, Huntingdon
☎ 0480 453492

Ferry Meadows
Ham Lane, Orton Waterville, Peterborough
☎ 0733 234418
➔A A605

Fishing

Grafham Water Reservoir
Trout fishing.
5 miles south-west of Huntingdon
☎ 0780 86 321

Hinchingbrooke Country Park
Brampton Road, Huntingdon
☎ 0480 451568

Tim's Tackle (Fishing permits)
18 High Street, Huntingdon
☎ 0480 450039

St Ives Angling Centre
5 Crown Street, St Ives
☎ 0480 301903

Stanjays
7 Old Court Road, Godmanchester
☎ 0480 453303

Information and licences from:

Anglian Water
☎ 0223 61561

National Rivers Authority
Bromholme Lane, Brampton
☎ 0480 414581

Golf

Ramsey Golf Club ⛳18
Ramsey
☎ 0487 813573

Walking

The Huntingdon Amble/Town Trails
i Leaflet from Tourist Office.

Ouse Valley Long Distance Footpath
Bluntisham to Eaton Socon.
Leaflets produced by Huntingdonshire District Council
☎ 0480 561561

Little Paxton Area
i Leaflets from Tourist Information Office or Huntingdonshire District Council.

Windsurfing and Sailing

Grafham Water Reservoir
Grafham Water Sailing Club, West Perry, Huntingdon
☎ 0480 810478

Mepal Outdoor Centre
Sailing, playpark, canoeing and windsurfing.
Chatteris Road, Ely
☎ 03543 2251

KELSO

Region: Borders

𝑖 Turret House, Roxburghshire

☎ 0573 23464

Early closing: Wednesday

Market day: Sunday, including crafts

Population: 5500

Kelso, a county town sited at the junction of the Rivers Teviot and Tweed, has only fragmentary remains of its once powerful abbey. Kelso Abbey, founded in 1128, was ravaged in the Border Wars and finally destroyed by Henry VIII. The town has an elegant square surrounded by gracious buildings, its five-arched bridge, built by Rennie over the River Tweed in 1803, was the prototype for London's Waterloo Bridge. There are a variety of historic buildings, castles and gardens in the area.

EQUESTRIAN

Riding and Pony Trekking

Easter Langlee Pony Trekking Centre

Easter Langlee Farm, Galashiels

☎ 0896 58234

Fernihurst Mill Lodge

Jedburgh, Roxburghshire

☎ 0835 63279

Nethorn Riding Stables

Nethorn, Kelso

☎ 0573 24073

HEALTH

Leisure Centres

Kelso Swimming Pool

Swimming and sunbeds.

Inch Road, Kelso

☎ 0573 24944

✖

The Tweedsider Sports Centre

Squash courts, sauna, jacuzzi, sunbeds, solarium, snooker and pool. Live music on Friday.

5 Vault Square, Kelso

☎ 0573 25777

🗑

LOCAL FEATURES

Architecture

Smailholm Tower

16th century tower-house with good views of the Border Country.

🗑

Art Galleries

Ancrum Gallery

Paintings by leading Scottish artists, monthly exhibitions.

Cross Keys Inn, Ancrum

☎ 08353 340

Off the A68, 3½ miles from Jedburgh

Stichill Smithy Gallery

Exhibitions of artists, designers and craftsmen's work.

The Smithy House, Ednam Road, Stichill,

☎ 05737 346

On the B6364, 3 miles north of Kelso

🖾

Arts and Crafts

Kelso Pottery

Domestic stoneware pottery.

The Knowles, Kelso

☎ 0573 24027

In the large car park behind Kelso Abbey

Water Lily Weavers

Rugs, tapestries and hand woven items.

Homestead Craft Centre, The Hirsel, Coldstream, Berwickshire

☎ 0890 2977

On the A697, west of Coldstream

Festivals and Fairs

February

Jedburgh Hand Ba'

June

Melrose Festival Week

July

Kelso Civic Week

August

Coldstream Civic Week

December

Masons Walk, Melrose, December 27

Gardens

Dundock Wood and the Hirsel Grounds

Museum and craft workshops, flowers through the year.

The Hirsel, Coldstream, Berwickshire

☎ 0890 2834

On the A697, 3 miles west of Coldstream

🖾 ✖

Mertoun Gardens

20 acres of beautiful garden walks, and a well-preserved dovecote, dated 1567.

St Boswells

☎ 0835 23236

🗑

Priorwood Garden

Alongside Melrose Abbey, picnic area, orchards and dried flower garden. National Trust of Scotland.

Melrose

☎ 089 682 2965

🖾

The Woodland Centre

Woodland walks, pinery, wood exhibits; bookshop with slide and tape programmes and a childrens play area.

Ancrum, nr Jedburgh

☎ 08353 306

3½ miles north of Jedburgh

🗑 ✖

KELSO

Heritage

Dryburgh Abbey
Abbey ruins; the grave of Sir Walter Scott.
By St Boswells
☎ 0835 22381
Off the A68, signposted
⌂

Ferniehurst Castle
Frontier fortress and 16th century home of
the Kerrs with a Great Hall and 17th
century chapel.
☎ 0835 62201
Off the A68, 1½ miles south of Jedburgh
⌂

Jedburgh Abbey
One of four Border monasteries founded by
David I.
☎ 0835 63925
Nr town centre
⌂

Kelso Abbey
A fragment of this 12th century abbey.
Town centre
⌂

Historic Buildings

Floors Castle
Home of the Duke and Duchess of
Roxburghe, the largest inhabited castle in
Scotland.
Kelso
☎ 0573 23333
⌂

Mellerstain House
Scotland's finest Adam mansion with
magnificent ceilings and decoration.
Gordon
☎ 057 381 225
On the A6089, 7 miles north-west of Kelso
⌂ ✗

Thirlestane Castle
Magnificent state rooms; family nurseries
with several thousand toys of bygone days;
woodland walk, picnic areas and country life
exhibitions.
Lauder
☎ 05782 430
⌂ ✗

Museums

Coldstream Museum
Market Square, Coldstream
☎ 0890 2630
⌂

Jedburgh Castle Jail
Local history museum.
Castlegate, Jedburgh
☎ 0835 63254
⌂

Kelso Museum
Award-winning museum of Kelso life.
Turret House, Abbey Court, Kelso
☎ 0573 25470
Town centre

Mary Queen of Scots House
Queen Street, Jedburgh
☎ 0835 63331
⌂

Melrose Motor Museum
Vintage cars, motorcycles, cycles,
automobilia.
Annay Road, Melrose
☎ 089682 2624
Town centre
⌂

Natural History

Yetholm Loch
A nature reserve of the Scottish Wildlife
Trust. A lowland loch with a rich fen and
many migratory birds. Permits from:
M. E. Braithwaite,
Cockspurs, Lilliesleaf, Melrose

Cycling

Coldstream Cycles
Tours and accommodation arranged.
The Lees Stables, Coldstream
☎ 0890 2709

Fishing

Salmon is the prime catch, but brown
trout, sea trout and coarse fishing are
popular. Local tackle shops will provide
information and permits.
i For detailed information ask the Tourist
Office for a brochure: *Angling in the
Scottish Borders*.

Golf

Hirsel Golf Club ⛳9
The Hirsel, Coldstream
☎ 0890 2351

Jedburgh Golf Course ⛳9
Dunion Road, Jedburgh
☎ 0835 22521

Kelso Golf Club ⛳18
Berrymoss, Kelso
☎ 0573 23259

Ice Skating

Border Ice Rink
Abbotseat Road, Kelso
☎ 0573 24774

Walking

Countryside Ranger Service
Guided walks available.
Borders Regional Council
Regional Headquarters, Newtown,
☎ 0835 23301
i Contact Tourist Offices or the above
address for information about local walks.

143

LEICESTER

WHAT TO DO AND SEE

County: Leicestershire
i 2—6 St Martin's Walk, Leicester
☎ 0533 511300
Early closing: Monday, Thursday
Population: 320,000
Leicester is a county town, busy commercial centre and cathedral city built on the site of a Roman settlement. St Nicholas Church has Roman and Saxon stones in its structure and is one of the oldest churches in the country. The market square is in daily use as it has been since the 13th century underlining Leicester's position in the heart of the shires in the centre of traditional agricultural and hunting country.

ADVENTURE

Clay Pigeon Shooting
Kibworth Shooting Ground
☎ 792007/692772
➡A A6

EQUESTRIAN

Riding and Pony Trekking
Limes Equestrian Centre
Hinckley Road, Sapcote
☎ 045527 2271

Thornhill Stud
Swinford Road, Walcote, Lutterworth
☎ 0455 4206

HEALTH

Health Farms
Ragdale Hall
Melton Mowbray
☎ 066475 831
☎ 066475 411

Leisure Centres
Granby Halls Leisure Centre
Roller skating, health and beauty suite; spectator sports events.
Walford Road, Leicester
☎ 0533 552644
P ✗ &

Leicester Leys Leisure Centre
Leisure pool, beach area, flume ride, wave machine; fitness studio and dry sports facilities.
Beaumont Way, Beaumont Leys
☎ 0533 366004
City centre
P ✗ &

LOCAL FEATURES

Arts and Crafts
Bosworth Crafts
Hand-made leather items including mediaeval shoes. Workshop area.
23 Main Street, Market Bosworth
☎ 0455 292061

Festivals and Fairs
August
Leicester Air Show
City of Leicester Show
City of Leicester Championship Dog Show

Food and Drink
Groby 'Pick Your Own' and Leisure Farm
Lake fishing, children's play area, craft demonstrations, puppet shows, pony rides, Shire horse displays plus pick your own fruit.
☎ 0533 311432
Off the A50, north of Leicester
P 🍴 ✗

Heritage
Bosworth Battlefield
Regular displays of mediaeval jousting.

Museums
Museum of Technology
Giant beam engines, horse-drawn vehicles, cycles and motorcycles.
Corporation Road, Leicester
☎ 0533 661330
🍴

Natural History
Desford's Tropical Bird Garden
Lindridge Lane, Desford
☎ 04557 4603
P ✗ &

Rutland Farm Park
Rare breeds of farm animals, Shetland/ Exmoor ponies, old farm implements/ vehicles. Parkland, wild flower meadow.
Catmose Farm, Uppingham Road, Oakham
☎ 0572 756789
Oakham town centre 5 mins walk
P ✗ &

LEICESTER

Parks

Abbey Park and Grounds
Formal Victorian park with lakes, fishing,
model railway, bandstand, aviary, pets'
corner, play area and tennis courts.
Abbey Park Road

Bradgate Park
Ruins of the mansion where Lady Jane
Grey, the '9 days Queen', was born.
6 miles north-west of the town

Braunstone Park
Large park with floral displays, woodland
and lakes; model boating lake and adventure
playground.
Braunstone Avenue

Western Park
Open parkland with roller skating rink,
BMX track, paddling pool and tennis courts,
adventure playground, large scale chess
game and bandstand.
Hinkley Road

Theatres

Leicester Haymarket Theatre
☎ 0533 539797
✗

Little Theatre
Dover Street
☎ 0533 542266

De Montfort Hall
Main venue for classical and pop concerts,
seating 2500.
Granville Road

Phoenix Arts
Multi-cultural events, visiting dance
companies, folk music and community
theatre.
Newarke Street
☎ 0533 554854

Zoos

Twycross Zoo
On the A444 Burton to Nuneaton road
P ✗ ♿

Cycling

Rutland Water
Whitwell Car Park
Off the A6060, nr Oakham

Fishing

Fly Fishing
At Rutland Water, Thornton Reservoir and
Eyebrook Reservoir.

Coarse Fishing
On the Grand Union Canal, River Soar, at
Stoney Cover quarry, and elsewhere.

Golf

Whetstone Golf Club ⛳₁₈
Cambridge Road, Cosby
☎ 0533 861424

Visitors welcome on weekdays at the
following clubs:

Birstall Golf Club ⛳₁₈
Station Road, Birstall
☎ 0533 675245

Humberstone Heights Golf Course ⛳₁₈
Gipsy Lane, Leicester
☎ 0533 764674

Leicestershire Golf Club ⛳₁₈
Evington Lane, Leicester
☎ 0533 738825

Western Golf Course ⛳₁₈
Scudamore Road, Braunstone Frith
☎ 0533 872339

Motor Sports

Mallory Park
Nr Hinckley
☎ 0455 42931

Dry-slope Skiing

Leicester Outdoor Pursuits Centre
Situated on the River Soar, courses are run
throughout the year in canoeing, skiing,
climbing, orienteering and abseiling.
Loughborough Road, Leicester
☎ 0533 681426
P ✗

Tennis

Hard courts may be hired on the spot at
Abbey Park and Western Park.

Boat Hire

Ashby Narrowboat Company
Dayboat hire to Bosworth Battlefield or
Market Bosworth along the Ashby Canal.
Canal Wharf, Station Road, Stoke Golding,
Hinkley
☎ 0455 212671

Leicester Boat Company
Explore the River Soar from Abbey
meadows to Mountsorrel. Self-steer
dayboats.
Abbey Meadows, Abbey Park Road, Leicester
☎ 0533 512334
☎ 0509 236362

Boat Trips

Abbey Park
Rowing boats and canoes for hire, river and
pleasure trips.

Sailing

Rutland Water
Sailing and windsurfing.

LIVERPOOL – AINTREE

Including Haydock Park

County: Merseyside
i 29 Lime Street, Liverpool
☎ 051 708 8854
Early closing: Wednesday
Population: 540,000
Liverpool, inhabited since the 1st century, is now a large, prosperous city and a major port for transatlantic shipping. The port has the largest docks in Britain with 7 miles of waterfront visible from the famous ferries across the Mersey. Liverpool has many galleries and museums with fine collections and is a vibrant cultural centre having produced many famous personalities, notably, the Beatles in the 1960s. Its two modern cathedrals hold prominent positions on Liverpool's skyline, both have been built on high ground overlooking the city; there are many impressive Victorian buildings around the city centre. Sport is another major feature in the city's life with its two famous football teams and the Aintree racecourse, home to the Grand National.

ADVENTURE

Shooting

Aintree Shooting Services Ltd
8 Grundy Street, Liverpool
☎ 051 207 2051

Altcar Rifle Range
Hightown
☎ 051 929 2539

EQUESTRIAN

Riding and Pony Trekking

Croxteth Riding Centre
Croxteth Hall Lane, Liverpool
☎ 051 220 9177

Longacres Riding School
290 Southport Road, Lydiate
☎ 051 526 0327

HEALTH

Leisure Centres

Spindles
Britannia Adelphi Hotel, Lime Street
☎ 051 709 7200

Everton Park Sports Centre
Excellent amenities plus international pool.
Greater Homer Street, Liverpool
☎ 051 207 1921

Oval Sports Centre
Bebington, Wirral
☎ 051 645 0551

LOCAL FEATURES

Art Galleries

Atkinson Art Gallery
19th and 20th century paintings, watercolours, prints and drawings; modern sculpture.
Lord Street, Southport
☎ 0704 33133
→A A565
P 🎨 🚌 ♿ ♿

Lady Lever Gallery
The first Lord Leverhulme's collection of English 18th century paintings, furniture, Wedgwood pottery, oriental porcelains and Pre-Raphaelite paintings.
Port Sunlight Village, Wirral
☎ 051 645 3623
→A A41
P 🎨 🚌 ✕ ♿ ♿

Sudley Art Gallery
Paintings by Turner and other 19th century British artists; furniture by Bullock
Mossley Hill Road, Liverpool
☎ 051 207 0001
P 🎨

Tate Gallery
Changing displays from the National Collection of Modern Art.
Albert Dock
☎ 051 709 3223
♿ ♿

Walker Art Gallery
One of the finest galleries in Europe; rich in early Italian and Flemish works; good coverage of European Art and Pre-Raphaelite pieces; striking modern collection and a new sculpture gallery.
William Brown Street, Liverpool
☎ 051 207 0001
🎨 ✕ ♿

Williamson Art Gallery
British paintings and watercolours, English porcelain and maritime history exhibits.
Slatey Road, Birkenhead
☎ 051 652 4177
P 🎨 🚌 ♿

Arts and Crafts

Bluecoat Chambers
Listed Queen Anne building with gallery, craft shop, film theatre, concert hall and artists studios.
Bluecoat Art Centre, School Lane, Liverpool
☎ 051 709 5297
M62, A5047 to city centre
🎨 🚌 ✕ ♿

Voirrey Embroidery
National embroidery centre, needlework supplies, courses and exhibitions.
Brimstage Hall, Wirral
☎ 051 342 3514
M53, jct 4, A5137
🎨

LIVERPOOL – AINTREE

WHAT TO DO AND SEE

Gardens

Botanic Gardens and Museum
Delightful gardens with an aviary, childrens playground, boating lake and museum display of Victoriana.
Churchtown, Southport
☎ 0704 27547
Off the B5244
P 🐕 ✕ ♿

Ness Gardens
Trees and shrubs, heather, rock and herb gardens.
University of Liverpool Botanic Gardens
Neston, Wirral
☎ 051 336 2135
🐕 ✕

Guided Tours

i Merseyside Tourism Board
Beatle Tour, Sightseeing Tour
☎ 051 709 2444

Heritage

Birkenhead Priory
The oldest building on Merseyside dating from the mid 12th century.
Priory Street, Birkenhead
☎ 051 666 1249
🏛

Historic Buildings

Croxteth Hall and Country Park
A 500 acre country park and Hall with displays, furnished rooms, a walled garden, rare breeds farm, miniature railway, gift shop and riding centre.
Muirhead Avenue East, Liverpool
☎ 051 228 5311
➔A A580
P 🐕 🚐 ✕ ♿ ♿

Liverpool Cathedral
Largest cathedral in Britain with the biggest Gothic arches ever built; excellent refectory.
St James Road, Liverpool
☎ 051 709 6271
Nr City Centre
🏛 🚐 ✕ ♿ ♿

Meols Hall
Ancestral home of the Fleetwood Hesketh family; fine paintings, silver and china. Game and Country Fayre held in May.
Churchtown, Southport
☎ 0704 28171
➔A A565, A570
P 🐕 ♿

Metropolitan Cathedral of Christ the King
Circular modern Cathedral made of concrete and glass with fine stained glass windows and modern fabric wallhangings.
Mount Pleasant, Liverpool
☎ 051 709 9222
➔A A5038, A5047
P 🏛 🚐 ✕ ♿

Port Sunlight Heritage Centre
Model garden village built by William Hesketh Lever for his soap factory workers.
PO Box 139, Greendale Road, Port Sunlight, Wirral
☎ 051 644 6466
➔A A41
P 🐕 🚐 ♿

Speke Hall
A Tudor manor house with rich Victorian interiors.
The Walk, Speke, Liverpool
☎ 051 427 7231
➔A A561
P 🐕 🚐 ✕ ♿ ♿

Museums

The Boat Museum
The largest floating collection of canal craft in the world.
Ellesmere Port, Cheshire
☎ 051 355 5017
P 🐕 ✕

Liverpool Museum and Planetarium
A fine museum with exhibits from all over the world.
William Brown Street
☎ 051 207 0001
P 🏛 🚐 ✕ ♿ ♿

Merseyside Museum of Labour History
Housed in the former County Sessions House built in 1884, the museum tells the story of working class life on Merseyside from 1840 to the present.
County Sessions House, Islington, Liverpool
☎ 051 207 0001
🏛 ♿ ♿

Merseyside Maritime Museum
A unique blend of floating exhibits, working displays and craft demonstrations, including a restored Victorian Dock.
Albert Dock, Liverpool
☎ 051 207 0001
➔A A565
P 🐕 🚐 ✕ ♿

Pilkington Glass Museum
The history and manufacture of glass.
Prescot Road, St Helens
☎ 0744 2888882
➔A A58
P 🏛 ✕ ♿ ♿

Prescot Museum of Clock and Watchmaking
History of clock and watchmaking.
34 Church Street, Prescot
☎ 051 430 7787
➔A A57
P 🏛 ✕ ♿

Music, Dance and Drama

Philharmonic Hall
Home of the Royal Liverpool Philharmonic Orchestra.
Hope Street, Liverpool
☎ 051 709 3789

LIVERPOOL – AINTREE

Natural History

Martin Mere Wildfowl Trust
Rare and exotic birds to hand feed.
Burscough, nr Southport
☎ 0704 895181

Parks

Wirral Country Park
Includes a 12 mile footpath through the
park with views across the Dee Estuary.
Station Road, Thurstaston
☎ 051 648 4371
☎ 051 648 3884
P &

Railways

Steamport Railway Museum
Fifteen steam and six diesel locomotives.
Derby Road, Southport
☎ 0704 30693
➔A A565
P ✕ &

Theatre

Playhouse Theatre/Studio
Williamson Square, Liverpool
☎ 051 709 8363

Everyman Theatre
Hope Street, Liverpool
☎ 051 709 4776

Liverpool Empire
Lime Street, Liverpool
☎ 051 709 1555

Neptune Theatre
Hanover Street, Liverpool
☎ 051 709 7844

Unity Theatre
1 Hope Place, Liverpool
☎ 051 709 4988

Royal Court Theatre
Roe Street, Liverpool
☎ 051 709 4321

Southport Theatre and Floral Complex
Promenade, Southport
☎ 0704 40004

Zoos

Knowsley Safari Park
A five mile drive through game reserves set
in 400 acres of parkland; childrens
amusement park.
Prescot, Merseyside
☎ 051 430 9009
P ☖ ⇰ ✕ & &

Southport Zoo
Including a breeding group of chimpanzees.
Princes Park, Southport
☎ 0704 38102
P ☖ ⇰ ✕ & &

OUTDOOR LEISURE

Fishing

Richards Fishing Tackle
42 Brunswick Street, Liverpool
☎ 051 236 2925

Liverpool Angling Centre
492 Smithdown Road, Liverpool
☎ 051 733 2591

Golf

Royal Birkdale Golf Club
Waterloo Road, Southport
☎ 0704 68857

Walking

The Wirral Way
Wirral Country Park Rangers
☎ 051 648 4371

Ainsdale Nature Trail
National Trust
☎ Fromby 78591

Sankey Valley Park
St Helens Rangers Centre
☎ 0744 39252

Stadt Moers Country Park
Knowsley Rangers Centre
☎ 051 443 3682

WATERSPORTS

Liverpool Watersports Centre
Tuition for sailing, canoeing, windsurfing;
narrowboat trips and canal walks are also
organised.
☎ 051 207 4026

LUDLOW

WHAT TO DO AND SEE

County: Shropshire
i Castle Street
☎ 0584 5053
Early closing: Thursday
Market day: Friday
Population: 8,000

Ludlow is often called 'the perfect historic town' with 500 listed buildings from the mediaeval, black and white Tudor and Georgian architectural periods. The ruins of its massive 11th century, red, sandstone castle stand out high over the River Teme, a border stronghold, it was finally abandoned in the 18th century. Striking hills, rugged castles, historic towns and a network of quiet, charming villages can be found in the countryside around Ludlow.

AERIAL SPORTS

Gliding
The Midland Gliding Club
The Longmynd, Church Stretton
☎ 058861 206

EQUESTRIAN

Riding and Pony Trekking
North Farm Riding Establishment
North Farm, Whitcliffe
☎ 0584 2026

HEALTH

Swimming
Public baths
Next to Dinham Bridge

LOCAL FEATURES

Festivals and Fairs
June
Ludlow Festival

Guided Tours
Town walks
Contact the Ludlow Historical Research Group.

Ludlow Guidelines
Greenacres, Ludlow
☎ 0584 4567

Historic Buildings
Dinham House
An elegant 18th century house once a residence, now a craft and exhibition centre with a programme of weekend tuition courses.

Ludlow Castle

A romantic ruined castle in the Welsh Marches; Norman, late 13th century and Tudor.
☎ 0584 3947
➔A A49 (town centre)

Shipton Hall
Exquisite Elizabethan house; dovecote, gardens.
Much Wenlock
☎ 074636 225
Off the B4378
P 🚌 ✗

Stokesay Castle
Only surviving example of 13th century fortified manor house; cottage gardens.
Craven Arms
☎ 0588 672544
➔A A49
P ♿

Wilderhope Manor
The house, unaltered since 1586, stands in remote wooded countryside. National Trust.
Much Wenlock
☎ 06943 363
Off the B4371

Museums

Acton Scott Working Farm Museum
Working farm demonstrating turn of the century agriculture; Shire horses and rare animals.
Church Stretton
☎ 06946 306
➔A A49
P 🚌 ✗ ♿

LUDLOW

Butter Cross Museum
History of Ludlow.
Church Street, Ludlow
☎ 0584 3857

Natural History

Wernlas Collection
The most extensive collection of large fowl
in the UK.
Green Lane, Onibury
☎ 058477 318
➔A A49
✗

OUTDOOR LEISURE

Archery

Archery Breaks
Tuition/accommodation packages offered to
beginners and established archers; fishing
and air rifle shooting.
Bush Farm, Clunton, Craven Arms
☎ 05887 330

Fishing

Mitre House
Lower Curve Street
☎ 0584 2138

Golf

Ludlow Golf Club ▶18
Bromfield
☎ Bromfield 334

Tennis

Visitors are welcome at the Burway and
Castle clubs.

Walking

Mortimer Forest
Forest trails and hides, route boards,
further details are available from the
Forestry Commission office.
☎ 0584 4542

Whitcliffe Common
A circular walk around the town for fine
panoramic views of Ludlow.

Ramblers Association
Regular walks are offered to members of the
Ramblers Association. Further details from:
Mrs D. Moore
☎ 058472 508

Carding Mill Valley and Long Mynd
Picturesque countryside. National Trust.
Church Stretton
Off the B4370
P ✗

Offa's Dyke Centre
Exhibitions and history of Offa's Dyke plus
information on walks; riverside park, picnic
area.
West Street, Knighton
☎ 0547 528753
➔A A488 west of Ludlow
P 🚌

WATERSPORTS

Boat Hire

River Teme
Small rowboats for hire, putting green,
picnic area and playground.

MARKET RASEN

WHAT TO DO AND SEE

County: Lincolnshire
i 9 Castle Hill, Lincoln
☎ 0522 512971
Early closing: Thursday
Market day: Tuesday, Friday, Saturday;
Indoor market Monday–Saturday
Population: 3,050
Market Rasen is an old market town set on
the River Rase with the Lincolnshire Wolds
nearby. Lincoln, a beautiful and historic city
with a fine mediaeval cathedral offers the
perfect base for a weekend in the area.

EQUESTRIAN

Riding and Pony Trekking
Mawers Farm Riding Centre
Long Leys Road
☎ 0522 545547

HEALTH

Leisure Centres
Lincoln City Sports Centre
Swimming, sunbeds, roller skating, tennis,
keep fit and squash.
☎ 0522 683946

LOCAL FEATURES

Archaeology
Roman Remains
From a military garrison established in
Lincoln and dating from 48AD; an
ingenious underground system of water
supply and sanitation, a canal and road
system.

Art Galleries
Usher Art Gallery
Paintings, ceramics, clocks and watches.
Lindum Road, Lincoln
☎ 0522 527980
🚌 ♿ ♿

Guided Tours
Guided Tours of Lincoln
Recreation and Leisure Department
City Hall, Beaumont Fee, Lincoln
☎ 0522 511511

Historic Buildings
Bishops Palace and Vineyard
Largely derelict, but the remains are still
impressive.
Minster Yard, Lincoln
☎ 0522 527468
🏠

Ellis Mill
Last surviving windmill in this area.
Mill Road, Lincoln
☎ 0522 541824
Off the B1398
🚌 🏠

Guildhall, Stonebow and Civic Insignia
15th century southern gateway to the city;
collection of treasures and regalia.
🚌 ♿ ♿

MARKET RASEN

Lincoln Castle
The castle occupies a superb hill top position west of the Cathedral and holds summertime activities such as jousting, archery, vintage vehicle rally and historic reconstructions.
Castle Manager, Lincoln Castle
☎ 0522 552222
→A A15
🏠 🚌 ✕ ♿

Lincoln Cathedral
Lincoln's 900 year old Cathedral dominates the city, probably the most spectacular setting for any English Cathedral. William the Conqueror ordered it built in 1072.
☎ 0522 544544
→A A46
P 🏠 🚌 ♿ ♿

St Mary's Guildhall
12th century building, the surface of the Roman Fosse Way is visible through a glass floor.
385 Lower High Street, Lincoln
☎ 0522 546422
🎫 🚌 ♿

Museums

City and County Museum
Natural history, prehistoric remains, Roman, Saxon and Viking finds.
Broadgate, Lincoln
☎ 0522 530401
🏠

Museum of Lincolnshire Life
Burton Road, Lincoln
☎ 0522 528448
→A A15
P 🏠 ✕ ♿ ♿

National Cycle Museum
Cycles dating from 1820.
Brayford Wharf, Lincoln
☎ 0522 545091
→A A57
P 🏠 🚌 ♿ ♿

Old Toy Show
Toys from the 1850s to the present.
26 Westgate, Lincoln
☎ 0522 520534

Parks

Elsham Hall Country Park
Arboretum, butterfly garden, tropical bird garden, crafts, adventure playground, animal farm and gallery.
Barnetby
☎ 0652 688698
→A A15/M180

Hartsholme Country Park
100 acres of parkland.
Skellingthorpe Road, Lincoln
☎ 0522 686264
Off the B1180
P 🎫 🚌 ✕

Theatres

Theatre Royal
Clasketgate, Lincoln
☎ 0522 525555

The Ritz Theatre
High Street, Lincoln
☎ 0522 522314

Skegness Embassy Centre
Grand Parade, Lincoln
☎ 0754 68333

Cycling

Arrow Cycles
2 Station Road, North Hykeham
☎ 0522 694564

F & J Cycles
Hungate, Lincoln
☎ 0522 545311

Fishing

Excellent local fishing on the River Witham and Fossdyke Canal and on nearby lakes and reservoirs.

Wheater Fieldsports
3–9 Tentecroft Street, Lincoln
☎ 0522 521219

Golf

Carholme Golf Club ⑱
Carholme Road, Lincoln
☎ 0522 523725

Southcliffe & Canwick Golf Club ⑱
Washingborough Road, Lincoln
☎ 0522 522166

Lincoln Golf Range ⑨
Washingborough Road, Lincoln
☎ 0522 522059

Walking

The Viking Way, a picturesque national footpath, passes through much of Lincolnshire.
ℹ The Tourist Board produces a series of excellent leaflets 'Lincolnshire Walks' which give detailed maps and excellent descriptions of the area.

Ramblers Association
☎ 0522 689367

Lincolnshire Tourist Guides
Daily walks.
☎ 0522 595114

Windsurfing

East Lincs Marine
Ashby Park, West Ashby, Horncastle
☎ 065 82 7966

NEWBURY

WHAT TO DO AND SEE

County: Berkshire
i Newbury District Museum, The Wharf
☎ 0635 30267
Early closing: Wednesday
Market day: Thursday and Saturday in
Market Place
Population: 31,000
Newbury, in the Kennet valley on the edge
of the Berkshire Downs, is famous as a
centre for horse training and racing. The
town, like Hungerford and Lambourn
nearby, has quaint old streets and houses.
The Kennet and Avon canal, used
commercially in the 18th century, is being
restored and provides barge trips and
towpath walks and rides. The ruins of
Donnington Castle beseiged and scarred by
the Civil War, lay on the northern outskirts
of Newbury.

ADVENTURE

Caving

Newbury District Caving Club
Mr D. Moisley, 9 Martin Place, Tilehurst,
Reading
☎ 0734 415520

AERIAL SPORTS

Ballooning

Mr Benest
7 Hampstead Marshall, nr Newbury, Berks
☎ 0635 253627

Smirk Balloon Group
Eling Hill Cottage, Eling Hill, Hermitage,
Newbury
☎ 0635 201007

Gliding

Mr Mackley
6 Maple Walk, Andover, Hants
☎ 0264 65176

Shalbourne Soaring Society
The Dell House, Charnwood Close, Newbury
☎ 0635 41803 evenings
☎ 0635 35544

Hang Gliding

Mr Fisher
Whitley Wood Road, Reading, Berks
☎ 0734 864066

Wiltshire Hang Gliding Club
The Old Barn, Rhyls Lane, Lockeridge, nr
Marlborough
☎ 0672 86 555

EQUESTRIAN

Riding

Newbury Riding Club
Pinchington Lane, Newtown
☎ 0635 41398

HEALTH

Leisure Centres

Northcroft Recreation Centre
Swimming, squash courts, sports hall,
solarium, multi-gym and health suite.
✗

Hungerford Swimming Pool
Bulpit Lane
☎ 0488 82287

Health Farms

Inglewood Health Hydro
Medically directed health hydro with a wide
range of accommodation and facilities.
Templeton Road, Kintbury, Berkshire
☎ 0488 82022

LOCAL FEATURES

Festivals and Fairs

January
The Icicle Meet
Hot air ballooning meet, first weekend in
January

May
Spring Festival

July
Summer Festival

September
Newbury Agricultural Show, third weekend
in September.
Newbury Carnival and Crafty Craft Race

Gardens

Hollington Nurseries
300 varieties of culinary, medicinal and
aromatic plants are grown in this award-
winning garden and nursery.
Woolton Hill
☎ 0635 253908
→A A343
P 🚐 ♿ ♿

Heritage

Combe Gibbet
A lonely landmark high above the scenic
village of Inkpen, erected in 1676 for a
double hanging.

Sandham Memorial Chapel
First World War Memorial; the walls are
covered in paintings of war scenes in
Salonica by Stanley Spencer.
☎ 063527 395
☎ 063527 292
→A A34

Silchester, Calleva Museum
The remains of a Roman town including an
entire circuit of the town wall and the walls
flanking the southern entrance to the
amphitheatre.
☎ 0734 700322
☎ 0734 700362

NEWBURY

Historic Houses

Donnington Castle
The ruins of the hilltop Castle that overlooks the village of Donnington.
→A A34
P ☒

Littlecote Park
A Tudor Manor House with a unique collection of Civil War armour, Roman excavations, museum, jousting exhibitions, falconry displays, steam train, craft village, herb garden, giant adventure playground, classic car collection and rare breeds farm.
Hungerford
☎ 0488 84000
P ☐ ✗ ⅏ ⅏

Ashdown House
A 17th century house with a monumental staircase rising from the hall to the attic; portraits from the Craven collection.
Lambourn
☎ 0488 71560
☎ 0488 72584
Off the B400
P ☐ ⊞

Highclere Castle
Built by Sir Charles Barry, builder of the Houses of Parliament.
Highclere park
☎ 0635 253210
→A A34
P ☐ ⊞ ✗ ⅏ ⅏

Museums

Newbury Museum
Housed in the 17th century Cloth Hall and 18th century Granary; local history, Civil War Battle and hot air ballooning displays.
The Wharf
☎ 0635 30511
Off the Newbury ring road
P ☒ ⅏

Parks

Snelsmore Common
A country park with picnic sites, nature trails, common, woodland, rare species and unusual birds.
Wantage Road
☎ 063521 618
Off the B4494
P ☐

Thatcham Moors
A site of special scientific interest located alongside the railway line between Newbury and Thatcham; the largest area of inland freshwater reed beds in England with boating facilities and a birdwatching area. Access from canal tow path from Lower Way, Thatcham.

Victoria Park
Tennis courts, bowling green, children's play area, boating lake and bandstand.
Nr town centre

Railways

Didcot Railway Centre
Large collection of locomotives, coaches and rolling stock; special steaming days
☎ 0235 817200
✗

Theatres

Watermill Theatre
Bagnor
☎ 0635 46044
P ⅏

Cycling

Cyclists Touring Club
Rosewood, The Ridge, Cold Ash, nr Newbury
☎ 0635 66278

Fishing

Field & Stream
Bartholomew Street, Newbury

Golf

Newbury & Crookham Club ⌐18
Bury Bank Road, Greenham
☎ 0635 40035

Bishopswood Golf Course ⌐9
Bishopswood Lane, Tadley, nr Basingstoke
☎ 07356 5213

Tennis

Greenacres Squash and Tennis Leisure Club
Pinchington Lane, Greenham
☎ 0635 41707

Walking

The Ridgeway Path
The oldest path in Britain. Contact the Ridgeway Officer:
☎ 0865 815718
_i_ Leaflet about town walks and local countryside walks available from the Tourist Information Centre.

Boat Hire

Kennet House Boat Co.
☎ 0635 44154
✗ ⅏ ⅏

Kennet Cruises
14 Beech Lane, Earley, Reading
☎ 0734 884065
☎ 0734 871115

Rose of Hungerford
7 Manor Park, Froxfields, Marlborough
☎ 0488 83006
✗

Dinghy Sailing

Newbury Yacht Club
Yew Tree House, High Street, Kintbury
☎ 0488 58258

NEWCASTLE UPON TYNE

County: Tyne and Wear
i Central Station, Newcastle, Tyne and Wear
☎ 091 230 0030
City Information Service
☎ 091 261 0691 ext 231
Early closing: Monday, Wednesday
Population: 290,000 (over a million in Greater Tyneside)
Newcastle a fort on Hadrian's Wall in Roman times, was known for its numerous religious houses in Saxon times and derives its name from the New Castle built in the 12th century. In the 1800s it was a great coal shipping port and the centre of George Stephenson's locomotive industry, it still remains a great industrial and engineering centre. The city centre was developed in Victorian times leaving many impressive buildings that now house some excellent art galleries and museums.

EQUESTRIAN

Riding

Lincoln Riding Centre
High Pit Farm, East Cramlington
☎ 0632 815376

HEALTH

Leisure Centres

There are 25 leisure centres in Newcastle, all with extensive facilities. For detailed information, contact the City Information Service.

LOCAL FEATURES

Archaeology

Arbeia Roman Fort
Roman Fort: remains of gateways, fort walls and defences; site museum and excavations.
Baring Street, South Shields
☎ 091 456 1369
➔A A183
&

Architecture

Bridges over the River Tyne
These are one of Newcastle's most notable features, amongst them are a 19th century, two level structure built by Robert Stephenson and the Tyne Bridge which has an arch span of 531 feet, the largest in Britain.

Art Galleries

Bede Gallery
Jarrow history; monthly exhibitions of local and international artists.
Springwell Park, Butcherbridge Road, Jarrow
☎ 091 489 1807
➔A A194
P ✕ &

Gambling Man Gallery
Bronzed sculpture made on the premises.
Wapping Street, South Shields
☎ 091 454 0360
➔A A194
P

Greys Gallery
Fortnightly exhibitions by local and national artists.
77/79 High Street, Gosforth
☎ 091 284 8735
➔A A1
P 🚌

Hatton Gallery
Contemporary art and a collection of 15th century paintings and drawings.
The University
☎ 091 222 6000
➔A A6127

WHAT TO DO AND SEE

Holly House Gallery
Ceramics, glass, textiles, jewellery, wood, pictures and prints sold and displayed.
14 Front Street, Tynemouth
☎ 091 259 2753
➔A A189

Laing Art Gallery
British paintings and watercolours; works by John Martin; textiles, ceramics, silver and glass.
Higham Place
☎ 091 232 7734
➔A A1
&. &.

Shipley Art Gallery
Victorian and Old Master paintings; traditional and contemporary crafts and temporary exhibitions.
Prince Consort Road, Gateshead
☎ 091 477 1495
➔A A6127
&. &.

Arts and Crafts

Washington Arts Centre
Galleries, theatre, workshops housed in 19th century farm buildings, meeting rooms for dance, music and drama.
Biddick Farm, Fatfield, Washington
☎ 091 416 6440
➔A A1231
P &. &.

Historic Buildings

Aydon Castle
A 13th century manor house converted to a farmhouse in the 17th century; captured by the Scots and English in turn.
On the A68 nr Corbridge
🏠

Castle Keep
A fine Norman keep with panoramic views of the city.
Saint Nicholas Street
☎ 091 232 7938
➔A A6125

Cathedral Church of Saint Nicholas
13th and 14th century cathedral with a famous lantern tower.
St Nicholas Square
☎ 091 232 1939
➔A A6127
✕ &. &.

Gibside Chapel
The mausoleum of the Bowes family, designed by James Paine. National Trust. Hosts the Flower Festival and Country Fayre in July.
Burnopfield
☎ 0207 542255
Off the B6314
P 🏠 ✕

Prudhoe Castle
Overlooking the River Tyne, Prudhoe Castle commanded the principal route through Northumberland and was a formidable obstacle in times of war. Home of the Dukes of Northumberland, it features a splendid 12th century gatehouse and keep.
Prudhoe
➔A A695
🏠

Washington Old Hall
A small, early 17th century English manor house, home of George Washington's ancestors.
Washington
☎ 091 4166879
➔A A1
P 🏠 &. &.

Museums

Greek Museum
Important collection of Greek and Etruscan antiquities from the Bronze age to the Hellenistic period. Appointment advised.
Dept. of Classics, the University
☎ 091 222600
➔A A696
&. &.

Grey's Monument
Grey Street
☎ 091 232 8520
➔A A1

Hancock Museum
Zoo room, bird room and geology gallery.
Great North Road
☎ 091 232 2359
➔A A1 to A6125
P

John George Joicey Museum
17th century almshouses depicting local history.
City Road
☎ 091 232 4562
➔A A6127
P 🚌 ✕

Military Vehicle Museum
The Pavilion, Exhibition Park, Great North Road, Jesmond
☎ 091 281 7222
➔A A6127
🚌 ✕ &.

Museum of Antiquities
The Quadrangle, The University
☎ 091 222 6000 ext 7844
➔A A6127
🚌

Museum of Science and Engineering
Blandford House, West Blandford Street
☎ 091 232 6789
➔A A6115
✕ &. &.

NEWCASTLE UPON TYNE

WHAT TO DO AND SEE

Newburn Hall Motor Museum
Vintage cars of the 1920s and 1930s.
Townfield Gardens, Newburn
☎ 091 264 2977
➔A A6085
P 🚌 🕭 ♿

Trinity Maritime Centre
Warehouse built in 1840 with models of
ships and quayside, as it was in 1775;
working models of winch, lifeboat and
capstan.
29 Broad Chare, Quayside
☎ 091 261 4691
➔A A6127
P 🏠 🚌 ✕ 🕭 ♿

Natural History

Bill Quay Farm
Smallholding of rare breeds, agriculture and
horticulture conservation.
Hainingwood Terrace, Bill Quay
☎ 091 438 5340
➔A A185
P 🚌 ✕ 🕭 ♿

St Mary's Lighthouse
Lighthouse and bird watching centre.
Trinity Road, Whitley Bay
☎ 091 252 0853
➔A A193
P 🚌 🕭 ♿

Shibdon Pond Local Nature Reserve
Off Shibdon Road, Blaydon, Gateshead
Off the B6317
P 🚌 🕭

Parks

Saltwell Park
55 acres of Victorian parkland with bowling
greens, tennis courts and a lake.
Saltwell Road, Gateshead
☎ 091 487 3311
➔A A1
P 🚌 ✕ 🕭 ♿

Railways

Bowes Railway
Rope-hauled standard gauge railway with
three steam locomotives.
Springwell Village, Gateshead
☎ 091 416 1847
➔A A1
P 🚌 ✕ 🕭 ♿

Stephenson Museum
Railway engines and rolling stock including
'Killingworth Billy' and 'Silver Link'.
Middle Engine Lane, North Shields
☎ 091 262 2627
➔A A1
P 🕭

Tanfield Railway
Oldest existing railway in the world, opened
in 1725; steam-hauled passenger trains,
vintage carriages and workshop; gala
weekends.
Marley Hill, Sunniside, Gateshead
➔A A6076
P 🚌 ✕ 🕭

Theatres

There are a large number of theatres in
Newcastle. For a list of events contact the
City Information Service.

OUTDOOR LEISURE

Birdwatching and Wildlife

The Leas and Marsden Rock
Spectacular coastline from Trow Rocks to
Lizard Point famous for kittiwakes,
cormorants etc; guided walks. National
Trust.
South Shields
☎ 067074 691
➔A A1300

Wildfowl and Wetlands Centre
Collection of 1250 wildfowl of 108 varieties;
hides, picnic areas, wildbird feeding station.
Washington, district 15
☎ 091 416 5454
➔A A1231
P 🏠 ✕ 🕭 ♿

Cycling

Glenbar Hire
217 Jesmond Road
☎ 091 281 5376

Walking

Derwent Walk Country Park
Rowlands Gill, Gateshead
➔A A694
P 🚌 🕭 ♿

The Heritage Way
110 km long distance footpath around Tyne
and Wear.
Mr J. C. Barford, Civic Centre, Regent
Street, Gateshead
☎ 091 477 1011

WATERSPORTS

Boat Hire

River Tyne Cruises
Scheduled trips, private charter and special
functions.
2nd Floor, Exchange Buildings, Quayside
☎ 091 232 8683
➔A A1 over Tyne Bridge
✕ 🕭

NEWMARKET

County: Suffolk
i The Library, Newmarket
☎ 0638 661216
Early closing: Wednesday
Market day: Tuesday and Saturday
Population: 16,000

Newmarket has been the centre of the 'Sport of Kings' since 1605 when James I and his nobles recognised that the springy turf of Newmarket Heath was ideal for horse racing. The Jockey Club, founded in 1751 is based in the High Street and Newmarket is home of the National Stud Museum and the National Horseracing Museum. Cambridge with its elegant, historic buildings is nearby as is Ely and the Fens making this a good centre for a wide variety of activities.

EQUESTRIAN

The National Stud
Booking essential for a tour of the stud.
☎ 0603 663464
Nr Newmarket July Racecourse
P 🏠 🚌 ✕ ♿

Riding
Sawston Riding School
Common Lane Farm, Common Lane, Sawston
☎ 0223 835198

LOCAL FEATURES

Architecture
Ely Cathedral
Mediaeval cathedral famous for its octagonal tower and its 14th century Lady Chapel.
Chapter House, The College, Ely
☎ 0353 667735
➔A A10
P 🏠 🚌 ♿ ♿

Kings College Chapel
Cambridge
☎ 0223 350411

Art Galleries
Kettle's Yard
1920s and 1930s art and works by Henri Gaudier-Brzeska.
Castle Street/Northampton Street, Cambridge
☎ 0223 352124
➔A A604
🎨 🚌

Festival and Fairs
May
Mildenhall Air Fete
Bury St Edmunds Festival

July
Cambridge Festival

Gardens
Chilford Hall Vineyard
Linton, Cambridge
☎ 0223 892641
Off the B1052

University of Cambridge Botanic Garden
Arboretum; rock, scented and winter gardens and glasshouses.
Covy Lodge, Bateman Street, Cambridge
☎ 0223 336265
➔A A10/A604

Guided Tours
Newmarket Equine Tours
Tours of the famous studs around Newmarket.
The National Horseracing Museum, 99 High Street, Newmarket
☎ 0638 667333
➔A A1304
P 🏠 🚌 ✕ ♿

Historic Buildings
Anglesey Abbey
13th century Augustinian priory, converted into a private house in 1591; European paintings and sculpture; 100 acres of world famous gardens.
☎ 0223 811200
➔A A1134

Cambridge Colleges
Visitors are welcome to walk through the courts and visit the chapels and some halls and libraries.

Ickworth
Oval house with flanking wings; fine paintings and Georgian silver; formal gardens and several waymarked walks.
The Rotunda, Horringer, Bury St Edmunds
☎ 028488 270
➔A A143
P 🏠 ✕ ♿ ♿

Wimpole Hall, Park and Home Farm
Imposing house with extravagant decoration, extensive gardens, children's corner, walks, adventure woodland, home farm and restored Victorian stable block with working Suffolk Punches.
Arrington, nr Royston
☎ 0223 207257
➔A A603
P 🏠 ✕ ♿ ♿

Museums
The National Horseracing Museum and Equine Tours
Five galleries packed with racing history.
99 High Street, Newmarket
☎ 0638 667333
Town centre
P 🏠 🚌 ♿

NEWMARKET

Fitzwilliam Museum
Outstanding collection of paintings, antiquities, ceramics and armour.
Trumpington Street, Cambridge
☎ 0223 332900
🛈 🚌 ✕ 🚻 ♿

Folk Museum
Fascinating array of bygones from Cambridgeshire.
Castle Street, Cambridge
☎ 0223 355159
🛈

Imperial War Museum
Largest collection of military and civic aircraft in Britain.
Duxford Airfield, Duxford, Cambs
☎ 0223 833963
☎ 0223 835600
➔A A505

Scott Polar Research Institute
Museum of polar life and exploration.
Lensfield Road, Cambridge
☎ 0223 336540
🛈

Sedgwick Museum
Extensive collection of geological specimens.
Downing Street, Cambridge
☎ 0223 333400
🛈 ♿

University Museum of Archaeology and Anthropology
Shrunken heads, totem poles and native dress as well as local finds.
Downing Street, Cambridge
☎ 0223 337733
🛈 ♿

Museum of Zoology
Birds, insects, mammals and sea animals stuffed and preserved.
Downing Street, Cambridge
☎ 0223 336650
🛈 ♿

Natural History

Wicken Fen
600 acres of wetland reserve; a remnant of the Great Fens rich in plant, insect and bird life; nature trail, bird hides and exhibitions.
Lode Lane, Wicken, Ely
☎ 0353 720274
➔A A1123
P 🛈 🚌 ♿ ♿

Theatres

The Arts Theatre, Cambridge
Professional theatre with a varied programme of drama, opera, ballet, music and films.
Peas Hill, Cambridge
☎ 0223 352000

Zoos

Linton Zoo
A varied collection of wildlife.
Hadstock Road, Linton
☎ 0223 891308
On the B1052 nr Cambridge
🛈 ✕

Cycling

Armada Cycles
47 Suez Road
☎ 0223 210421

Fishing

Information from National Rivers Authority, Cobham Road, Ipswich.
☎ 0473 727712

Thorton & Son (Tackle shop)
46 Burleigh Street, Cambridge
☎ 0223 358709

Golf

Gog Magog Golf Club ⛳18 ⛳9
Advanced booking essential.
Babraham Road, Cambridge
☎ 0223 246058

Newmarket Golf Course ⛳18
☎ 0638 663000

Skiing

Bassingbourn Ski Club
Hitchin
☎ 0462 434107

Walking

Devil's Dyke Walk
Early Saxon ditch embankment between Reach and Stetchworth. Leaflet from Cambridgeshire Wildlife Trust
☎ 0223 880788

Gog Magog Hills and Wandlebury Ring
Woods and open grassland.
➔A A1307

Icknield Way Long Distance Footpath
Follows the oldest road in Britain along the chalk spine of southern England. Walkers guide available from the Icknield Way Association.
☎ 0279 505602

Wicken Walks
Two interlinked waymarked walks passing through the Fenlands.
Leaflet from the Cambridgeshire County Council Rural Management Division
☎ 0223 317404

Punting

Scudamore's
Granta Place, Cambridge
☎ 0223 359750

NEWTON ABBOT

County: Devon
i Tourist Office, 8 Sherborne Road
☎ 0626 67494
Market day: Saturday
Population: 9000

Newton Abbot is a busy market town with a perfect situation for touring enjoying both its proximity to the coast and a number of popular holiday resorts, and inland the 365 square miles of Dartmoor National Park, high moorland with some of the wildest open space in England. An area steeped in history, it offers some of the most beautiful scenery at any time of year with picturesque rural villages reflecting the slow pace of Devon Life.

The seaside resorts of Torbay include nearby Teignmouth with its sandy beach and pretty walks around Dawlish. One of the best beaches in the area, Dawlish Warren is also an important nature reserve. Backed by dunes, the beach runs for 2 miles along the southern bank of the Exe estuary.

EQUESTRIAN

Riding and Pony Trekking

Elliotts Hill Riding Centre
Buckland-in-the-Moor
☎ 0364 53058

Smallacombe Farm Riding Stables
Ilsington
☎ 03646 265

HEALTH

Leisure Centres

Dyrons Leisure Centre
Pool with fun slide, sauna, sunbeds, squash and tennis.
Highweek Road, Newton Abbot
☎ 0626 60426
Close to town centre

Trago Mills Shopping and Leisure Centre
Huge shopping complex; Edwardian penny arcade, miniature railway, cinema, adventuredome and coarse fishing lakes.
Stover, nr Newton Abbot
☎ 0626 821111
➔A A38/382
P ✕ ⅃

LOCAL FEATURES

Arts and Crafts

Dartington Cider Press Centre
Craft shops and visitor centre.
Shinners Bridge, Dartington
☎ 0803 864171
➔A A384
P ⅃

The Devon Guild of Craftsmen
Museum, demonstrations and changing craft exhibitions.
Riverside Mill, Bovey Tracey
☎ 0626 832223
➔A A382
P ✕ ⅃

Food and Drink

Whitestone Vineyard
Bovey Tracey, nr Moretonhampstead
☎ 832280
➔A old A382

Gardens

Plant World
4 acres of gardens, unique 'map of the world gardens', plant nursery and panoramic views.
St Mary Church Road, Newton Abbot
☎ 0803 872939
➔A A380
P

Historic Buildings

Bradley Manor
Mediaeval manor house and chapel set in woodland and meadows. National Trust.
Newton Abbot
☎ 0626 4513
➔A A381

Buckfast Abbey
Founded nearly a thousand years ago, the abbey was rebuilt earlier this century by the present community. Today it is a living Benedictine monastery well-known for its beekeeping, stained glass and tonic wine.
Buckfastleigh
☎ 0364 42519
➔A A38
P ⅊ ⍩ ⅃

Compton Castle
Fortified manor house. National Trust.
Marldon, nr Paignton
☎ 08047 2112
➔A A381
P

Ugbrooke House and Park
Ancestral home of the Lords Clifford of Chudleigh; fine furniture and paintings; Capability Brown landscaped park.
Chudleigh
☎ 0626 852179
➔A A38
P ⍩ ✕ ⅃

Natural History

Buckfast Butterfly Farm and Otter Sanctuary
Tropical butterflies and moths; otter pools and underwater viewing.
Buckfast Steam and Leisure Park, Buckfastleigh
☎ 0364 42916
➔A A38/A384
P ⍩ ✕ ⅃

NEWTON ABBOT

WHAT TO DO AND SEE

Miniature Pony Centre
Collection of rare miniature ponies;
adventure playground.
Wormhill Farm, nr Bovey Tracey
☎ 06473 2400
On the B3212 nr Moretonhampstead
P ⛺ ✗ ♿

Rare Breeds Farm
Farm trails, river walks and rare breeds of
farm animals.
Parke, nr Bovey Tracey
☎ 0626 833909
Off the B3387
P ✗ ♿

Parks

River Dart Country Park
Adventure playgrounds, bathing lake, grass
sledges, pony rides, nature trails and fly
fishing.
Holne Park, Ashburton
☎ 0364 52511
Nr Ashburton
P ✗ ♿

Stover Country Park
14 acre lake with a wide variety of birds and
wildlife.
Newton Abbot

Decoy Park
100 acres of woodland, a boating lake and
playgrounds.
Newton Abbot

Railways

Dart Valley Light Railway
Buckfastleigh to Totnes steam trips; leisure
park and museum.
The Station, Buckfastleigh
☎ 0364 42338
➔A A38
P ✗

Gorse Blossom Miniature Railway
Small gauge passenger trains; picnic area,
woodland walks and gardens.
Nr Bickington
☎ 0626 821361
➔A old A38
P ♿

Zoos

Paignton Zoo
Totnes Road, Paignton
☎ 0803 527936
P ♿

OUTDOOR LEISURE

Birdwatching and Wildlife

Dawlish Warren Nature Reserve
500 acres of mixed dune, saltmarsh and
sandy shores.
i The Tourist Office can provide details of
accompanied weekend breaks.
⛺

Shaldon Wildlife Trust
Rare and endangered small mammals;
exotic birds and reptiles; breeding centre.
Ness Drive, Shaldon
☎ 0626 872234
➔A A379
♿ ⛺ ✗

Fishing

Trago Mills Nature Reserve
Fishing stretch for carp, rudd, roach, bream
and tench.
Between Newton Abbot and Bovey Tracey

Decoy Lake
Stocked with tench, perch and rudd.

Rackerhayes Ponds
5 lakes stocked with bream, carp, tench,
roach, rudd, perch, pike and eels. Available
to day ticket holders.
Between Newton Abbot and Kingsteignton

Golf

Warren Golf Club ⛳18
Dawlish
☎ 0626 862255

Newton Abbot (Stover) Golf Club ⛳18
Newton Abbot
☎ 0626 52460

Walking

Becky Falls Estate
70 foot waterfall in lovely woodland, picnic
areas and nature trails.
Manaton, nr Bovey Tracey
☎ 064722 259
On the B3344
P

Canonteign Falls and Water Park
The highest falls in southern England set in
natural woodland in the Teign valley,
lakeside picnic areas and barbecue centre.
Canonteign, nr Chudleigh
☎ 0647 52666
➔A A38
P

Short Walks
i The Tourist Office can provide
information about varied walks in the area.

NOTTINGHAM

County: Nottinghamshire
𝑖 Nottingham Tourist Office,
  16 Wheeler Gate
☎ 0602 470661
Early closing: Thursday
Population: 275,000
Nottingham, a historic university city, grew around an important bridging point on the River Trent. It is well known for its links with the legendary Robin Hood and Sherwood Forest, for its connections with the lace, tobacco and pharmaceutical industries, for the oldest pub in England, for its honeycomb of over 400 caves as well as its theatres, museums and modern shopping centres. It also has ties with two great literary figures. D H Lawrence was born at Eastwood, near Nottingham, and Lord Byron made his home at Newstead Abbey, its glorious surroundings providing the inspiration for some of his poetic works.

LOCAL FEATURES

Festivals and Fairs

August
Monsters of Rock Festival
Castle Donington

October
Goose Fair

Guided Tours

Mortimer's Hole Tour
300 ft long ancient passageway.
𝑖 16 Wheeler Gate
☎ 0602 470661

The Nottingham Story
25 minute audio-visual show: the story of Nottingham.
𝑖 16 Wheeler Gate
☎ 0602 470661

Historic Buildings

Belvoir Castle
Home of the Duke and Duchess of Rutland; staterooms, furniture, tapestries and paintings. Regular displays of mediaeval jousting and falconry.
Nr Grantham
☎ 0476 870262
→A A607/A52
P ✕

Newstead Abbey
Home of Lord Byron, 800 year old priory, converted into a country mansion in the 16th century, set in 300 acres of parkland.
Linby
☎ 0623 793557
→A A60
P ✕ ♿

Nottingham Castle
The site of the royal mediaeval castle, now houses the city's art gallery and museum in the 17th century residence built by the Dukes of Newcastle; ceramics, silver, glass and paintings.
☎ 0602 483504
→A A52 (city centre)
🎫 small charge Sun 🚐 ✕

Museums

Aeropark and Visitor Centre
12 acre park of exhibits, play area.
East Midlands International Airport
☎ 0332 810621 ext 3361
→A A453 nr Castle Donnington
P ♿

Brewhouse Yard Folk Museums
Museum of daily life housed in converted 17th century town houses; period rooms.
Castle Boulevard
☎ 0602 483504
Town centre
🎫 ♿

Canal Museum
A waterway museum situated within a former canal warehouse.
Canal Street
☎ 0602 598835
🎫

Castle Gate Costume Museum
An elegant row of Georgian terraced houses now containing the city's costume, lace and textile collections.
51 Castle Gate
☎ 0602 483504
→A A52
🎫

Green's Windmill and Science Centre
The home of mathematical theorist and miller George Green, the restored mill and adjoining science centre displays hands-on exhibits of light, magnetism and electricity.
Belvoir Hill, Sneinton
☎ 0602 503635
→A A612
P ♿

Lace Hall
The story of Nottingham's lace industry with demonstrations of hand and machine lace-making.
High Pavement
☎ 0602 484221
🚐 ✕ ♿

D H Lawrence's Birthplace
Sons and Lovers cottage is at 28 Garden Road, Eastwood and was also the home of the family for a few years.
8a Victoria Street, Eastwood
☎ 0773 763312
→A A610, M1, exits 26 or 27
🚐 ✕

NOTTINGHAM

Natural History and Industrial Museum

In Elizabethan mansion set in 500 acres of parkland.
Wollaton Hall, Wollaton Park
☎ 0602 281333
➔A A609
P 🏛 🚐 ✕ ♿
Small charge Sun and Bank Hols

Tales of Robin Hood

The story of Robin Hood.
Maid Marian Way
☎ 0602 414414
➔A A52 (city centre)
♿

Natural History

White Post Modern Farm Centre
Working farm with most farm animals and crops, llamas, quail and ostriches too, lake picnic area and country walk.
White Post Farm, Farnsfield, nr Newark
☎ 0623 882977
On the A614, 12 miles from Nottingham
P 🚐 ✕ ♿

Parks

Colwick Country Park
250 acre park adjacent to the Nottingham racecourse. Dinghy hire; fishing areas; nature reserve; cycle and horse riding trails.
Colwick Road
☎ 0602 870785
Off the B686
P ♿

Sherwood Forest Country Park
450 acres of ancient Sherwood Forest; Information centre; Robin Hood exhibition and Major Oak.
Edwinstowe
☎ 0623 823202
Off the B6034
P ✕ ♿

Theatres

Co-operative Arts Theatre
George Street
☎ 0602 476096

Nottingham Playhouse
Wellington Circus
☎ 0602 419419
➔A A52 (city centre)
✕

Nottingham Theatre Club
Halifax Place
☎ 0602 507201

Theatre Royal and Royal Concert Hall
Theatre Square
☎ 0602 472328
P ✕ ♿

Birdwatching

Wetlands Waterfowl and Exotic Bird Park
Many species of birds, wildflowers and fungi; children's farmyard and rare breeds.
Off Loundlow Road, Sutton-cum-Lound, nr Retford
☎ 0777 818099
➔A A638
P 🚐 ✕

Cycling

Olympic Cycles
43 Radford Road, Hyson Green, Nottingham
☎ 0602 702616

Golf

Bulwell Forest Municipal Golf Course ⛳₁₈
Bulwell Common
☎ 0602 278008

Ice Skating

Ice Stadium
Lower Parliament Street
☎ 0602 501938

Skiing

Carlton Forum
Foxhill Road, Carlton, Nottingham
☎ 0602 872333

Tenpin Bowling

Nottingham Bowl
Barker Gate
☎ 0602 505588

Colwick and Holme Pierrepont National Watersports Centre
Two landscaped water parks offering many watersports, fishing, nature reserves, walks and picnic areas. Rowing, canoeing and power boat events are held at Holme Pierrepont.
Adbolton Lane
☎ 0602 821212

PERTH

County: Tayside
i The Round House, Marshall Place, Perth
☎ 0738 38353
Early closing: Wednesday
Market day: Monday and Friday for livestock
Population: 42,000
Perth, set on the River Tay and bounded by parks, is a former mediaeval burgh. It has fine Georgian crescents and terraces and many antique shops. Its landmarks include Smeaton's Bridge built in 1771 and St John's Kirk, the 15th century cruciform church where John Knox delivered his momentous sermon in 1559.

Excellent golf courses, good riding and fishing are all available in the area around Perth which is also rich in historic places to visit.

EQUESTRIAN

Riding and Pony Trekking

Caledonian Equestrian Centre
Pitskelly, Balbeggie, by Perth
☎ 08214 426

HEALTH

Leisure Centres

Bell's Sports Centre
Wide range of sports facilities including tennis, badminton and table tennis.
Hay Street, Perth
☎ 0738 22301
✕

Perth Leisure Pool
Leisure pool with flumes, wild water, outdoor lagoon, bubble beds and a 25 metre training pool; health suite, fitness room and childrens pool.
Glasgow Road, Perth
☎ 0738 30535
✕

LOCAL FEATURES

Arts and Crafts

Perth City Mills
Restored grain mill with Scotland's largest working waterwheel; several craft workshops and an exhibition.
West Mill Street, Perth
☎ 0738 30572
🛍 ✕

Factory Visits

Caithness Glass
See production and visit the factory shop.
Inveralmond
☎ 0738 37373
On the A9, 1 mile north of Perth
P

Dewar's Whiskey Bottling Plant
Free guided tour and tasting.
Inveralmond
☎ 0738 21231
On the A9, 1 mile north of Perth
P 🚌

Festivals and Fairs

May
Festival of Fine Arts

August
Highland Games

Gardens

Bell's Cherrybank Gardens
18 acres of gardens; the Bell's National Heather collection, waterfall pools, an aviary, sculptures and children's play area.
Off Glasgow Road, Perth
☎ 0738 27330
P 🛍 ✕

Branklyn Garden
Outstanding collection of alpines.
Perth
☎ 0738 25535
Off the A85 Dundee road
🛍

Guided Tours

Nine signposted tourist trails are available in Perthshire.
i All are described in detail in a leaflet, *Car Touring in Perthshire*, available from the tourist office.

Heritage

Dunsinane Hill Vitrified Fort
Hilltop fort with views of Strathmore and the Tay valley.
➔A A94

Historic Buildings

Abernethy Round Tower
An 11th century tower, 74 feet high, is in a conservation village, once an important Pictish settlement.
On the A913, 8 miles south-east of Perth

Elcho Castle
The ancestral seat of the Earls of Wemyss, notable for its tower-like jambs or wings.
4 miles south east of Perth
🛍

Huntingtower Castle
A 15th century castellated mansion and the scene of the raid of Ruthven in 1583, known as Ruthven Castle until 1600.
Off the A85, 3 miles west-north-west of Perth
🛍

WHAT TO DO AND SEE

Scone Palace

The famous Stone of Scone was brought here in the 9th century, then taken to Westminster Abbey by Edward I. Fine collections of furniture, china, needlework, clocks and ivories. Moot Hill, the crowning place for the Scottish kings is in the grounds.
☎ 0738 52300
Off the A93, nr Perth
♿

Museums

Black Watch Museum
Balhousie Castle, Hay Street, Perth
☎ 0738 21281 ext 30

Perth Museum and Art Gallery
Award-winning exhibitions of the plants, animals and geology of the district.
George Street, Perth
☎ 0738 32488

Tourist Island
Motor museum, shop and restaurant.
☎ 0738 87696
Off the A9 at Bankfoot, 8 miles north of Perth
♿

Natural History

Fairways Heavy Horse Centre
Clydesdale horses, dray rides, vintage horse implements and a blacksmith.
Walnut Grove, Kinfauns, Perth
☎ 0738 25931
☎ 0738 32561
♿ ✗

Parks

North Inch
Site of the famous "Battle of the Clans" in 1396, now a park bordering the River Tay with a golf course, bowling green, and sports centre.
Perth

South Inch
Large public parks with many facilities.
Perth

Theatre

Perth Theatre
High Street, Perth
☎ 0738 21031

OUTDOOR LEISURE

Fishing

Perthshire contains a wealth of salmon, sea trout and brown trout waters with an increasing number of rainbow trout fisheries. The game species are the major attraction for the visiting angler, but there is also excellent grayling, pike, perch and roach fishing. The predominant fishing water is the River Tay, one of the principal salmon rivers in Europe; there are stillwater fishing opportunities in the many lochs.
i For detailed information see *Fishing in Perthshire*, a comprehensive leaflet available from the Tourist Board.

Tayside Tackle and Guns
259 Old High Street, Perth
☎ 0738 32316

M. G. Guns and Tackle
51 York Place, Perth
☎ 0738 25769

Golf

All Perthshire's golf courses welcome visitors.
i For details of the 29 Perthshire courses see *Golfing in Perthshire* a leaflet available from the Tourist Board. They can also arrange a "Perthshire Highlands Golf Ticket" allowing you to play at five courses.

King James VI Golf Club ⛳18
Moncrieffe Island, Perth
☎ 0738 32460

North Inch ⛳18
Leisure and Recreation Dept, 3 High Street, Perth
☎ 0738 36481

Walking

i *Walk Perthshire* available from the Tourist Board gives details of 45 popular and varied walks in the district. It includes forest walks, nature trails, riverside walks and hill walks some of which are strenuous.

PONTEFRACT

County: West Yorkshire
i Wakefield Tourist Office,
   Town Hall, Wood Street
☎ 0924 370211
Population: 32,000
Pontefract is a pleasant market town with a history that spans 900 years. It gave its name to the well known liquorice cakes that are produced locally and exported worldwide. They were made originally from locally grown liquorice fields.

An area noted for its fine rugby league teams, brass bands and coal mining heritage, visitors can attend the traditional Yorkshire galas held throughout the district in the summer. Leeds and Wakefield, both shopping and entertainment centres are nearby.

LOCAL FEATURES

Art Galleries

Elizabethan Gallery
16th century building housing a wide-ranging programme of exhibitions featuring contemporary works of craft, design and photography by nationally known artists.
Brook Street, Wakefield
→A A650 (town centre)
☎ 0924 370211

Wakefield Art Gallery
20th century painting and sculpture.
Wentworth Terrace, Wakefield
☎ 0924 375402
→A A650 (town centre)
占

Yorkshire Sculpture Park
Set in beautiful parkland, open-air sculpture displays include works by Henry Moore and Barbara Hepworth, both born locally, as well as other internationally famous sculptors.
Bretton Hall, West Bretton, nr Wakefield
☎ 0924 830302
1 mile from exit 38 of M1
P 🕎 🚌 占 占

Bowling

Superbowl 2000
Ten-pin bowling alley.
180 Doncaster Road, Wakefield
☎ 0924 382222
City centre
✕

Festivals and Fairs

Wakefield Waterways Festival (Fall Ing Lock, Wakefield) annual display of boats and barges.

Historic Buildings

Carlton Towers
A Victorian Gothic house, the Yorkshire home of the Duke of Norfolk.
✕

Kirkstall Abbey
Substantial remains of massive Cistercian abbey.
Kirkstall Road, Leeds
☎ 0532 755821
A65 Ilkley–Leeds road
P 🕎 占

Lotherton Hall
An Edwardian country house with portraits, furniture, silver; period gardens, deer park and bird garden.
Aberford, nr Leeds
☎ 0532 813259
Off the B1217
🚌 ✕ 占

Nostell Priory
A Palladian house, and stately home; paintings, Chippendale furniture and state rooms; lake and gardens. National Trust.
Doncaster Road, Nostell, nr Wakefield
☎ 0924 863892
→A A638
P 🚌 ✕ 占

Pontefract Castle
Romantic ruins of a once formidable fortress, Shakespeare's 'Pomfret' where Richard II met his death.
Pontefract
☎ 0977 600208
→A A645 (town centre)
占 占

Sandal Castle
Excavated mediaeval castle above Wakefield, site of the Battle of Wakefield in 1460, finds are displayed in the Wakefield Museum, Wood Street.
Manygates Lane, Sandal, nr Wakefield
P 🕎

Wakefield Cathedral
The historic Church of All Saints has a 247 foot spire.
Northgate, Wakefield
☎ 0924 373923
A1/M1 (town centre)
🚌

Museums

Pontefract Museum
Local history museum housed in an extravagant Art Deco building.
Salter Row, Pontefract
☎ 0977 797289
→A A645 (town centre)
🕎

Top Farm Agricultural Museum
Working farm where visitors can see traditional wheat threshing, butter making, farm machinery and animals.
West Hardwick, nr Nostell
☎ 0977 611165
Off the B6428 Featherston to Royston road
P 🚌 ✕ 占

PONTEFRACT

WHAT TO DO AND SEE

Yorkshire Mining Museum
Award-winning museum traces the history
of mining. Underground guided tours
available (not for the under-fives).
Caphouse Colliery, New Road, Overton,
nr Wakefield
☎ 0924 848806
➔A A642
P 🚌 ✕

Music, Dance and Drama

Wakefield Arts Centre
Regularly changing programme of jazz, rock
and cabaret events.

Parks

Bretton Country Park
100 acres of parkland with nature trails.
Adjacent to Yorkshire Sculpture Park and
Yorkshire Wildlife Trust Nature Reserve
(reserve by permit only).
West Bretton, nr Wakefield
☎ 0924 830550
➔A A637
P ♿

OUTDOOR LEISURE

Birdwatching and Wildlife

Fairburn Ings Nature Reserve
Once an open-cast coal mining site, now a
600 acre wetland wildlife reserve with many
rare species.
Off the A1, north of Pontefract

Cricket

Headingley County Cricket Ground
Test and County ground. Contact for
fixtures.
St Michaels Lane, Headingley

Walking

Wakefield's Countryside Service organise
walks and rambles in the area including a
popular orienteering course at
Newmillerdam.

WATERSPORTS

Pugneys Country Park
UK's best water park award in 1988.
Introductory courses in dinghy sailing,
windsurfing and canoeing. Approved by the
Royal Yachting Association.
Asdale Road, Wakefield
☎ 0924 386782

REDCAR

WHAT TO DO AND SEE

County: Cleveland

i Tourist Office, Regent Cinema Building, Newcomen Terrace

☎ 0642 471921

Population: 85,000

Redcar is a large family seaside resort with safe, sandy beaches and a wide variety of traditional entertainment from fishing boats to the indoor funfair. It lies close to the entrance of the River Tees and is England's second largest port. This area has a history of invasion, devasted by the Norman Conquest, it was described in the Domesday Book of 1086 as "waste". Guisborough Priory, also mentioned is one of Cleveland's most ancient landmarks.

The sea has a dominant influence over the area. The coast south of Saltburn is designated as Heritage Coast in recognition of its outstanding natural beauty and the views from the highest cliffs at Boulby, overlooking Staithes, are spectacular.

The discovery of ironstone during the 1850s led to the development of industry as mines were opened and introduced another episode in the regions long history.

ADVENTURE

Go-karting

Wheels Motor Sports Complex

Kart circuit with kart hire available.

A1053, between Redcar and Middlesborough

☎ 0642 24417

HEALTH

Leisure Centres

Redcar Leisure Centre and Baths

Large pool, snooker and squash.

Majuba Road, Redcar

☎ 0642 480636

LOCAL FEATURES

Arts and Crafts

Glass Engraver

Liverton Grange, Liverton Mines, Loftus, nr Saltburn-by-Sea

☎ 0287 43888

Festivals and Fairs

July

Hartlepool Sea Angling Festival, 7–15 July

Cleveland County Show, 28 July

August

Kirkleatham Country Fayre, early Aug

Saltburn Victorian Celebrations, 11–18 Aug

October

Captain Cook's Birthday Celebrations, 20–27 Oct

Middlesbrough Beer Festival, late Oct

Historic Buildings

Guisborough Priory

Ruins of a 12th century Augustinian priory with beautifully kept gardens and octagonal dovecote.

Church Street, Guisborough

☎ 0287 38301

Ormesby Hall

Elegant 18th century house, until recently the ancestral home of the Pennyman family. National Trust.

Off the B1380, 3 miles south-east of Middlesbrough

☎ 0642 324188

Saltburn Cliff Lift

The oldest remaining water-balanced cliff railway in Britain, dating from 1884.

On the A174 at Saltburn Bank

Upleatham Church

12th century and reputedly the smallest stone-built church in England, measuring only 17'9" x 13'. Set in open countryside outside the village of Upleatham.

Off the B1268 Saltburn to Guisborough road

Museums

Kirkleatham Old Hall Museum

Displays on local history of Langbaurgh and the Turner family. Gardens and playground.

➔A A1042

☎ 0642 479500

Tom Leonard Museum

Exhibits depict the history and practice of ironstone mining in east Cleveland.

Off the A174

☎ 0287 42877

Zetland Lifeboat Museum

The history of sea rescue. Exhibits include a reconstruction of a fisherman's cottage and the 'Zetland', the oldest lifeboat in the world.

Old Lifeboat House, Redcar Esplanade

☎ 0642 471813

🛞

OUTDOOR LEISURE

Walking

Cleveland Way

107 miles long, the Cleveland Way passes through the North York Moors and the North Yorkshire and Cleveland Heritage Coast.

Information Centre at Saltburn

☎ 0287 22422

RIPON

County: North Yorkshire
i Tourist Office, Minster Road
☎ 0765 4625 (Apr–Sep)
Early closing: Wednesday
Market day: Thursday
Population: 13,000

Ripon, one of the oldest boroughs in England, was granted its first Charter of Incorporation in 886 by Alfred the Great. Its cathedral has a Saxon crypt, and in the town's old Market Place a tricorn-hatted Hornblower sounds a horn each night at 9pm to 'set the watch', thereby continuing a 1000 year-old tradition.

The beauitiful Yorkshire Dales can be explored using Ripon as a base, an ideal centre for walking or cycling holidays. For those with an interest in James Herriot's Yorkshire, suggested routes are available from the Tourist Office to take the motorist through the picturesque villages used for the popular TV serial.

ADVENTURE

Multi-activity Centres

John Bull School of Adventure
Expert instruction in canoeing, rock climbing, mountain walking, caving, cross-country skiing and windsurfing for families, individuals, novices or experts.
12 Littlethorpe Park, Ripon
☎ 0765 4071
☎ 0765 690074

Shooting

Yorkshire Gun Room
Private tuition and practice with professional instructors.
Bishop Thornton, nr Harrogate
☎ 076586 602
Off the B6165

AERIAL SPORTS

Ballooning

Airborne Adventures
Champagne balloon flights.
4 North View, Lothersdale, Keighley
☎ 0535 33431

EQUESTRIAN

Riding and Pony Trekking

Swinton Riding and Trekking Centre
Home Farm, Swinton, nr Ripon
☎ 0765 89636

LOCAL FEATURES

Arts and Crafts

Grewelthorpe Hand Weavers
Hand loom workshop.
At Grewelthorpe village between Ripon and Masham
☎ 0765 83209

Littlethorpe Potteries
Country pottery using local clay.
Off the B6265, 2 miles from Ripon
☎ 0765 3786
✗

T & R Theakston Brewery
Brewers of Yorkshire ale since 1827, visitor centre shows the brewing process and the skills of the cooper. Steep stairs prohibit children under 16 years.
Masham
☎ 0765 89057
🚐

Uredale Glass
Viewing gallery to watch glass making.
Market Place, Masham
☎ 0765 89780

Festivals and Fairs

May
International Youth Music Festival, May 9–11

July
Great Yorkshire Show, July 10–12
Steam Engine and Fair Organ Rally, July 21–22

Fun Parks

Lightwater Valley Theme Park
Acres of parkland with children's amusements, rides, boating lake, steam railway and working farm. Picnic areas, golf, bowls, double loop rollercoaster, go karts and roller skating.
North Stainley
☎ 0765 85321
Off the A6108 Ripon to Masham road, 3 miles north of Ripon
P ✗ ♿

Gardens

Harrogate Valley Gardens
Recreational facilities and bandstand concerts.

Ripon Spa Gardens
Gardens and recreational facilities.

Guided tours

Ripon Civic Society
i Evening tours depart from the Ripon Tourist Office.

RIPON

Historic Buildings
Fountains Abbey

Founded by Cistercian monks in 1132, Fountains Abbey is the largest monastic ruin in Europe. The ruins stand in the midst of the 18th century landscaped gardens of Studley Royal, on the banks of the River Skell. Water gardens; ornamental temples; follies; deer park and lake. National Trust.
☎ 0765 86333
Off the B6265, 4 miles west of Ripon
P ✕ ♿

Knaresborough Castle
14th century ruins high on a cliff overlooking the River Nidd.
Knaresborough

Newby Hall
Adam House with fine furnishings and extensive gardens; woodland walks, lake trips and a miniature railway.
☎ 0423 322583
4 miles south-east of Ripon

Norton Conyers
Fine Jacobean house set in parkland with an 18th century walled garden. Reputedly the inspiration for Thornfield House in Charlotte Bronte's *Jane Eyre*.
Wath, nr Ripon
☎ 076584 333

Museums
Ripon Prison and Police Museum
☎ 0765 3706

Cycling
John Donoghue
1 Westgate, Ripon
☎ 0765 701395

Golf
Ripon City Golf Club ⚑18
Palace Road
☎ 0765 3640

Skiing
Harrogate Ski Centre
Yorkshire Showground, Hookstone Wood Road
☎ 0423 505457
➔A A661
✕

Walking
Brimham Rocks
Millstone grit rock formations set in open moorland overlooking Nidderdale.
Nr Pateley Bridge
☎ 0423 780688
P ✕

How Stean Gorge
Spectacular limestone gorge best explored from Pateley Bridge, referred to as England's 'Little Switzerland'.
Nr Pateley Bridge
☎ 0423 75666
P ✕

Nidd Gorge Nature Trail
A refuge for wildlife, the trail follows the River Nidd from Bilton, Harrogate to Knaresborough.

Boat Hire
Blenkhorns Boat Builders
Rowing boats, punts and canoes for hire.
High Bridge, Knaresborough
☎ 0423 862105

Canoeing
Sleningford Water Mill
Canoe hire on the River Ure.
North Stainley
☎ 0765 85201

SALISBURY

WHAT TO DO AND SEE

County: Wiltshire
i Fish Row, Salisbury
☎ 0722 334956
Early closing: Wednesday
Market day: Tuesday, Saturday
Population: 37,000
Salisbury is a fine old cathedral city whose roots can be traced back to Old Sarum, an Iron Age settlement, two miles north of the present city. The Cathedral is built in the shape of a double cross and has a beautiful spire rising to 404 feet. The Cathedral is surrounded by many interesting old buildings and the area has many fine gardens and historic houses, castles, museums and wildlife parts to visit. The famous Megalithic monument of Stonehenge is nearby.

AERIAL SPORTS

Gliding
Dorset Gliding Club
Old Sarum Airfield
Mr R. Witheridge, 123 Runnymeade Avenue, Bearwood, Bournemouth
☎ 0202 577701
☎ 0202 338479

Hang Gliding
White Sheet Hill at Mere is popular for hang gliding.

EQUESTRIAN

Hunting
South and West Wiltshire Hunt
Major T. P. Wootton, Milton House, East Knoyle, Salisbury
☎ 0747 83397

Riding and Pony Trekking
Brympton Riding School
Mrs S. Near, Whiteparish, Salisbury
☎ 0794 884386

HEALTH

Leisure Centres
Salisbury Swimming Pool, Health and Fitness Centre
Swimming pool, sauna, spa bath, sunbeds. multi gym, Turkish bath.
College Street, Salisbury
☎ 0722 25284

LOCAL FEATURES

Falconry
The Hawk Conservancy
Birds of prey and demonstrations.
Weyhill, Nr Andover, Hants
Off the A303, 4 miles west of Andover
P ✗

Festivals and Fairs
May
Downton Cuckoo Fair
Wishford Oakapple Day

July
Southern Cathedrals Festival

September
Salisbury Festival

October
Salisbury Charter Fair

Gardens
Fitz House Garden
Teffont Magna
→A A30

Heale House Gardens and Nursery
Early Carolean manor house where King Charles II hid during his escape. Beautiful gardens with an authentic Japanese tea house.
Woodford
☎ 072 273 207
→A A345/A360
🚌 ♿

Guided Tours
Countryside Tours
Round trips from Salisbury to Avebury Stone Circle, Stonehenge, Dorset coast, the New Forest, the Longleat Stately Home, Wells and Glastonbury.
i Contact Alison Fenwick at the Tourist Office
☎ 0722 29983
March to October

Guided City Tours
i Contact the Tourist Office

SALISBURY

WHAT TO DO AND SEE

Heritage

Stonehenge
An awe-inspiring stone circle dated between 2700 BC and 1400 BC. It is linked with midsummer sunrise, fertility rites, astronomy and the solar calendar.
Nr Amesbury
Off the A303/A344, 10 miles from Salisbury
P 🛈 ♿ ♿

Woodhenge
Believed to date from 1700 BC, the position of the wooden structure is now marked by concrete pillars.
Off the A345, 9 miles from Salisbury
🖈

Historic Buildings

Breamore House
Elizabethan Manor House with a fine collection of paintings, tapestries and furniture; countryside museum and carriage museum.
Nr Fordingbridge, Hampshire
☎ 0725 22270
➔A A338
🛈 ✗

Mompesson House
Built in 1701, a perfect example of a Queen Anne house. National Trust.
Choristers' Green, The Close, Salisbury
☎ 0722 335659
🛈

Mottisfont Abbey
A 12th century Augustinian priory with a fine collection of roses, set beside the River Test. National Trust.
Mottisfont
☎ 0794 40757
Nr Romsey
🛈 🚍 ♿

Newhouse
Jacobean 'Trinity' house built about 1619 with two Georgian wings; contents include Nelson relics.
Redlynch
☎ 0725 20055
9 miles south of Salisbury
🛈 ✗

Wilton House
Home of the Earls of Pembroke for over 400 years; superb 17th century state rooms by Inigo Jones; dolls houses and model soldiers, adventure playground and a model railway.
☎ 0722 743115
On the A30 west of Salisbury
P 🚍 ✗ ♿ ♿

Museums

Museum of Army Flying
Many historic aircraft on display.
Middle Wallop
➔A A343
P 🛈 ✗

Salisbury and South Wiltshire Museum
The story of Stonehenge and Early Man; the history of the area; archaeological treasures.
The Close, Salisbury
☎ 0722 332151

Music, Dance and Drama

There are a considerable number of musical events throughout the year including organ recitals, Saturday morning concerts, orchestral concerts, opera, chamber music, singers, live bands and pub music. For a detailed list of events contact: The Library, Salisbury Cathedral or the Tourist Office.

Parks

Paultons Park
Wide range of activities available including fun park and wildlife.
Ower, Romsey, Hampshire
☎ 0703 814442

Theatres

Salisbury Playhouse
☎ 0722 20333

Salisbury Arts Centre
☎ 0722 21744

OUTDOOR LEISURE

Cycling

Wiltshire Cycleway
160 miles of cycle routes through glorious landscape.
i Leaflet from the Tourist Information Centre.

Hayballs
Rollestone Street, Salisbury
☎ 0722 411378

Fishing

John Eadie Sports
Catherine Street, Salisbury
☎ 0722 28535
☎ 0722 335585 after hours

Golf

High Post Golf Club ⛳₁₈
Includes leisure club facilities.
Great Durnford, Salisbury
☎ 072273 356
➔A A345

Walking

i Guided tours of Salisbury from the Tourist Information Centre.

SEDGEFIELD

County: Durham
i Market Place, Durham City
☎ 091 384 3720
i The Dolphin Centre, Market Place, Darlington
☎ 0325 382698
Market day: Friday, Saturday (Durham) Monday, Saturday (Darlington)
Population: 4500

Sedgefield is known as a village but is in fact a small market town. The church has dominated the Green for seven hundred years and the Bishops have been landlords dominating the town of Sedgefield for even longer. Set in the midst of County Durham, between Darlington and Durham, this is the land of the Bishop Princes who once had the power and independence normally held only by a king. The limestone cliffs of the coastline and the Pennine Moors offer a range of pleasures to suit all tastes within easy reach.

ADVENTURE

Multi-activity Centres

Hudeway Centre
For families, groups and individuals; canoeing, windsurfing, abseiling, riding, caving, orienteering.
Hudegate Farm East, Middleton-in-Teesdale, Barnard Castle
☎ 0833 40012

EQUESTRIAN

Riding and Pony Trekking

High Pennine Rides
Brook Villa, The Green, Lanchester, Durham
☎ 0207 521911

Hoppyland Trekking Centre
Hoppyland Farm, Hamsterley, Bishop Auckland
☎ 038 888 617

LOCAL FEATURES

Architecture

Bowes Castle
12th century stone keep built on the site of a Roman Fort.
On the A67, 4 miles west of Barnard Castle
🏛

Egglestone Abbey
Ruined late 12th century abbey; nearby is a fine mediaeval pack-horse bridge.
Off the A67 1½ miles south-east of Barnard Castle
🏛 &

Art Galleries

Darlington Art Gallery
Crown Street, Darlington
☎ 0325 462034

Gardens

Durham College of Agriculture and Horticulture
Gardens are used as training grounds for students; questions answered at a gardening clinic.
On the A177, 1 mile south-east of Durham
☎ 091 386 1351
P 🏛 🚌 &

Durham University Botanic Gardens
Hollingside Lane
☎ 091 374 2671
➜A A1050
P 🏛 🚌 ✕ & &

Eggleston Hall Gardens
Eggleston village
☎ 0833 50378
South of Eggleston Village
P 🏛 🚌 ✕ &

Heritage

Binchester Roman Fort
Notable Roman military bath-suite.
Bishop Auckland
☎ 0388 663089
1 mile north of Bishop Auckland
P 🏛 🚌

Historic Buildings

Auckland Castle
Principal country residence of the Bishops of Durham since Norman times; magnificent chapel built from the ruins of the 12th century banqueting hall in 1665.
Bishop Auckland
☎ 091 386 4411 ext 2698
🏛 🚌 &

Barnard Castle
Norman stronghold, extensively renovated, includes Bowes Museum which has an important art collection.
☎ 0833 38212
🏛

Durham Castle
The Norman castle of the Prince Bishops of Durham founded in 1072; now a conference and banqueting centre.
Durham City
☎ 091 374 3800
P 🏛 🚌

Rokeby Park
Palladian style country house with a unique collection of 18th century needlework pictures.
Barnard Castle
☎ 0833 37334
On the A66 between A1(M) and Bowes
P 🏛 🚌

SEDGEFIELD

WHAT TO DO AND SEE

Museums

Beamish, North of England Open Air Museum
A top tourist attraction; vivid reconstruction of Northern life in the early 1900s.
4 miles west of Chester le Street
☎ 0207 231811
➔A A1(M)
P 🎁 ✗ 🚻 ♿

Parks

Hardwick Hall Country Park
18th century landscaped park with lake.
Sedgefield
➔A A177

Railways

Darlington Railway Centre and Museum
Historic engines 'Locomotion' and 'Derwent' are displayed.
North Road Station, Darlington
☎ 0325 460532
➔A A167 north of town centre
P 🎁 🚌 🚻 ♿

Fishing

Northumbrian Water own 11 reservoirs operated as fisheries.
Contact the Recreation Dept, Northumbrian Water, Abbey Road, Pity Me, Durham City
☎ 091 384 4222

Golf

All 21 courses in the county welcome visitors.

Walking

The Durham Dales offer a wide range of walking opportunities including the long-distance Pennine Way.
Information from the County Environment Department's guided walk programme.
☎ 091 386 4411

SOUTHWELL

County: Nottinghamshire
i The Ossington, Castlegate, Newark
☎ 0636 78962
Early closing: Wednesday
Market day: Saturday
Population: 7000

Southwell is a small market town in an attractive belt of Nottinghamshire countryside. Southwell Minster with its magnificent spires dominates the town. The rich heritage of the area is reflected in its association with many famous events and names. The Saracen's Head, the town's oldest inn, is where Charles I gave himself up to the Scots in 1646. Lord Byron's mother lived in Burgage Manor, facing the Green. Robin Hood's forest home, once a huge, ancient, royal hunting forest is now encompassed in the 450 acre Sherwood Forest Country Park.

A region of rich variety, farmland and forests, market towns and mining communities to explore and appreciate.

LOCAL FEATURES

Arts and Crafts

Church Farm Craft Workshops
Mansfield Road, Edwinstowe, nr Sherwood Forest Visitor Centre
P 🏠 ✗

Festivals and Fairs

April–October
International Antique and Collectors Fair, 3 Apr, 5 Jun, 14 Aug, 23 Oct.

July
Robin Hood Festival, 20–29 July

Fun Park

Center Parcs, Sherwood Forest
Award-winning holiday village set in hundreds of acres of woodland. Swimming; golf; riding; walking; cycling and watersports. Self-contained villas and evening entertainment.
Rufford, Newark
☎ 0623 411411

Historic Buildings

Kelham Hall
Victorian mansion set in 42 acres of gardens and parkland.
Newark
☎ 0636 605111
✗

Newark Castle
12th century ruined castle, overlooks the River Trent.
Castle Gate, Newark
☎ 0636 79403
🏠

Southwell Minster
The 12th century Minster, with its world famous foliage carvings and three Norman towers, dominates the small town.
Church Street, Southwell
☎ 0636 812649
➜A A612
P 🏠 🚌

EQUESTRIAN

Riding and Pony Trekking

Trent Valley Riding and Holiday Centre
Tanyard Farm, Westgate, Southwell
☎ 636 813588

HEALTH

Leisure Centres

Southwell Leisure Centre
Pool, sauna and solarium.
Nottingham Road, Southwell
☎ 0636 813000
➜A A612

Museums

Vina Cooke Museum of Dolls and Bygone Childhood
The history of dolls from 1750–1950 featuring doll's houses and dolls in wood, wax, porcelain and plastic.
The Old Rectory, Cromwell, nr Newark
☎ 0636 821364
Off the A1, 6 miles north of Newark
P ✗

Millgate Folk Museum
48 Millgate, Newark
☎ 0636 79403
🏠

SOUTHWELL

WHAT TO DO AND SEE

Newark Air Museum
Collection of American and European jet fighters and bombers.
The Airfield, Winthorpe
☎ 0636 707170
Off the A46, north-west of Newark
P ♿

Natural History

Laxon Visitor Centre
Exhibition of mediaeval strip farming.
Laxton village, on a minor road 6 miles east of Ollerton
☎ 0777 871586

Sherwood Forest Farm Park
Rare breeds collection.
Lamb Pens Farm, Edwinstowe
☎ 0623 822255
Between Old Clipstone and Warsop, 2 miles west of Edwinstowe
P ✗ ♿

White Post Farm Centre
Modern working mixed farm, lakeside picnic area, no dogs, kennels provided.
Farnsfield
☎ 0623 882977
On the A614, 12 miles north of Nottingham
P ✗

Parks

Clumber Park
3800 acre 18th century landscaped park.
Nr Worksop
☎ 0909 476592

Rufford Country Park
25 acre lake, woodland walks, picnic areas, craft centre and sculpture gardens.
Rufford
☎ 0623 824153
On the A614, 2 miles south of Ollerton
✗

Sherwood Forest Country Park
Ancient royal hunting forest where Robin Hood and his band are said to have gathered by the **Major Oak** – a huge hollow 400-year-old oak tree. 450 acre park with marked trails, picnic areas, a nature trail for the blind and a visitor centre.
Rufford Mill
☎ 0623 823202
Off the B6034 nr Edwinstowe
P ⌂ ✗

OUTDOOR LEISURE

Fishing

Coarse Fishing
Day tickets for the Trent can be purchased on the bank for most Newark Federation waters. Contact:
John Garland, Secretary
58 Riverside Road, Newark
☎ 0636 702962

Newark Angling Centre (Tackle shop)
29 Albert Street
☎ 0636 77055

Golf

Newark Golf Club ⛳18
Visitors welcome weekdays only.
Coddington, Newark
☎ 0636 626282

Oxton Golf Course ⛳18
Visitors welcome, advance booking required.
Forest Farm, Oaks Lane, Oxton, Nottingham
☎ 0602 653545

WATERSPORTS

Boat Trips

Green's Passenger Cruisers
☎ 0636 706479

Lock and Castle Line
Lock Entry Cottage, Castlegate
☎ 0636 707939

STRATFORD-UPON-AVON

WHAT TO DO AND SEE

County: Warwickshire
i Tourist Office, High Street
☎ 0789 293127
☎ 0789 67522
Early closing: Thursday
Market day: Friday
Population: 23,000

Stratford-upon-Avon, a lovely old market town, is the birthplace of Shakespeare and has become a world famous tourist centre. Holy Trinity Church, Shakespeare's burial place, his birthplace, Ann Hathaway's cottage and the world famous Royal Shakespeare Theatre are all easily found on foot. Stratford itself and many olf the small 'wool' towns of the Cotswolds such as Chipping Camden offer excellent shopping and accommodation. The gentle, green countryside of Warwickshire, seemingly untouched by time, provides wooded walks and many river bank picnic spots.

AERIAL SPORTS

Ballooning
Heart of England Balloons
Champagne flights.
Cross Lanes Farm, Walcote, nr Alcester
☎ 0789 488219

Gliding
Avon Soaring Centre
Bidford Airfield
☎ 0789 772606

EQUESTRIAN

Riding and Pony Trekking
Pathlow Riding Centre
Pathlow
☎ 0789 292451

HEALTH

Leisure Centre
Bridgefoot Leisure Centre
Tennis, squash, pool, sauna and sun beds.
Bridgefoot, town centre
☎ 0789 67751

LOCAL FEATURES

Arts and Crafts
Brass Rubbing Centre
The Summer House, Avonbank Gardens, Waterside
☎ 0789 297671
Just beyond the Royal Shakespeare Theatre

Festivals and Fairs
April
Shakespeare's Birthday Celebrations

July
Stratford Arts Festival

October
Mop Fair

Guided Tours
Guide Friday
Guided tours of the Shakespeare properties and surrounding area.
14 Rother Street
☎ 0789 294466

Historic Buildings
Charlecote Park
The Lucy family's home since 1247, the present house dates from 1550.
☎ 0789 840277
5 miles east of Stratford
P ✕ ♿

Bagley Hall
A Palladian manision owned by the Marquess of Hertford, many attractions.
Alchester
☎ 0789 762090
→A A435
P 🚌 ✕ ♿

Shakespeare Trust Properties
Reduced charge tickets are available for those intending the visit the following 5 properties:

Shakespeare's Birthplace
Childhood home of the playwright; furnished in period style.
Henley Street
☎ 0789 204016
→A A34 (town centre)
🚌

Ann Hathaway's Cottage
A thatched farmhouse, early home of Shakespeare's wife.
Shottery
☎ 0789 292100
1 mile from the town centre
P 🚌 ✕

STRATFORD-UPON-AVON

Mary Arden's House
Farmhouse home of Mary Arden,
Shakespeare's mother.
Wilmcote
☎ 0789 293455
On the A34, 3 miles out of Stratford
P 🚌 ✕ ♿

New Place
Local history museum and gardens at the
site of Shakespeare's last home. Adjacent is
Nash's House, home of Shakespeare's
grand-daughter.
Chapel Street
☎ 0789 292325
➤A A439 (town centre)
🚌

Hall's Croft
A Tudor house occupied by Shakespeare's
elder daughter.
Old Town
☎ 0789 292107
➤A A439 (town centre)
🚌

Natural History

Butterfly Farm
Swan's Nest Lane
☎ 0789 299288
➤A A422/A34 (town centre)

Parks

Broadway Tower Country Park
Panoramic views; animals, nature trails,
picnic areas, and an adventure playground.
Broadway
➤A A44
✕

Theatres

Royal Shakespeare Theatre
Home of the world-famous Royal
Shakespeare Company.
Waterside
☎ 0789 295623
➤A A34/A46 (town centre)
P 🚌
♿ Seats available with able-bodied escort
(Specify when booking)

Swan Theatre
Jacobean style theatre with a permanent
theatrical exhibition.
Waterside
☎ 0789 295623
➤A A34/A46

Fishing

Coarse Fishing
Day tickets and tackle available from:
The Avon Pet Store, 37 Greenhill Street
☎ 0789 292778

The Old Mill Fisheries
Anglers lake.
Clifford Chambers
☎ 0789 295389
A34, 2 miles south of Stratford

Golf

Stratford Golf Club ⛳
Welcomes weekday visitors by arrangement.
Tiddington Road
☎ 0789 205749
➤A A34

Stratford Oaks Golf Club ⛳
Bearley
☎ 0789 731571
➤A A34

Welcombe Hotel ⛳
Private course and hotel.
Warwick Road
☎ 0789 295252

Walking

Rambers Association
Contact:
J. A. Smith, No 3 Preston-on-Stour,
Stratford-upon-Avon.

Short Walks
ℹ Detailed publications available from the
Tourist Office.

Boat Hire

River Avon
Rowing boat, canoe, motor boat hire, and
short sightseeing trips on barges.

TAUNTON

County: Somerset
i Taunton Tourist Information Centre,
The Library, Corporation Street
☎ 0823 274785
Early closing: Thursday
Market day: Saturday
Population: 50,000

Taunton, the county town of Somerset is a thriving and historic market town well known for its cider industry. Its restored Norman castle was, in 1685, the scene of Judge Jeffrey's Bloody Assizes, the trial of over 500 supporters of the Duke of Monmouth; it is now a museum open to the public. Taunton became a centre for textile manufacture in the 13th century and still has a lively craft community. It is an excellent centre from which to explore the beautiful Somerset countryside.

ADVENTURE

Multi-activity Centres

Taunton Summer School
Over 50 summer courses in arts, sports and special interests, age range 7–70, full board available.
Taunton School, Staplegrove Road
☎ 0823 276543

AERIAL SPORTS

Ballooning

Taunton Hot Air Balloon Co. Ltd.
60 Bridge Street, Taunton
☎ 0823 333137

EQUESTRIAN

Riding and Pony Trekking

Curland Equestrian Enterprises
Crosses Farm Stud, Curland
☎ 046034 234

HEALTH

Leisure Centres

Taunton Pools
Station Road, Taunton
☎ 0823 284108

LOCAL FEATURES

Arts and Crafts

Aller, The Pottery
Bryan and Julia Newman, The Pottery, Aller, Langport
☎ 0458 250244
On the A372, 2 miles north of Langport

E. J. Hill & Son Basketmakers
Unit 10–12, Wireworks Estate, Bristol Road, Bridgwater
☎ 0278 424003
On the A38 nr Bridgwater

Willow Craft Industry
P. H. Coates & Son, Meare Green Court, Stoke St Gregory, nr Taunton
☎ 0823 490249
➔A A361/A378
🚌

Festivals and Fairs

October
Taunton's traditional Cider Barrel Race and Carnival Procession, third Saturday in October.

November
Bridgwater Carnival, the Thursday nearest 5th November

Food and Drink

Perry Brothers Cider Mills
Museum, shop and traditional farmhouse cider.
Dowlish Wake, Ilminster
☎ 0460 52681
On the A303 and the A30, 2 miles from Ilminster
P ♿ ♿

Sheppys Cider
Three Bridges, Bradford on Tone, Taunton
☎ 0823 461233
On the A38 between Taunton and Wellington

Gardens

Hestercombe House Gardens
Designed by Sir Edwin Lutyens and Miss Gertrude Jekyll.
Cheddon Fitzpaine
☎ 0823 337222
➔A A361
P 🏠 🚌

Tintinhull House Garden
Modern formal garden with borders and ponds.
☎ 0935 822509
South of the A303, 5 miles north-east of Yeovil
P 🏠

Guided Tours

Guided Tours of Taunton
Louise Murrell, Spyspot, Staplehay, Taunton
☎ 0823 331527

Historic Buildings

Barrington Court
A model estate and farm buildings complex designed to support a large Tudor manor house. Estate trail and farm exhibition.
☎ 0460 40601
Off the A303, 5 miles north-east of Ilminster
P 🏠 🚌 ♿ ♿

179

TAUNTON

Brympton D'Evercy House
House, gardens and vineyard.
Brympton Estate Office, Yeovil
☎ 0935 862528
→A A30
P 🏠 🚌 ✕ ♿

Combe Sydenham Manor Hall
Elizabethan house with gardens, deer park,
waymarked walks, trout ponds, fly fishing
and childrens play area.
Monksilver, nr Taunton
☎ 0984 56284
Off the B3188
P 🏠 🚌 ✕

Gaulden Manor
Tolland, Lydeard St Lawrence
☎ 09847 213
Off the B3188
P 🏠 🚌 ✕

Lyte's Cary Manor and Gardens
Mediaeval manor house and chapel of local
stone, with an excellent garden.
Charlton Mackrell, Somerton
☎ 04582 23297
On the A38, 4 miles north of Ilchester
P 🏠 🚌

Montacute House
16th century house with an H-shaped
houseplan, surrounded by a formal garden
and landscaped park.
☎ 0935 823289
South of the A3088, 4 miles west of Yeovil
P 🏠 🚌 ♿

Museums

Hornsbury Mill and Museum of Bric-a-Brac
Chard
☎ 04606 3317
P 🏠 ✕ ♿ ♿

Somerset County Museum
Taunton Castle
☎ 0823 275893
P 🏠 🚌

Somerset Cricket Museum
Priory Avenue, Taunton
☎ 0823 275893

Natural History

Widcombe Bird Gardens
Culmhead, Blagdon Hill
☎ 082342 268
Off the B3170
P 🏠 ✕ ♿

Parks

Exmoor National Park
600 miles of public footpaths in this area of
wild moorland and deep wooded combes.
Exmoor House, Dulverton, Somerset
☎ 0398 23665

Railways

West Somerset Railway
Britain's longest preserved railway.
The Railway Station, Minehead
☎ 0643 704996
→A A39
P 🏠 ✕

Theatres

Brewhouse Theatre and Arts Centre
Coal Orchard, Taunton
☎ 0823 283244

Cycling

Taunton Holiday Cycle Hire
Bridgwater Road, Bathpool, Taunton
☎ 0823 73016
On the A38 at Bathpool

Fishing

Detailed fishing information may be
obtained from:
Area Fisheries and Recreation Officer
Wessex Rivers, King Square, Bridgwater
☎ 0278 457333

Golf

Vivary Park and Golf Course ⛳
Ideal for the serious golfer and beginner
alike. Walks, playgrounds, tennis, putting,
gardens and wildlife.
Vivary Park, Taunton
☎ 0823 333875

Skiing

Wellington Sports Centre
Corams Lane, Wellington
☎ 082347 3010

Tennis

Vivary Park
Book at Golf Course
☎ 0823 333875

Walking

For information on walking in the
Quantock Hills, telephone the Warden.
Fyne Court, Broomfield, Bridgwater
☎ 082345 526
P ⛳ ✕

Boat Trips

Trips on the 'IWA Ruby' on the Bridgwater
and Taunton Canal.
Mr & Mrs Rymell, Crewkerne
☎ 0460 72509

Windsurfing

Windsurfing Centre
13 Upper High Street, Taunton
☎ 0823 251729

THIRSK

County: North Yorkshire
i Thirsk Tourist Office, 14 Kirkgate
☎ 0845 22755
Early closing: Wednesday
Market day: Monday
Population: 7000
Thirsk is a traditional, Yorkshire market town with a cobbled square and coaching inns. An area set between the North York Moors and the Yorkshire Dales and crossed by many great Yorkshire rivers, this is excellent walking country offering the visitor a wide range of accommodation and interest.

AERIAL SPORTS

Gliding
Yorkshire Gliding Club
Sutton Bank, Thirsk
☎ 0845 597237

EQUESTRIAN

Riding and Pony Trekking
Bedale Riding Centre
Exelby Road, Bedale
☎ 0677 24891
On the B6285, 1 mile from Bedale

Belle Vue Farm Riding Centre
Fullicar Lane, Brompton, Northallerton
☎ 0609 774719
Off the A684 Northallerton to Teeside road, nr Brompton village

Boltby Pony Trekking Centre
Johnstone Arms, Boltby
☎ 0845 537392

Over Stilton Riding and Trekking Centre
North Cottage, Over Stilton, Thirsk
☎ 060983 344
Off the A19, 7 miles north of Thirsk

HEALTH

Leisure Centres
Hambleton Leisure Pool
Wave pool with chute.
Northallerton
☎ 0609 779977

LOCAL FEATURES

Arts and Crafts
Clark Farm
A small-scale dairy farm producing yoghurt and ice-cream.
Aiskew, Bedale
☎ 0677 22125

Treske Furniture
Furniture workshop, craftsmen at work.
Station Road, Thirsk
☎ 0845 22770

Gardens
Thorp Perrow Arboretum
Nr Snape, Bedale
☎ 0677 22480
Off the B6268, 2 miles south of Bedale

Historic Buildings
Newburgh Priory
Founded in 1145 by the Augustinian order and reputedly the burial place of Oliver Cromwell, it is now a private family home.
Coxwold
☎ 03476 435
Off the A19 Thirsk to Easingwold road
P 🚌 ✗ ♿

Rievaulx Abbey
Beautiful monastic ruins.
Rievaulx, nr Helmsley
☎ 04396 228
Off the B1257, 3 miles north-west of Helmsley
P ♿

THIRSK

Shandy Hall
The home of Laurence Sterne, author of
Tristam Shandy between 1760–67; walled
gardens.
Coxwold
☎ 03476 465
Off the A19 Thirsk to Easingwold road
P 🚌

Sion Hill Hall
Neo-Georgian country house; large
collection of furniture and paintings.
Kirby Wiske, Thirsk
☎ 0845 587206
Off the A167, 4 miles north-west of Thirsk
P 🚌 ✕

Museums

Thirsk Museum
Cricket memorabilia, James Herriot's
original manuscripts housed in the
birthplace of Thomas Lord, founder of
Lord's Cricket Ground.
16 Kirkgate
☎ 0845 22755
➔A A61/A19 (town centre)

Thirsk Bird Museum
87b Market Place
☎ 060983 362
➔A A19 (town centre)

OUTDOOR LEISURE

Cycling
The Cycle Centre
Kirkgate
☎ 0845 23248

Park House Outdoor Centre
☎ 0845 567435
☎ 060982 571

Fishing

Thirsk Anglers Centre
Specialists in coarse, game and sea tackle.
Tuition in fly fishing.
Sowerby Road, Thirsk
☎ 0845 24684

Low Osgodby Lake
Mr Fawcett, Alma House, Low Osgodby,
Thirsk
☎ 0845 597601

Golf

Bedale Golf Club ⛳
Leyburn Road, Bedale
☎ 0677 22451

Easingwold Golf Club ⛳
Stillington Lane, Easingwold
☎ 0347 21964

Thirsk and Northallerton Golf Club ⛳
Non-members welcome on weekdays.
Thornton-le-Street, Thirsk
☎ 0845 22170

Tennis

Courts for hire at Bedale.
i Details from the Tourist Office, Bedale
Hall

Walking

North York Moors Information Centre
Sutton Bank 2 mile nature trail.
Sutton Bank, nr Thirsk
☎ 0845 597426

Cleveland Way
Join the Cleveland Way long-distance
footpath.

County: Northamptonshire
i Towcester Library
☎ 0327 50794
Population: 5000
Towcester, built on Watling Street, has sections of the Roman town of Lactodorum still visible as well as some fine Victorian and Georgian buildings. The 13th century church of St Lawrence has an interesting collection of chained books.

The nearby Silverstone Motor Racing Circuit hosts the British Grand Prix every year.

EQUESTRIAN

Riding and Pony Trekking

Holdenby Riding School
Holdenby, Northants
☎ 0604 770003
Off the A50/A428
P

LOCAL FEATURES

Gardens

Castle Ashby
Parkland landscaped by Capability Brown, Victorian gardens and lakes surrounding an Elizabethan mansion.
Yardley Hastings
☎ 060 129 234
Off the A428 at Castle Ashby village
P 🏠 🚌 ♿

Coton Manor Gardens
Old English garden, 17th century manor house.
Coton
☎ 0604 740219
Off the A50 nr Guilsborough village
P 🏠 ✕ ♿

Holdenby House Gardens
Remains of a large Elizabethan garden; Charles I's prison after the battle of Naseby in 1645; small museum, rare breeds, falconry.
☎ 0604 770786
Off the A50/A428 at Holdenby village
P 🏠 🚌 ✕ ♿ ♿

Historic Buildings

Althorp House
The 16th century home of the Earl Spencer, the father of the Princess of Wales. Some fine paintings, porcelain and rare French and English furniture.
☎ 0604 770209
On the A428 nr Harlestone
P 🏠 🚌 ✕ ♿

Cannons Ashby House
A 15th century manor house, once home to the Dryden family; Elizabethan wall paintings, Jacobean plasterwork, small park and gardens.
Blakesley
☎ 0327 860044
Off the B4525 at Canons Ashby village
P 🏠 ✕ ♿ ♿

TOWCESTER

WHAT TO DO AND SEE

Sulgrave Manor
Tudor manor house.
☎ 029576 205
Off the B4525 at Sulgrave village
P 🏠 🍴 ✕ 🚻

Museums

Abington Museum
Former 15th century manor house which
houses the museum of Northamptonshire
Regiment and Northamptonshire Yeomanry.
Fire fighting equipment, furniture, pottery,
porcelain and displays of childrens toys.
Northampton
☎ 0604 31454
Off the A45 in Abington Park
🏠

Central Museum and Art Gallery
Unique collection of footwear through the
ages, paintings, and ceramics; museum of
leathercraft nearby.
Guildhall Street, Northampton
☎ 0604 39415
Town centre
🏠 🚻 🚻

Stoke Bruerne Waterways Museum
200 years of life on the canals and
waterways.
Stoke Bruerne, Towcester
☎ 0604 862229
Off the A508 in Stoke Bruerne village
P 🏠 🍴 ✕ 🚻 🚻

Turner's Musical Merry-go-Round
Collection of mechanical musical
instruments; fairground and carousel.
Queen Eleanor Vale, Newport Pagnell Road,
Wootton
☎ 0604 763314
Off the A508, nr Wootton village
Admission by booking
P 🏠 🚻 🚻

Natural History

Old Dairy Farm Craft Centre
Working farm with craft centre.
Weedon
☎ 0327 40525
Off the A5 in Upper Stowe village
🏠

Parks

Billing Aquadrome
Swimming, boating, fishing, pleasure park,
amusements, watermill and milling
museum.
Northampton
☎ 0604 408181
Off the A45, nr Cogenhoe village
P 🏠 ✕ 🚻 🚻

Theatres

The Royal Theatre
Northampton
☎ 0604 24811
☎ 0604 32533

OUTDOOR LEISURE

Fishing

Pitsford Water
Reservoir with trout fishing and boats for
hire.
☎ 0604 781350
Off the A508 nr Holcot village

Anglian Water
Rod licences.
Oundle Division, North Street, Oundle
☎ 0832 73701

WATERSPORTS

Boat Hire

UK Waterway Holidays Ltd
Welton Hythe, Daventry
☎ 0327 843773

UTTOXETER

County: Staffordshire
i Town Hall, King Edward Square,
Burton on Trent
☎ 0283 45454
Early closing: Thursday
Market day: Wednesday (livestock and street)
Population: 10,000
Uttoxeter, an historic market town, lies in the richly scenic countryside of the Vale of Trent with forests and picturesque villages, heathland and historic towns to explore. Alton Towers, a popular fun park, is also within easy reach.

EQUESTRIAN

Riding and Pony Trekking

Hilltop Farm Riding Stables
Hilltop Farm, Main Road, Anslow, Burton on Trent
☎ 00283 520024

HEALTH

Leisure Centres

Uttoxeter Leisure Centre
Swimming pool, sports hall, squash courts.
Oldfields Road, Uttoxeter
☎ 0889 562844

LOCAL FEATURES

Architecture

Croxden Abbey
Founded in 1176 for Cistercian monks; a fine west front still stands with walls 40 feet high.
Croxden
Off the A50, 3 miles north-west of Uttoxeter
🏛

Art Galleries

Stafford Art Gallery and Craft Shop
Leading Midlands gallery for crafts and contemporary visual arts.
Lichfield Road, Stafford
☎ 0785 57303
🏛

Factory Visits

Tutbury Crystal Glass Ltd
Burton Street, Tutbury, Burton on Trent, Staffs
☎ 0283 813281
P 🏛

Wedgwood Visitor Centre
Museum, art galleries and crafts people at work.
Barlaston, nr Stoke-on-Trent, Staffs
☎ 0782 204141
☎ 0782 204218
P 🏛 ⛐

Festivals and Fairs

April–May
Burton on Trent Competitive Festival of Music and Drama

July
Burton Regatta and Riverside Show
Uttoxeter Carnival

August
Burton Carnival, Bank Holiday Monday

September
Burton Beer Festival

Guided Tours

Deetours
Guided tours of the Vale of Trent
Cathedral View, 9 Beacon Street, Lichfield
☎ 0543 255086

Village Tours
Don Coxon, 1 Marston Lane, Rolleston-on-Dove, Burton on Trent
☎ 0283 814470

Heritage

Uttoxeter Heritage Centre
Restored 17th century timber framed building with local history exhibitions.
34–36 Carter Street, Uttoxeter
☎ 08893 67176
🏛 🚌 ⛐

Historic Buildings

Sudbury Hall
Richly decorated Charles II house, formerly belonging to the Lords Vernon.
Sudbury, Derby
☎ 028378 305
Off the A50, 6 miles east of Uttoxeter
🏛 ✕ ⛐

Shugborough
18th century mansion house, ancestral home of Lord Lichfield; county museum, working farm museum and restored mill, beautiful gardens and parkland with neo-classical monuments.
Milford, nr Stafford
☎ 0889 881388
➔A A513
P 🏛 🚌 ✕ ⛐ ♿

Tutbury Castle
Ruined 15th century stronghold, twice the prison of Mary Queen of Scots.
Tutbury, Staffs
☎ 0283 812129
On the A50, 4 miles north-west of Burton on Trent
P 🏛 🚌 ✕ ⛐ ♿

UTTOXETER

Museums

Bass Museum
Visitor Centre, Shire Horse Stables and museum of the history of Bass, brewing and beer.
Horninglow Street, Burton on Trent
☎ 0283 45301
➔A A50
P 🏠 🚌 ♿ ♿

Heritage Brewery Museum
Working brewery museum.
Angelsey Road, Burton on Trent
☎ 0283 69226
➔A A5121
P 🏠 🚌 ♿ ♿

Puppet Theatre Museum
Edinburgh House, Bagot Street, Abbots Bromley
☎ 0283 840348
Off the B5013
🏠 🚌 ✗ ♿

Natural History

Fisher Pit Rare Breeds Open Farm
Abbots Bromley, nr Rugeley
☎ 0283 840204
On the B5234, 1 mile east of Abbots Bromley

Parks

Branston Water Park
40-acre lake used by anglers, windsurfers and model boaters.
Nr Burton on Trent
☎ 0283 45454 (amenities manager)
➔A A38

Alton Towers
Top leisure park.
Alton, Staffs
☎ 0538 702200
On the B5032, signposted from the M1/M6
P 🏠 🚌 ♿ ♿

Birdwatching and Wildlife

JCB Lakes and Nature Reserve
42 acres of landscaped lakes.
Rochester, nr Uttoxeter

Fishing

Angling on the Rivers Trent and Dove, the Trent and Mersey Canal in Branston Water Park and Blithfield Reservoir near Abbots Bromley.

Golf

Uttoxeter Golf Club ♟18
Wood Lane, Uttoxeter
☎ 0889 564884

Skiing

Swadlincote Ski Centre
Hill Street, Swadlincote, nr Burton
☎ 0283 217200

Walking and Rambling

The Staffordshire Way
A long distance footpath that spans the county of Staffordshire.

The Johnson Trail
Starting in Lichfield and designed so that the visitor can join or leave it at convenient points along its 260 miles.
i Details from the Tourist Information Centre.

WARWICK

County: Warwickshire
i The Court House, Jury Street, Warwick
☎ 0926 492212
Early closing: Thursday
Market day: Saturday
Population: 22,000

Warwick, situated on the River Avon, is dominated by the magnificent castle of the Earls of Warwick. A small market town, existent since Norman times, it has several mediaeval buildings and sections of the old walls that survived a great fire in 1694. The tall tower of Collegiate College of St Mary's dominates the skyline, it houses the beautiful Beauchamp Chapel. A very inviting and attractive town to visit and explore.

EQUESTRIAN

Riding and Pony Trekking

Warwick School of Riding
Guy's Cliffe, Coventry Road
☎ 0926 494313

LOCAL FEATURES

Festivals and Fairs

July
Royal Show, 2–5 July
Arts Festival, 5–15 July

October
Mop Fair, mid-October
follows on from Stratford-upon-Avon

Historic Buildings

Coventry Cathedral
A masterpiece of modern architecture designed by Sir Basil Spence in 1962 next to the cathedral bombed and ruined during World War II.

Kenilworth Castle
Dramatic Civil War ruin.
Kenilworth
☎ 0926 52078
Off the B4103
P

Lord Leicester Hospital
A home for military veterans, founded in 1571 by Robert Dudley, the Earl of Leicester.
High Street, Warwick
☎ 0926 494122
→A A46 (town centre)
P ⛙ ✕

Packwood House
Timber-framed Tudor house; collections of tapestry, needlework and furniture; yew garden. National Trust.

Stoneleigh Abbey
Georgian mansion linked to a 16th century manor house in park and gardens landscaped by Repton. Playground, model railway and nature trail.
Stoneleigh village
☎ 0926 52116
Off the B4115
P ⛙ ✕ ♿
Note: Abbey currently closed for redevelopment

Upton House
Dates from 1695; a fine private art collection, Brussels tapestries, 18th century furniture, Sèvres porcelain and Chelsea figures, gardens, a lake and a ha-ha.
Edgehill, nr Banbury
☎ 029587 266
On the A422, 1 mile south of Edgehill, 7 miles north-west of Banbury
P ⛙ ✕

Warwick Castle
A fine mediaeval castle set in 60 acres of grounds with a mediaeval dungeon, torture chamber, armour collection, the Madame Tussaud's waxworks, river and woodland walks.
Warwick
☎ 0926 495421
→A A41
P ⛙ ✕ ♿

Museums

County Museum
The history of Warwickshire, a branch at St John's House, Coten End features folk life, crafts and costumes.
Market Place
☎ 0926 410410
Town centre
🗹

Doll Museum
Dolls, toys and bygones.
Castle Street
☎ 0926 495546
Town centre
🗹

OUTDOOR LEISURE

Golf

Warwick Municipal Golf Course ⛳9
Open only when there are no race meetings as access crosses the course.
☎ 0926 494316

Newbold Comyn Municipal Course ⛳18
Leamington Spa
☎ 0926 21157

Tennis

Courts to hire at St Nicholas Park, close to the river.

WETHERBY

County: West Yorkshire
i Tourist Office, Council Offices,
24 Westgate
☎ 0937 62706
Early closing: Wednesday
Market day: Thursday
Population: 9500
Wetherby, an attractive and historic market town, was mentioned in the Domesday Book as Wedrebi. It acts as the business centre for the surrounding farming district and still holds a weekly market first chartered in 1240. The many old inns remind the visitor of Wetherby's past importance as a staging post stop on the old Great North Road.

The Wharfe and Washdale valleys offer superb scenery to the walker and motorist with Plumpton Rocks, a renowned beauty spot, being within reach of the town.

EQUESTRIAN

Riding and Pony Trekking

Dairy Farm Riding Stables
Sicklinghall
☎ 0937 62262

HEALTH

Leisure Centres

Wetherby Swimming Pool and Health Suite
Pool, sauna, sunbeds, gym.
The Ings
Town centre
☎ 0937 65125

LOCAL FEATURES

Festivals and Fairs

April/May
Wetherby Agricultural Show (Whit Tuesday)
Otley Agricultural Show

Historic Buildings

Bramham Park
Queen Anne house with 66 acre French Baroque garden, Versailles on a smaller scale. Host to the International Horse Trials in June.
☎ 0937 844265
→A A1
P 🚐

Harewood House
Family home of the Earl and Countess of Harewood; fine Chippendale furniture and works of art, magnificent grounds, adventure playground, garden centre, bird garden and tropical rain forest exhibition.
Harewood, nr Leeds
☎ 0532 886225
On the A61 Harrogate road, 5 miles from Wetherby
P 🚐

Stockeld Park
Palladian villa by James Paine in attractive gardens with childrens play area.
Wetherby
☎ 0937 62376
→A A661
P 🚐 ✕ ♿

Parks

Golden Acre Park
76 acres of gardens.
→A A660
✕

Mother Shipton's Historic Park
Part of the ancient Forest of Knaresborough; riverside walks, petrifying well (where cascading water turns everyday objects into stone) and Mother Shipton's cave.
The High Bridge, Knaresborough
☎ 0423 864600
P ✕ ♿

OUTDOOR LEISURE

Birdwatching and Wildlife

Stainburn Gate
Bird sanctuary and forest park by Lindley Wood reservoir.

Swinsty Reservoir
Bird sanctuary and fishing.

Fishing

Coarse fishing
The rivers Wharfe, Nidd and their tributaries are well stocked with trout and coarse fish. Contact:
Wetherby Angling Club
☎ 0937 62171

Boston Spa Angling Club
☎ 0937 842664

Golf

Wetherby Golf Club ▶18
Linton Lane
☎ 0937 63375

Skiing

Harrogate Ski Centre
Ski centre and dry slope.
Yorkshire Showground, Hookstone Wood Road, Harrogate
☎ 0423 505457
☎ 0423 505458
→A A661
P ✕

WATERSPORTS

Boat Hire

River Wharfe
Rowing boats for hire.

WINCANTON

WHAT TO DO AND SEE

County: Somerset
i The Library, 7 Carrington Way,
    Wincanton
☎ 0963 32173
Early closing: Thursday
Population: 3600
Wincanton, a thriving market town, was once an important staging post on the London–Plymouth coach route. The market place has many fine 18th century hotels and coaching inns, reminders of this era; there are several fine Georgian buildings also.

AERIAL SPORTS

Ballooning

Somerset Balloon Safaris
Wheathill
☎ 096 324 468

Hang Gliding

British Hang Gliding Association
Damian Robinson
☎ 0303 68052

EQUESTRIAN

Riding and Pony Trekking

Folly Field Stables
Parsonage Lane, Charlton Musgrove
☎ 0963 32103

Pevlings Farm
Cabbage Lane, Charlton Musgrave
☎ 0963 70990

HEALTH

Leisure Centres

Gillingham Leisure Centre
Swimming pool, sports hall, squash and badminton.
☎ 0747 82206

LOCAL FEATURES

Festivals and Fairs

June
Castle Cary Street Market

August
Wincanton Horse Show

Gardens

Hadspen Garden and Nursery
Sheltered 8 acre garden with rare plants in an 18th century setting.
Hadspen House, Castle Cary
☎ 0963 50200
→A A371
P 🛏 🚐 ✕ 🚹 🚺

Heritage

Cadbury Castle
Iron Age Fort site covering 18 acres with extensive views.
6 miles south-west of Wincanton

Historic Buildings

Cutterne Mill
17th century working watermill, craft shop and rural museum.
Evercreech, Shepton Mallet
→A A371
P 🛏 🚐 ✕

Longleat House

Elizabethan House, important libraries and Italian ceilings. Safari Park
Warminster
☎ 09853 551
→A A362
P 🛏 🚐 ✕ 🚹 🚺

Sherborne Castle
16th century castle, home of the Digby family since 1617.
Sherborne, Dorset
☎ 0935 813182
On the A30, 5 miles east of Yeovil
🛏 ✕

Stourhead House and Garden
18th century house, Chippendale and Younger furniture; exotic garden.
Stourton, nr Mere, Wiltshire
☎ 0747 840348
Off the B3092
P 🛏 🚐 🚹 🚺

Museums

Haynes Sparkford Motor Museum
A collection of classic, veteran and vintage motor cars and motor cycles; motoring memorabilia.
Sparkford, nr Yeovil
☎ 0963 40804
→A A359
P 🛏 🚐 ✕ 🚹 🚺

WINCANTON

Castle Cary and District Museum
The Market House, Castle Cary
☎ 0963 50277
→A A371
P 🛝 🚌

Railways

East Somerset Railway
Replica of a Victorian engine shed, 9 steam
engines, historic coaches, wagons, a
standard gauge steam railway, museum and
art gallery.
The Station, Cranmore, Shepton Mallet
→A A361
P 🏠 🚌 ✕

Zoos

Lions of Longleat
Safari park, boat trips on the lake, wild
animals on view including the only white
tigers of Britain.
Warminster, Wiltshire
☎ 09853 328
→A A362
P 🏠 ✕ ♿ ♿

Cycling

i The Tourist Information Office publish a
leaflet *Cycling in South Somerset* which
gives routes, places to see, places to stay
and cycle repair shops in this lovely cycling
county.
Mr B Hockey
Torbay Road, Castle Cary
☎ 0963 50559

Yeovil Cycle Centre
8–10 South Western Terrace, Yeovil
☎ 0935 22000

Fishing

i The local Tourist Information Office
issues leaflets on the local rivers and
reservoirs. Wincanton is well placed for
access to river salmon, trout and coarse
fishing.

Stourhead and Gasper
For bream and coarse fish. Licences at the
entrance to Stourhead Gardens.
Mr Trussler Bourton
☎ 2984 300

Redlynch Lake
10 acre lake renowned for carp fishing.
Mrs H. N. Heal, Redlynch Farm, Redlynch,
nr Bruton
☎ 0749 2235081
Off the B3081, north of Wincanton

Rod Licence Distributor
Petfood Stores,
47a High Street, Wincanton

Golf

Sherborne Golf Club ⛳
Higher Clatcombe, Sherborne
☎ 0935 814431

Dry–Slope Skiing

Yeovil Ski Centre
Addlewell House, Ninesprings, Yeovil
☎ 0935 21702

Tennis

Horsington House Hotel
Horsington, Templecombe
☎ 0935 70721

Holbrook House Hotel
Castle Cary Road, Wincanton
☎ 0963 32377

Walking

i Booklets on walks in and around
Wincanton are available from the Tourist
Information Office, as is a *Town Trail*.
Organised walks are arranged at various
times:
Mr H. Craig
☎ 0749 812491

Ramblers Association
Mr H. Dowers
☎ 0460 30443

WOLVERHAMPTON

County: West Midlands
i 18 Queen Square, West Midlands
☎ 0902 312051
Early closing: Thursday
Market day: many excellent markets in the area
Population: 260,000

Wolverhampton lies in the heart of the Black Country, an area rich in industrial heritage. Traditional crafts can still be seen at work in a variety of different industries, including glass making, leather, lock making and enamels. There are canals to explore on narrowboats, museums to visit, an excellent zoo and numerous markets where you can browse through everything from Victorian artefacts to modern porcelain. Nearby the visitor will find some marvellous countryside and some outstanding pubs – the Black Country is famed for its beer and its humour.

AERIAL SPORTS

Ballooning

Heart of England Balloons
Cross Lanes Farm, Walcote, nr Alcester, Warks
☎ 0789 488219

EQUESTRIAN

Riding and Pony Trekking

Sandwell Valley Riding Centre
Wigmore Farm, Wigmore Lane, West Bromwich
☎ 021 588 2103

HEALTH

Leisure Centres

Bilston Leisure Centre
Swimming, solarium, squash and snooker.
Prouds Lane
☎ 0902 353836

LOCAL FEATURES

Art Galleries

Bilston Art Gallery and Museum
Displays 18th century painted enamels and pottery; exhibitions by leading local artists.
Mount Pleasant, Bilston
☎ 0902 409143
🖾 ⛓

Wolverhampton Art Gallery
British and American Pop Art; displays of local history and major exhibitions.
Lichfield Street
☎ 0902 312032
🖾 ✕ ⛓

Arts and Crafts

Wyvern
Crystals, minerals, natural gemstones, stones, jewellery and gifts.
5 Polly Brooks Yard, Pedmore Road, Lye Cross, Stourbridge

Factory Visits

Mushroom Green Chainshop
Restored chainmaking workshop c.1860, demonstrations.
Mushroom Green, Quarry Bank, Dudley
☎ 021 557 9643
☎ 0384 67411 (evenings)
🖾

Royal Doulton Crystal
Webb Corbett Glassworks, Coalbourn Lane, Amblecote, Stourbridge
☎ 0384 440442
🖾 🚌

Stuart Crystal
Famous Redhouse Cone, museum shop and glass repair service.
Redhouse Glassworks, Wordsley
☎ 0384 71161
On the A491, 1½ miles north of Stourbridge
🖾 🚌 ✕

Food and Drink

Many Black Country pubs were established in the 19th century in any building available near to the factories. Beer was usually brewed on the premises and small independent breweries still remain, producing "real ales". Among the best known are 'The Old Swan' at Netherton, 'Daniel Batham' at Brierley Hill, 'Holdens' of Dudley and 'Holts' of Oldbury. Famous Black Country Pubs include 'The Vine' at Brierley Hill, the 'Glynne Arms' or 'Crooked House' at Gornal Wood, 'The Old Swan' or 'Ma Pardoes' at Netherton, the magnificent 'Waterloo Inn' at Smethwick and the 'Royal Exchange' at Bilston. Many pubs are popular venues for local comedians and musicians.

Historic Buildings

St Peters Church
Standing on the site of the ancient monastery of St Mary, the church dominates the centre of the town. The Anglo-Saxon cross in the grounds is a surviving monument to the times of Lady Wulfruna's Charter in 985 which led to the naming of the town "Wulfrun Hampton".

Wightwick Manor
This house is a notable example the work of William Morris, with many original wallpapers, fabrics and Pre-Raphaelite works of art; fine gardens, a pottery studio and antiquarian bookshop.
Wightwick Bank
☎ 0902 761108
🕀

WOLVERHAMPTON

WHAT TO DO AND SEE

Museums

Bantock House Museum
19th century house, parkland; displays of 18th century English enamels and Midland japanned wares, dolls, toys and Worcester porcelain.
Bantock Park, Finchfield Road
☎ 0902 312132
🏠 &

Natural History

Cotwall End Nature Centre
Catholic Lane, Sedgley, Dudley
☎ 09073 74668
➔A A459
🏠 ✕

Parks

Valley Park
A rural pathway and park developed from the disused Kingswinford branch railway; includes the towpath of the nearby canal.
Off Tettenhall Road, Compton Road or Castlecroft Road
☎ 0902 744736 for ranger service
🏠 & &

West Park
Victorian Park, two lakes, a conservatory, bandstand, extensive floral displays, tennis courts and other amenities.
Park Road East/Park Road West
🏠

Railways

Severn Valley Railway
Britain's premier steam railway it runs from Bridgnorth to Kidderminster.

The Railway Station, Bewdley, Wolverhampton
☎ 0299 403816
☎ 0299 401001

Theatres

Grand Theatre
Lichfield Street
☎ 0902 714775

Zoos

Dudley Zoological Gardens and Castle
Mediaeval castle ruins; 40 acres of woodlands and gardens, amusement park and chairlift.
2 The Broadway, Dudley
☎ 0384 52401
➔A A459
🎁 ✕

OUTDOOR LEISURE

Golf

Himley Hall Golf Centre 🏌
Himley
☎ 0902 895207

WATERSPORTS

Boat Hire

Dudley Tunnel Trips Limited
Electric narrowboat trips through the man-made caverns under Dudley Castle Hill.
Unit 44, High Street, Tipton
☎ 021 5205321
🎁 ✕

WORCESTER

WHAT TO DO AND SEE

County: Hereford and Worcestershire
i Guildhall, High Street,
  Worcester
☎ 0905 723471
Early closing: Thursday
Population: 75,500
Worcester, an ancient riverside city, proudly bears the title of "the faithful city" for its loyalty to the King during the Civil War. Elgar's statue looks towards the lovely cathedral from the High Street and just beyond is the Guildhall with its magnificent Queen Anne facade. Several streets contain fine half-timbered buildings, particularly Friar Street. Worcester is famous for its Royal Worcester Spode porcelain factory and its famous spicy sauce.

EQUESTRIAN

Riding and Pony Trekking

Hallow Mill Equestrian Centre
Hallow, nr Worcester
☎ 0905 640373

HEALTH

Leisure Centres

Worcester Swimming Pool and Fitness Centre
Swimming pool, Turkish baths, saunas, sunbeds and fitness room.
Sansome Walk, Worcester
☎ 0905 20241
🏠

The Splash
A complete tropical resort with wave machines and water slides.
Priory Park, Malvern
☎ 0684 893423
✗ ⴕ ⴕ

LOCAL FEATURES

Art Galleries

Dysom Perrins Museum
A collection of Royal Worcester porcelain from 1751.
Severn Street, Worcester
☎ 0905 23221
➔A A44
P 🏠 ⴕ

Factory Visits

Royal Worcester Spode
Complete factory tours; factory shop with seconds.
☎ 0905 23221
🚌

Festivals and Fairs

March
Spring Music Festival

August
Worcester Entertains Festival
☎ 0905 723471
Three Choirs Festival

Gardens

Spetchley Park
30 acre garden, collection of rare trees, shrubs and plants.
Worcester
☎ 090565 213
➔A A422
P 🏠 ✗ ⴕ

Guided Tours

The Faithful City Guides
Guided walks in the city start from the Guildhall.
☎ 0905 726311

Historic Buildings

Guildhall
Restored 18th century building of distinction.
High Street, Worcester
☎ 0905 723471
🏠 ✗

Hanbury Hall
Wren style red brick house built in 1701, with outstanding painted ceilings.
Hanbury
☎ 052784 214
Off the B4090/B4091
P 🏠 🚌 ⴕ ⴕ

Hartlebury Castle State Rooms
15th and 18th century restored castle, home of the Bishop of Worcester. Great Hall, chapel and library; Hereford and Worcester County Museum.
Hartlebury
☎ 0299 250410
➔A A449
🏠 🚌 ✗ ⴕ

Little Malvern Court
14th century Prior's Hall once attached to a 12th century Benedictine Priory; fine paintings, furniture and needlework.
Malvern
☎ 0684 892988
➔A A4014
P 🏠 🚌 ✗

Museums

The Commandery
A 15th century timbered building by the canals, the Royalist headquarters in the Battle of Worcester; audiovisual display on the Civil War.
Sidbury
☎ 0905 355071
➔A A422
P 🚌 ✗ ⴕ

WORCESTER

Elgar's Birthplace
Original manuscripts and photographs
displayed.
Lower Broadheath, nr Worcester
☎ 090566 224
→A A44
P 🚌

Tudor House Museum
Social and domestic history of Worcester,
period room settings.
Friar Street, Worcester
☎ 0905 20904
🚻 ♿

Worcester Museum and Art Gallery
Local geology, prehistory and natural
history.
Foregate Street, Worcester
☎ 0905 25371
🚻 ✗ ♿

Parks

Worcester Woods Country Park
Activities and countryside centre in 100
acres of broad leaved woodland.
County Hall, Spetchley Road, Worcester
☎ 0905 350770
→A A422
P 🚻 🚌 ✗ ♿ ♿

Theatres

The Swan
21 Sansome Street, Worcester
☎ 0905 27322

OUTDOOR LEISURE

Cycling

Cadence Cafe Cycle Hire
Platform 1, Foregate Street Railway Station,
Worcester
☎ 0905 613501
Worcester (city centre)

Golf

Tolladine Golf Club 🏌
Tolladine Road, Worcester
☎ 0905 21074

Worcester Golf and Country Club 🏌
No public at weekends.
Broughton Park, Branstard Road, Worcester
☎ 0905 422044

**Worcester Golf Range/Pitch and Putt
Course**
Weir Lane, Worcester
☎ 0905 421213

Walking and Rambling

Worcester Town Trail
A "behind the scenes" tour of the historic
landmarks of Worcester.
i Details available from the Tourist
Office.

The Wychavon Way
A 40 mile waymarked walk through
attractive countryside stretching from Holt
Fleet in Worcestershire to Winchcombe in
the Cotswolds.
i Route available from the Tourist Office.

WATERSPORTS

Boat Hire

Viking Afloat Ltd
Narrowboat hire.
Lowesmoor Wharf, Lowesmoor Terrace,
Worcester
☎ 0905 28667

Seaborne Yacht Company Ltd
Narrowboat hire.
Court Meadow, Kempsey
☎ 0905 820295

GREAT YARMOUTH

County: Norfolk
i Marine Parade, Great Yarmouth, Norfolk
☎ 0493 842195
i Town Hall, Great Yarmouth, Norfolk
☎ 0493 846345
☎ 0493 846344
Early closing: Thursday
Market day: Wednesday, Friday (summer only), Saturday
Population: 87,000
Great Yarmouth, an interesting and historic market town and port is also a major holiday centre and touring base for the Norfolk Broads. It has 15 miles of soft, white sandy beach and a wide variety of events, holiday attractions and sporting activities to offer the visitor. There are wildlife parks, stately homes, castles, gardens and archaeological sites to explore in the surrounding East Anglian countryside.

EQUESTRIAN

Riding and Pony Trekking
Hillcrest Riding School Ltd
Filby Heath, Great Yarmouth
☎ 0493 730394

HEALTH

Leisure Centres
Marina Leisure Centre
Marine Parade, Great Yarmouth
☎ 0493 851521
Open daily from 10am
P 🏠

LOCAL FEATURES

Architecture
Berney Arms Windmill
Tall, late 19th century marsh windmill accessible only by boat or rail from Vauxhall station.
Halvergate Marshes
☎ 0493 700605
3 miles west of Great Yarmouth
🏠

Nelson's Monument
144 feet high monument, built in 1819.
☎ 0493 855746
🏠

Art Galleries
Museum Exhibition Galleries
Modern galleries with changing programmes.
Central Library, Tolhouse Street, Great Yarmouth
☎ 0493 858900

Festivals and Fairs
July
Carnival Week

October/November
St Andrew's Festival

Gardens
Fairhaven Garden Trust
Woodland and water gardens, 174 acres including private Inner Broad and Bird Sanctuary.
South Walsham
☎ 060549 449
On the B1140, 13 miles west of Great Yarmouth
P 🏠 🚌 ✕ ⚹ ⚹

Fritton Lake and Gardens
Old-world gardens and 2 mile long lake. Boats for fishing and rowing, windsurfing school, childrens assault course, pitch and putt, wildfowl reserve.
☎ 0493 488208
Off the A143, 6 miles south-west of Great Yarmouth
P 🏠 ⚹ ⚹

Historic Houses
Anna Sewell House
A 16th century cottage, the birthplace of the authoress of *Black Beauty*.
26 Church Plain
☎ 0493 850437
➜A A12/A47
P

Old Merchant's House
17th century dwelling, with three other houses renovated as examples of small town houses and Greyfriars Cloisters.
Row 111, South Quay, Great Yarmouth
☎ 0493 857900
➜A A149
🏠 🚌

Somerleyton Hall and Gardens
Mansion in Anglo-Italian style with Tudor-Jacobean origins. Maze and miniature railway.
Off the B1074, 8 miles south-west of Great Yarmouth
☎ 0502 730224

Museums
Caister Castle Car Collection
Largest collection of motor vehicles in the country.
West Caister
3 miles north of Great Yarmouth
P 🏠 ✕ ⚹ ⚹

Elizabethan House Museum
Toys, games, china and civic plate.
4 South Quay, Great Yarmouth
☎ 0493 855746
➜A A47
🏠

GREAT YARMOUTH

WHAT TO DO AND SEE

Maritime Museum for East Anglia
Historic shipwrecked sailors' home
containing models, paintings, and other
local maritime history items.
Marine Parade Central, Great Yarmouth
☎ 0493 842267

Strumpshaw Hall Steam Museum
A collection of working steam vehicles
including steam wagon and beam engine.
Off the A47, 13 miles from Great Yarmouth
☎ 0603 714535

Tolhouse Museum
Once a courthouse and gaol, with original
dungeons. Now the museum of local history
and a brass rubbing centre.
Tolhouse Street, Great Yarmouth
☎ 0493 858900

Natural History

Butterfly Farm
Marine Parade
☎ 0493 842202

Parks

The Bygone Village
40 acres of park and woodland with railway,
adventure playground, working steam
exhibits and craft centre, music from
Compton organ, farm animals and pets'
paddock.
Burgh Hall Estate, Fleggburgh
☎ 0493 369770
On the A1064, 7 miles from Great
Yarmouth

Pleasurewood Hills American Theme Park
Pay once to choose from over 60 free rides.
☎ 0502 513626
Off the A12 at Corton, 8 miles south of
Great Yarmouth

Theatres

Britannia Theatre
The Pier, Great Yarmouth
☎ 0493 842914

Hippodrome Circus
St George's Road, Great Yarmouth
☎ 0493 844172

Gorleston Pavilion
Pavilion Road, Gorleston
☎ 0493 662832

Royalty Theatre
Marine Parade, Great Yarmouth
☎ 0493 842043

St George's Theatre
Deneside, Great Yarmouth
☎ 0493 858387

Wellington Theatre
Wellington Pier, Great Yarmouth
☎ 0493 844945

Zoos

Suffolk Wildlife and Rare Breeds Park
Selection of animals set in 70 acres of
parkland.
☎ 0502 740291
On the A12, 11 miles south of Great
Yarmouth

Thrigby Hall Wildlife Gardens
Collection of Asian mammals, birds and
reptiles.
Filby
☎ 0493 369477
Off the A1064, 7 miles from Great
Yarmouth

OUTDOOR LEISURE

Birdwatching and Wildlife

Breydon Water Nature Reserve
Guided walks are organised in the season.
Access from Haven Bridge or North Bridge

Broadland Conservation Centre
A floating gallery for birdwatching moored
at Ranworth.
Inner Broad. Norfolk Naturalists' Trust
☎ 060549 479
Off the B1140, 15 miles west of Great
Yarmouth

Horsey Mere
Extensive reed beds; migratory birds and
winter wildfowl. National Trust.
Horsey, 11 miles north of Great Yarmouth

North Beach
Successful RSPB breeding colony of little
terns.
Opposite Iron Duke Public House

Winterton Dunes
National Conservancy Council.
Winterton, 8 miles north of Great Yarmouth

Cycling

Lawfords
224 Northgate Street, Great Yarmouth
☎ 0493 842741

Fishing

The Broads, Fritton Lake and the sandy
beaches provide good fishing. Permits from:
National Rivers Authority, Aqua House,
London Road, Peterborough
Information from: National Rivers
Authority, 79 Thorpe Road, Norwich,
Norfolk
☎ 0603 662800

GREAT YARMOUTH

WHAT TO DO AND SEE

Fishing Trips
Bishop Boat Services, 48 Warren Road,
Gorleston, Great Yarmouth
☎ 0493 664739

Mr Dyble
13 St Margaret's Way, Fleggburgh, Great
Yarmouth
☎ 0493 369582 (after 6pm)

Mr L Read
17 Wellington Road, Great Yarmouth
☎ 0493 859653

Golf

The Great Yarmouth and Caister Golf
Club ⌐18
Yarmouth Road, Caister-on-Sea, Great
Yarmouth
☎ 0493 720421

Gorleston Golf Club ⌐18
Warren Road, Gorleston
☎ 0493 662103

Tennis

Hard courts on the promenade at Great
Yarmouth and cliffs at Gorleston; grass
courts at Gorleston.

Dinghy Sailing

Great Yarmouth and Gorleston Sailing Club
Merlin-Rockets, Ospreys, 505s, Javelins and
Lasers. Class racing.

Yacht Cruising

Norfolk Sailing Centre
Trips or lessons among the nature reserves.
31 Riverside, Martham
☎ 0493 653597

Sea Cruises

Haven Cruiser
Mr K. Duffy, 13 Highfield Road, Gorleston,
Great Yarmouth
Daily, south side Britannia Pier

Glenda Margaret
Mr D Wells, 105 North Denes Road,
Great Yarmouth
Daily, north side Britannia Pier

Windsurfing

Fritton Lake Country Park
Great Yarmouth
Tuition and hire.
Peter Leggett
☎ 0493 488378

YORK

County: North Yorkshire
i De Grey Rooms, Exhibition Square, York
☎ 0904 621756
Population: 125,000

York is an exceptionally beautiful cathedral city, and the ecclesiastical capital of the Church of England. The city is still surrounded by the original walls and is one of Europe's best preserved mediaeval cities, the Minster has some spectacular mediaeval stained glass. "The Shambles", York's famous street of butchers, dates back over 1000 years. A fascinating city in which to wander, it is also a modern city with an international range of shops, good entertainment and sports facilities.

AERIAL SPORTS

Gliding

Rufforth Gliding Club
Rufforth Airfield, York
☎ 090483 694
On the B1224 York to Wetherby road, 5 miles west of York

EQUESTRIAN

Riding and Pony Trekking

Moor House Riding Centre
Surron Road, Wigginton
☎ 0904 769029

Naburn Grange Riding Centre
Naburn, nr York
☎ 090487 283
Off the A19, 4 miles south-west of York

Tenthorne Farm
Knapton, nr York
☎ 0904 798130
3 miles from York

LOCAL FEATURES

Art Galleries

York City Art Gallery
European and British painting spanning seven centuries.
Exhibition Square
☎ 0904 623839

Festivals and Fairs

May
Early Music Festival, York

Guided Tours

Qualified guides take free daily walking tours starting from the Exhibition Square throughout the year.

Yorktour
Sightseeing tours both of the city and surrounding area (Whitby and Castle Howard, Fountains Abbey, Yorkshire Dales and Herriot Country) book through the Tourist Information Centre, hotels and guest houses. All coaches non-smoking. Private guides also available.
3 St Sampson's Square
☎ 0904 641737

Historic Buildings

Beningbrough Hall
Fine Baroque house with collection of paintings on loan from the National Portrait Gallery; Victorian kitchen; adventure playground. National Trust.
Shipton-by-Beningbrough
☎ 0904 470666
Off the A19 York to Thirsk road, 8 miles north-west of York
✗

Castle Howard

Thousands of acres of parkland with a plant centre, rose gardens and nature walks.
☎ 065384 333
Off the A64, 15 miles north-east of York
✗

Fairfax House
Fine town house with 18th century furniture and clock collection.
Castlegate
☎ 0904 655543
City centre

Harewood House
Leeds
20 miles west of York

Newby Hall
Nr Ripon
20 miles north-east of York

Ripley Castle
Ripley
24 miles west of York

YORK

WHAT TO DO AND SEE

Sutton Park
Attractive Georgian house with Chippendale, Sheraton and French furniture; Capability Brown gardens; woodland walks.
Sutton-on-the-Forest
☎ 0347 810249
On the B1363, 8 miles north of York
✗

York Minster
The largest mediaeval cathedral in northern Europe.

Museums

Jorvik Viking Centre
Visitors sit in 'time cars' and are whisked back 1000 years in history to witness sight, sound and smell reconstructions of the city of Jorvik (Viking name for York); displays of archaeological artefacts.
Coppergate
☎ 0904 643211
&

National Railway Museum
Display covering 150 years of British railway history.
Leeman Road
☎ 0904 621261
P &

Rail Riders World
Model railway recreates the modern British rail scene over an area of 2000 sq ft.
York Station
☎ 0904 30169
City centre

Yorkshire Museum
Displays of Roman, Anglo Saxon, Viking and mediaeval treasures of Britain; wildlife gardens.
Museum Gardens
☎ 0904 629745

York Castle Museum
Popular museum of everyday life; exhibition of children's games and toys.
Kirkgate
☎ 0904 653611
✗

Theatres

York Theatre Royal
Georgian theatre, opened in 1740 offers a varied programme.
✗

OUTDOOR LEISURE

Cycling

Cycle Scene
2 Ratcliffe Street, Burton Stone Lane
☎ 0904 653286

York Cycleworks
14–16 Lawrence Street
☎ 0904 626664

Auto Discount Cycling Tours
Touring holidays organised.
Ings Vie, Shipton Road
☎ 0904 30692

Fishing

Local fishing tackle shops can provide information on fishing in the Ouse and other rivers.

Golf

Fulford (York) Golf Club ⚑₁₈
Visitors welcome by prior arrangement.
Heslington Lane
☎ 0904 413579

Heworth Golf Club ⚑₉
Visitors welcome except Sun mornings.
Muncastergate, Malton Road
☎ 0904 422389

Pike Hills Golf Club ⚑₁₈
No visitors at weekends.
Tadcaster Road, Copmanthorpe
☎ 0904 708756

Walking

40 miles of dramatic upland scenery stretches across to the Yorkshire coast, for information on North York Moors contact:

National Park Visitor Centre
Town Hall, Market Place, Helmsley
☎ 0439 70173

WATERSPORTS

Boat Hire and Trips

Castle Line Cruises
Skeldergate Bridge
☎ 0836 739357

Hills Boatyard
Lendal Bridge
☎ 0904 623752

White Rose Line
King's Staith
☎ 0904 628324

Chester Racecourse

HORSE RACING

THE FAMILY LEISURE GUIDE

Thank you for buying this Guide, we hope that it has proved informative, colourful and enjoyable to use.

Our researchers are constantly up-dating their files both on the **courses** and the **leisure listings**. If there are any major leisure facilities that you feel should be included in future editions of this Guide please write to:

The Editor
The Family Leisure Guides
Whitwell Chambers
Ferrars Road
Huntingdon
Cambridgeshire
PE18 6DH

Please give us the name and address or telephone number of the leisure facility so that we can contact them for further information.

Do also write to us to let us know if there is any new feature or additional information you would like to see included either under the **courses** or in the **leisure listings** of future editions of this Guide.

If you have found this Guide has helped you to enjoy a sporting break then you will be pleased to know that we are publishing further Guides in the same series covering other popular sporting and leisure activities. Please look out for them!

CROWN CLASSIFICATION

Your Sign of Confidence

Over 16,000 hotels, guesthouses, motels, inns, B&Bs and farmhouses throughout England, Scotland and Wales are now inspected by the tourist boards each year. Those that are found to meet our standards are given the official endorsement of a Crown classification.

The classification given depends on the range of facilities and services provided. There are six classification bands: 'Listed' and from One to Five Crown. The more Crowns, the wider the range of facilities and services.

Specified requirements are laid down for each classification band. For example, all bedrooms in a One Crown establishment—be it a farmhouse, B&B or hotel—will have a washbasin in the room or in a private bathroom and a light controlled from the bed. In a Four Crown establishment you will always find a TV, radio and telephone in your bedroom and a lounge service until midnight at least. Whilst in a Five Crown establishment all bedrooms will have an en suite bathroom with both bath and shower and there will be a comprehensive range of services.

All Crown classified places to stay are clean, well-maintained and provide comfortable accommodation. Those that have been found to offer higher quality standards are distinguished by the term Approved, Commended or Highly Commended alongside their classification.

A Listed or One Crown B&B or guesthouse may still be Commended or even Highly Commended if its facilities and services, although limited in range, are provided to a high quality standard.

The Crown classifications - and the quality commendations - are designed to help you find places to stay that match your needs and pocket. We believe that if you are happy with your accommodation you will be happy with your holiday. You can be confident in the accommodation that carries our sign.

CORAL

A comprehensive service - wherever you are!

Credit Betting

With a Coral Credit betting account, CORAL offer you the widest range of betting opportunities even on a Sunday!

A simple telephone call puts you in touch with our specially trained team, always on hand to provide you with:

- The very best personal attention

- The widest variety of betting opportunities combined with great value

- Fast efficient transactions

SPORTING BREAKS

- over 130 golf courses
- sports and leisure pursuits around the courses
- places to visit in each area
- location maps and a colour atlas

Combine a round of golf with a weekend break
or short holiday for all the family

£9.95 from all major bookshops

English Tourist Board
Quality Books & Guides

Where To Stay

(1991 series) Best-selling England guides to: *Hotels & Guesthouses* £6.95, *Bed & Breakfast, Farmhouses, Inns & Hostels* £5.95. *Self-Catering Holiday Homes* £4.95. Also in the *Where to Stay* series: *Camping & Caravan Parks in Britain* £4.95. With descriptions of towns, comprehensive indexes, maps and features on the English regions. (Available January 1991).

Let's Do It!

(In association with William Curtis Ltd.) Hundreds of ideas for holidays and breaks in England. Discover new interests or improve existing skills - from action and sport, study courses, special interests, holidays afloat and children's holidays. (Price £2. 95)

Visit Britain at Work

(In association with Visitor Publications.) A unique guide to hundreds of fascinating workplaces to visit from breweries and broadcasting studios to piano workshops and power stations. (Price £2.95)

Hotels & Guesthouses and *Bed & Breakfast, Farmhouses, Inns & Hostels* feature the national Crown ratings. The classifications, from Listed to ⌂⌂⌂⌂⌂ indicate the range of facilities and services. Those offering higher quality standards have the term APPROVED, COMMENDED or HIGHLY COMMENDED alongside the classification.

All the holiday homes featured in the *Self-Catering Holiday Homes* guide are inspected by the tourist boards. The classifications to indicate the range of facilities and equipment provided. Those offering higher quality standards have the term APPROVED, COMMENDED or HIGHLY COMMENDED alongside the classification.

Camping & Caravan Parks in Britain gives details of the national British Graded Holiday Parks Scheme. Parks participating in the scheme are graded from 1-5 ✓ symbols according to the relative quality of what is offered.

Journey Through Britain

(In association with Ravensburger Fisher-Price.) Have fun getting to know Britain with this family game. A race through Britain's towns and cities answering questions based on places of interest. Beautifully illustrated. (Price £12.99 from all good toyshops)

Stay On A Farm

(In association with the Farm Holiday Bureau UK and William Curtis Ltd.)
Official guide to nearly 1,000 farms in membership of the Farm Holiday Bureau. All inspected and approved by the national tourist boards. Accommodation includes B&B, half-board, self-catering. Enjoy the countryside from the unique hospitality of a working farm. (Price £4. 50)

The Countryside Directory

(In association with Sphere and The Royal Agricultural Society of England.) From farming museums to pick your own fruit and vegetable farms, agricultural shows to afternoon teas - whatever you need to know about countryside activities. (Price £4.99)

Let's Go!

(1990-91edition)The English Tourist Board's free guide to short breaks throughout England. Take advantage of reduced rates at hundreds of hotels from autumn 1990 to summer 1991. *Let's Go!* is available FREE from most Tourist Information Centres.

Home From Home

(1990-91edition) The English Tourist Board's new guide to hundreds of self-catering holiday homes in England open from October 1990 to March 1991. Available FREE from most Tourist Information Centres.

For the best choice in books on England, look for the English Tourist Board logo.

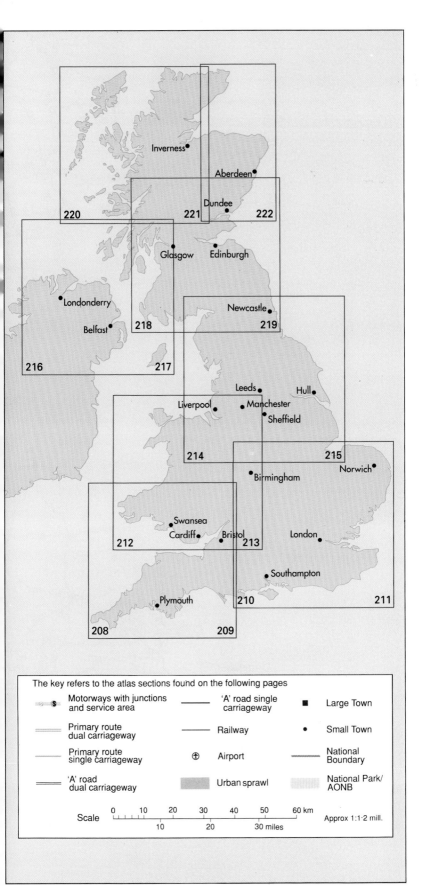

The key refers to the atlas sections found on the following pages

Motorways with junctions and service area	'A' road single carriageway	Large Town
Primary route dual carriageway	Railway	Small Town
Primary route single carriageway	Airport	National Boundary
'A' road dual carriageway	Urban sprawl	National Park/ AONB

Scale
0 10 20 30 40 50 60 km
10   20   30 miles

Approx 1:1·2 mill.

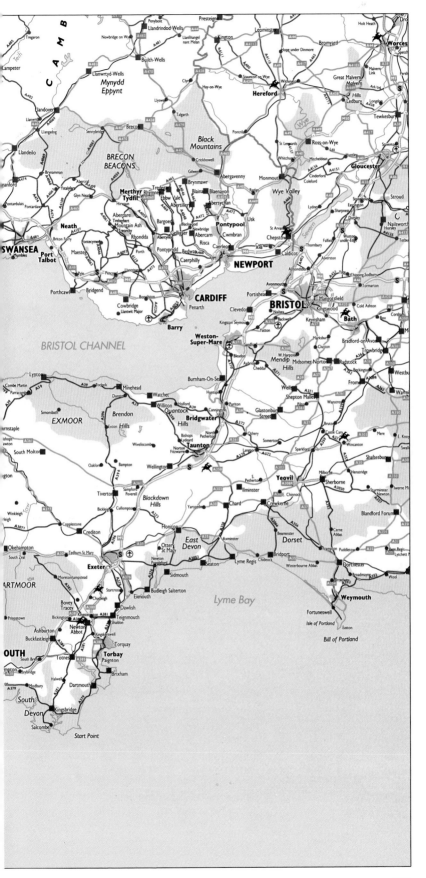

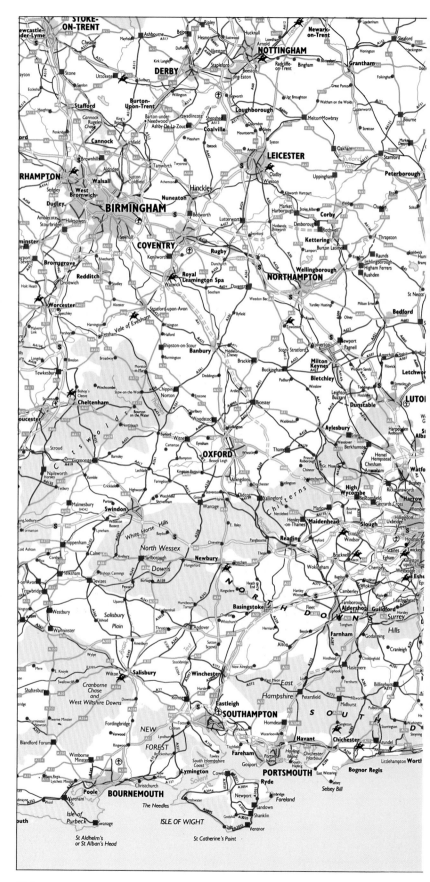

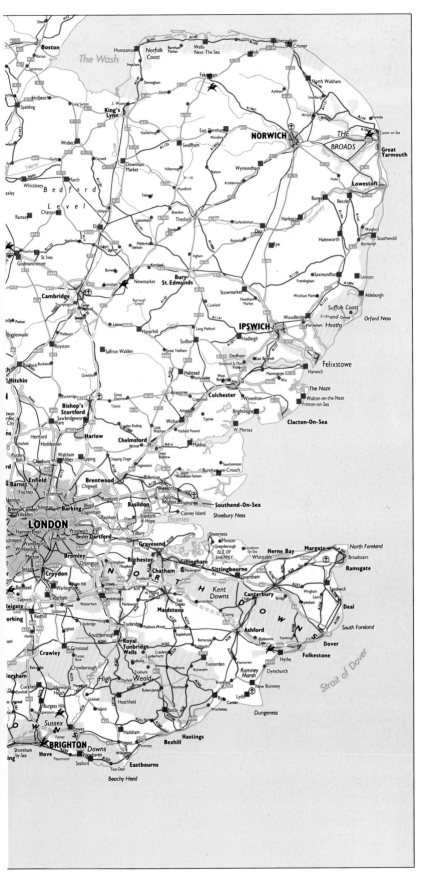

211

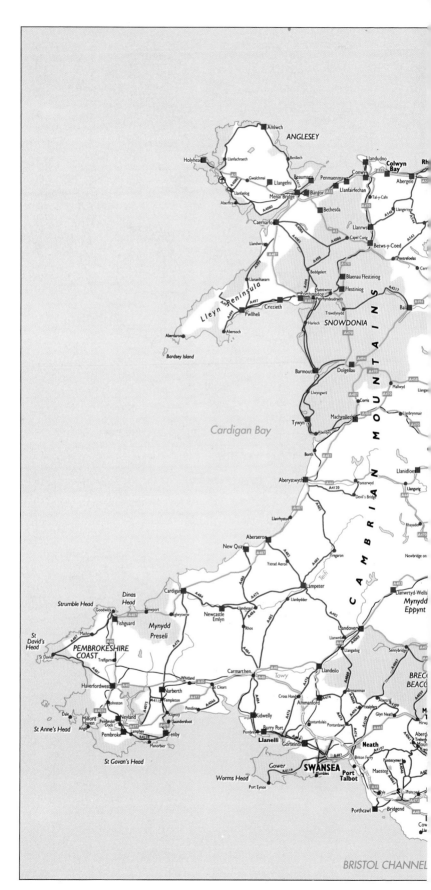

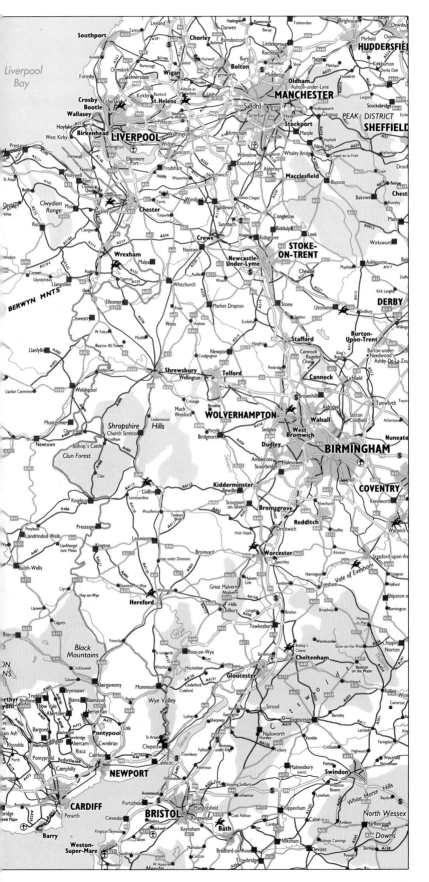

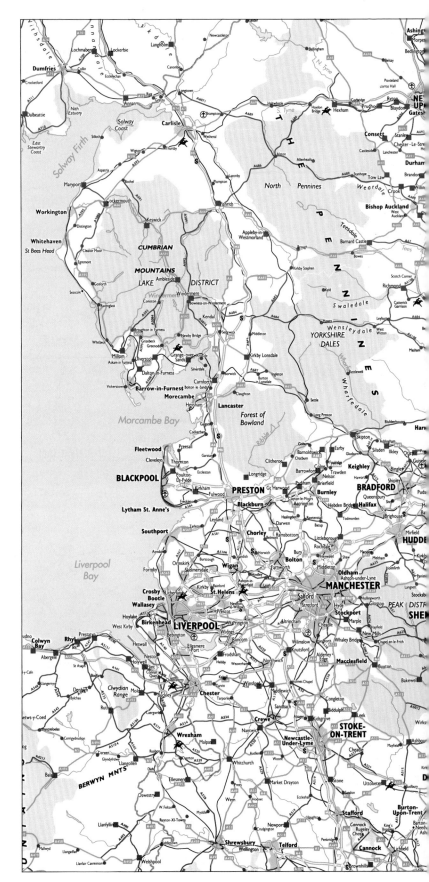

NORTH SEA

Newbiggin-by-the-Sea
Blyth
Seaton Delaval
Whitley Bay
Tynemouth
ASTLE TYNE
South Shields
SUNDERLAND
Washington
Seaham
Hetton-le-Hole
Easington
Peterlee
Hartlepool
ennymoor
Sedgefield
Wolviston
Newton Aycliffe
Billingham
Stockton-on-Tees
MIDDLESBROUGH
Redcar
Coatham
Marske-by-the-Sea
Saltburn-by-the-Sea
Skelton
Brotton
Loftus
Thornaby-on-Tees
Darlington
Guisborough
Stokesley
Whitby
Cleveland Hills
NORTH YORK MOORS
Ravenscar
Northallerton
Cloughton
Lockton
Helmsley
Scalb
Scarborough
Pickering
Vale of Pickering
Derwent
Brompton
Filey
Staxton
Filey
Reighton
Flamborough Head
Sherburn
Howardian Hills
Malton
Norton
Rillington
Bridlington
The Wolds
Burton Agnes
Wetwang
Gt Driffield
Barmston
Stamford Bridge
Wilberfoss
Hutton Cranswick
York
Middleton-on-the-Wolds
Escrick
Hayton
Leven
Hornsea
Market Weighton
Leconfield
LEEDS
Holme-on-Spalding-Moor
Beverley
KINGSTON UPON HULL
Cottingham
Hessle
Hedon
Withernsea
Castleford
Goole
Barton-Upon-Humber
Patrington
Wakefield
SFIELD
Crowle
Scunthorpe
Immingham
Ulcer
Grimsby
Cleethorpes
Spurn Head
Barnsley
Bentley
Belton
Messingham
Brigg
Waltham
Humberston
Doncaster
Ludborough
Saltfleet
Rotherham
Finningley
Gainsborough
Glenham
Market Rasen
Louth
Lincolnshire Wolds
Mablethorpe
ELD
Maltby
Langold
Carlton in Lindrick
Marton
Saxilby
East Barkwith
Maltby le Marsh
Sutton on Sea
Chesterfield
Worksop
E. Retford
Newton on Trent
Washingborough
Horncastle
Alford
Chapel St Leonards
Bolsover
Warsop
Carlton-on-Trent
Lincoln
Barton
Spilsby
Skegness
Staveley
Clay Cross
Sutton in Ashfield
Kirklington
Waddington
Woodhall Spa
Wainfleet All Saints
Matlock
Mansfield
Kirkby in Ashfield
Southwell
Billinghay
Sibsey
Alfreton
Ravenshead
Ripley
Hucknall
Newark-on-Trent
Leadenham
Heanor
Eastwood
Sleaford
Boston
Hunstanton
RBY
Ilkeston
Arnold
NOTTINGHAM
Heckington
Kirton
The Wash
Stapleford
Radcliffe-on-Trent
Bingham
Grantham
Honington
Sutterton
Long Eaton
Folkingham
Donington
Keyworth
Upr Broughton
Great Ponton
Holbeach
Loughborough
Waltham on the Wolds
Colsterworth
Pinchbeck
Spalding
Long Sutton
S. Wootton
King's Lynn
Swadlincote
Shepshed
Melton Mowbray
Bourne
Coalville
Quorndon
Mountsorrel
Stretton
Market Deeping
Crowland
Wisbech
Syston
Oakham
Anstey
LEICESTER
Stamford
Outwell

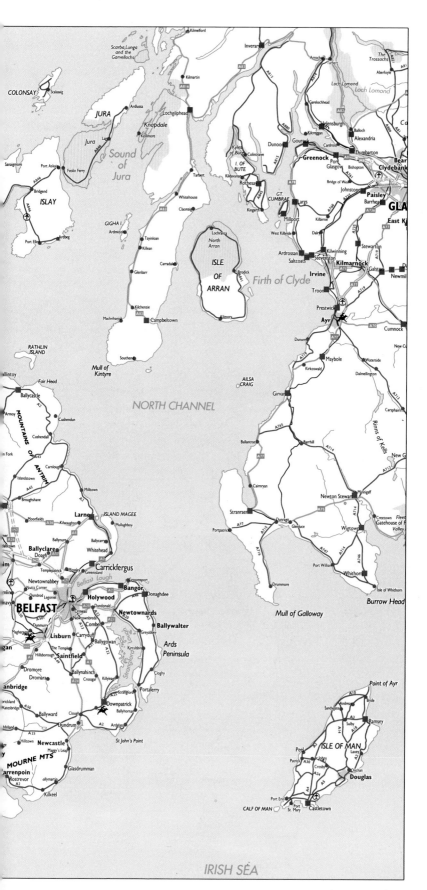

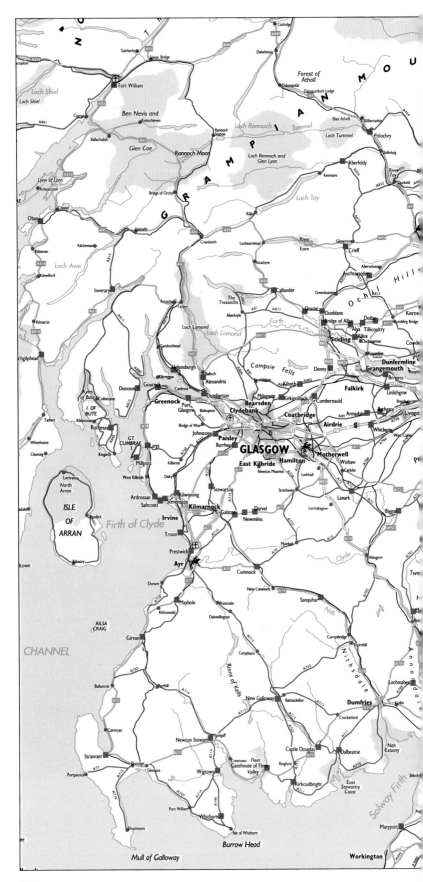

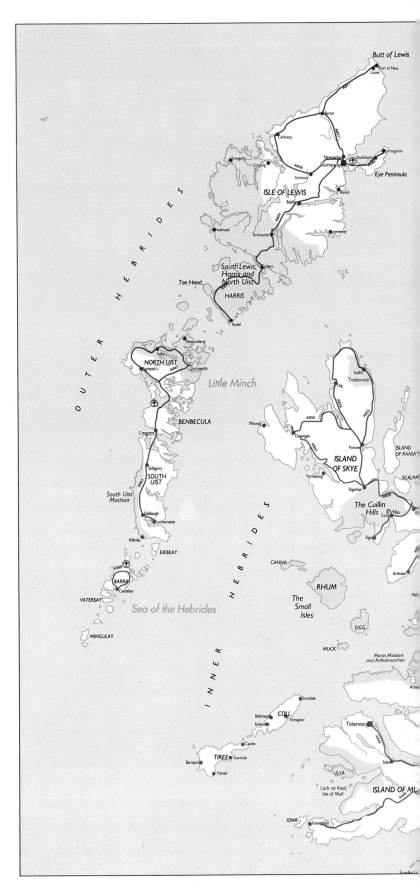

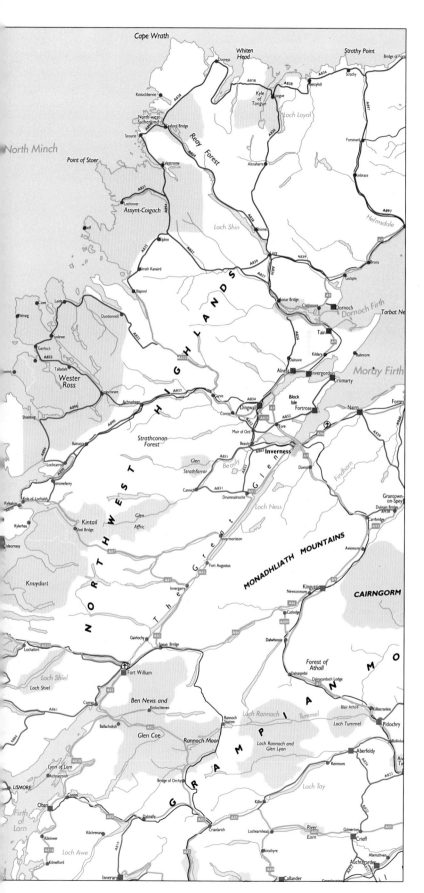

221

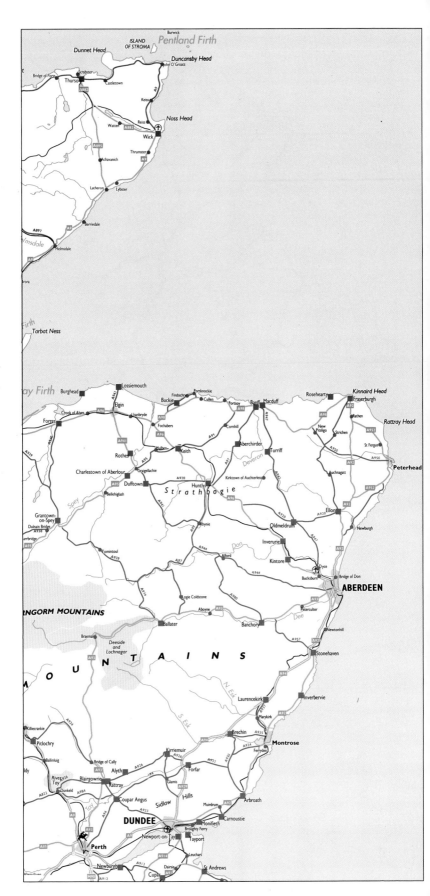